# PRINCESS MONONOKE

Original story and screenplay written and directed by
## HAYAO MIYAZAKI

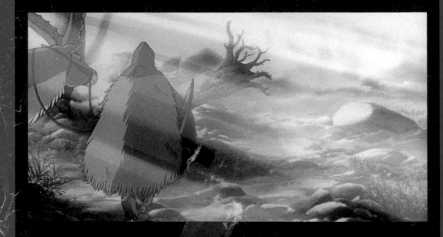

1

# ❰ *Character Introductions* ❱

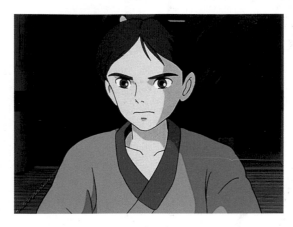

## Ashitaka
■ A young village prince of a tribe hidden away in the northern mountains. He is cursed as a result of fighting a demon god. He takes a journey out west in order to lift the curse.

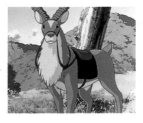

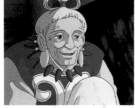

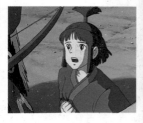

## Yakul
■ Named "Akashishi" by the Yamato villagers, it is equal parts elk and horse. Ashitaka rides it on his westward journey.

## The Wise Woman
■ The village's medium. A senior leader who also performs the rites of a priestess.

## Kaya
■ She is a member of Ashitaka's tribe and cares deeply for him. Upon his departure from their village she gives him her crystal dagger.

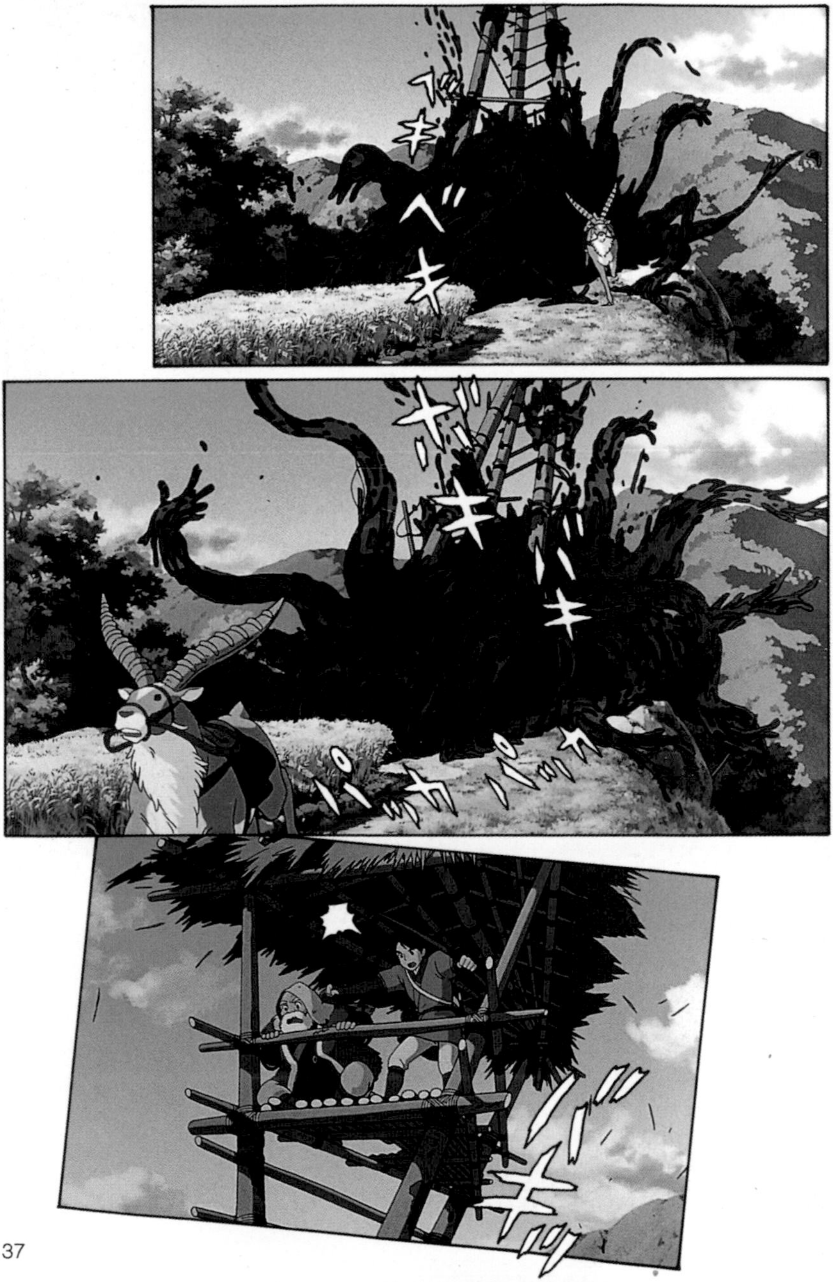

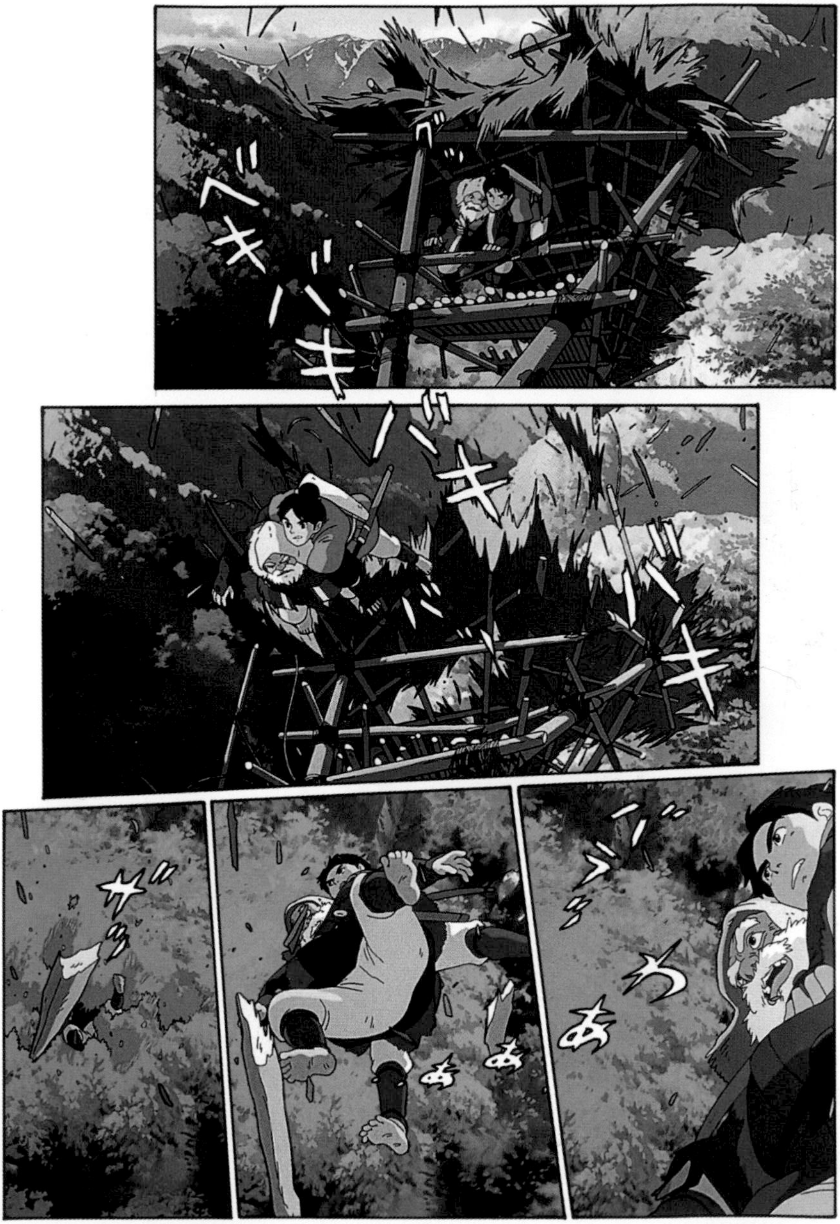

ベキ
バキ
バキ
バキ
わ
あ
あ
あ

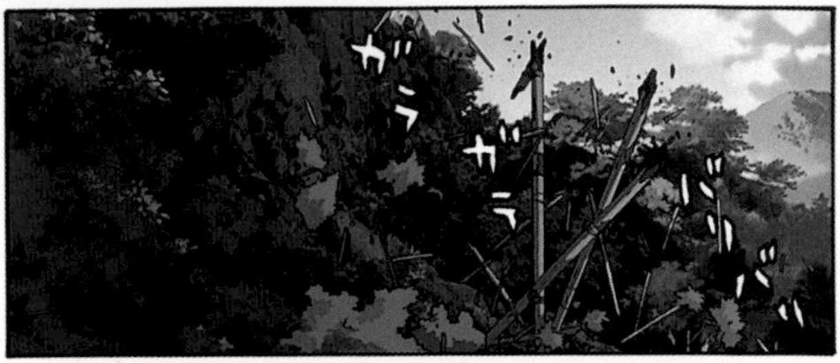
ガラ
ガラ
バリ
バリ
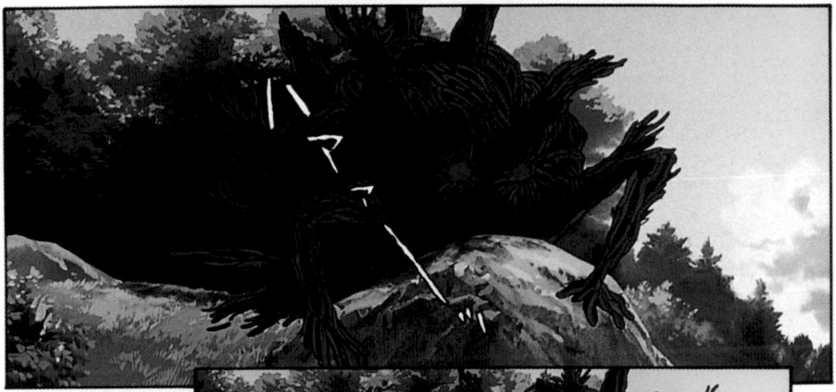
ハア
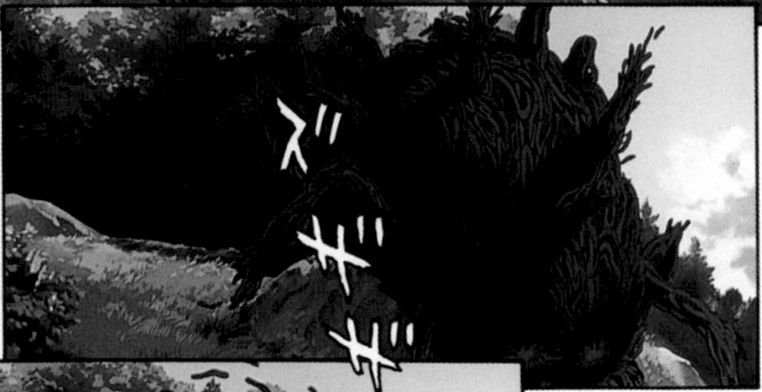
ズザザ
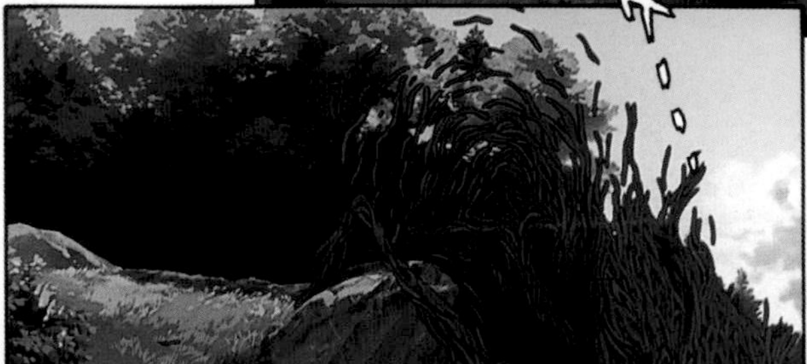

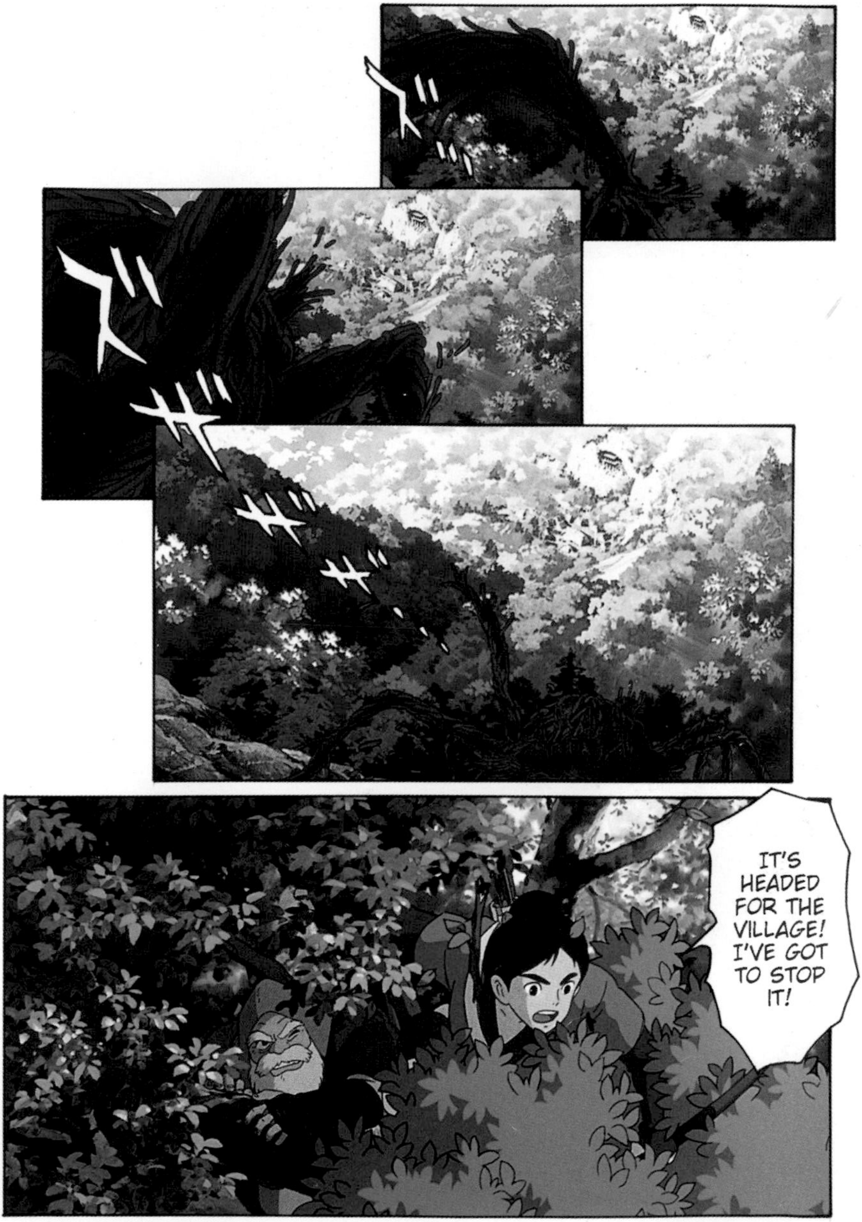
IT'S HEADED FOR THE VILLAGE! I'VE GOT TO STOP IT!

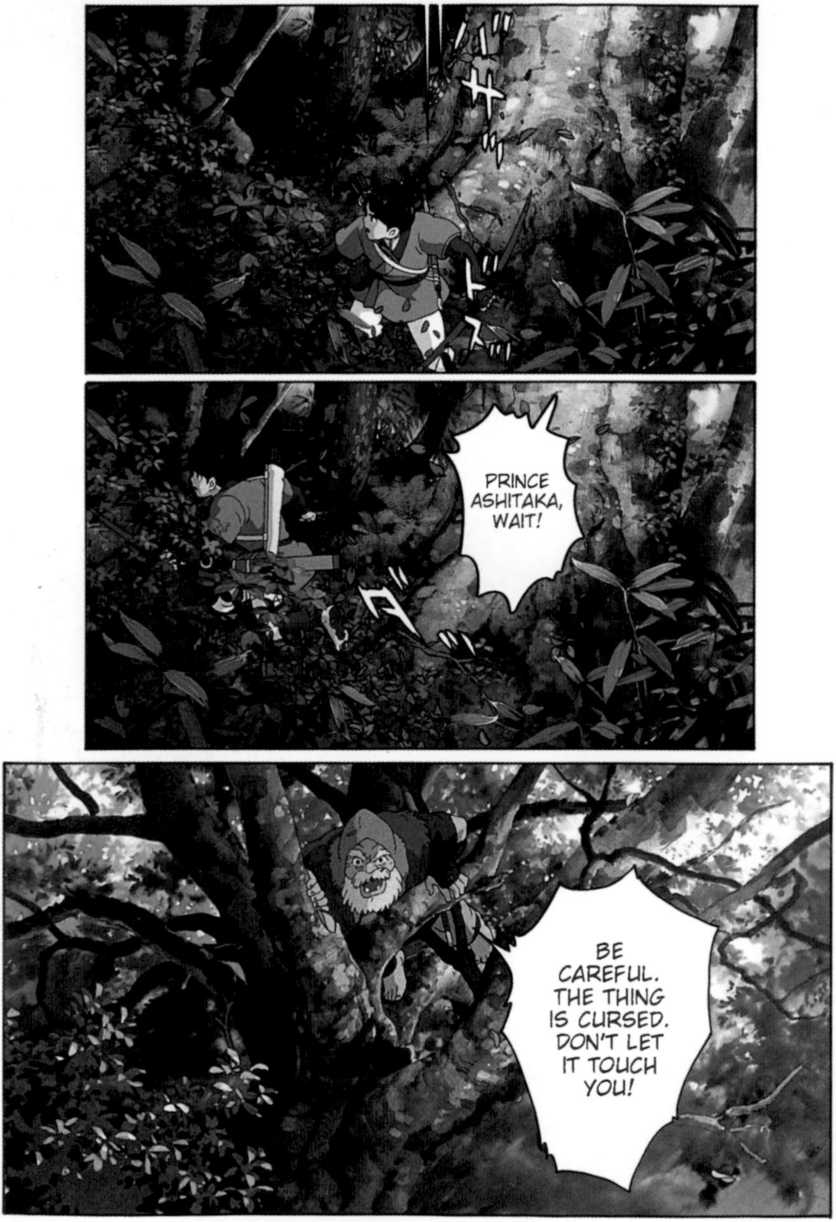
PRINCE ASHITAKA, WAIT!
BE CAREFUL. THE THING IS CURSED. DON'T LET IT TOUCH YOU!

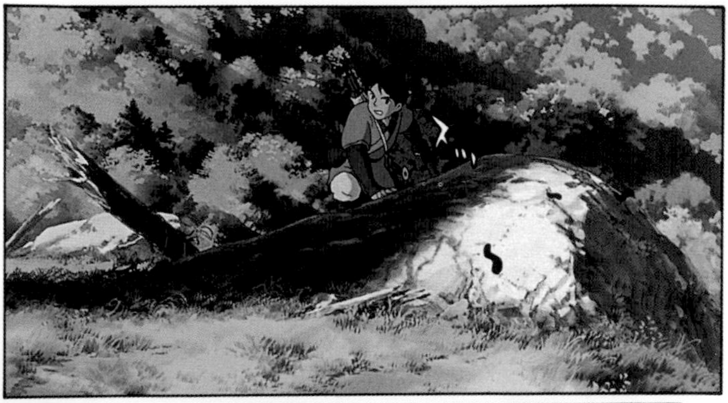

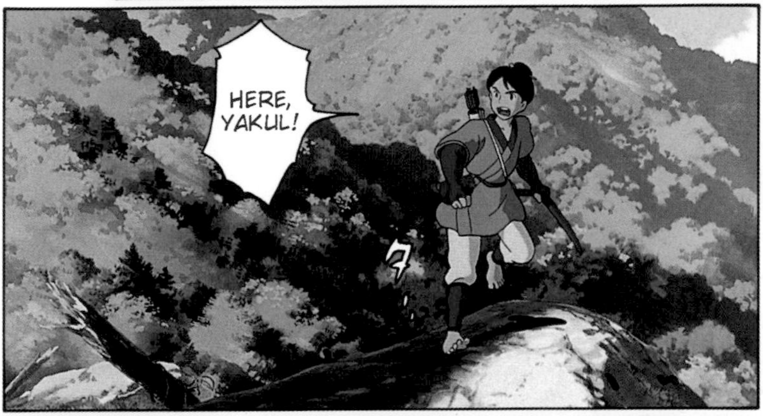
HERE, YAKUL!

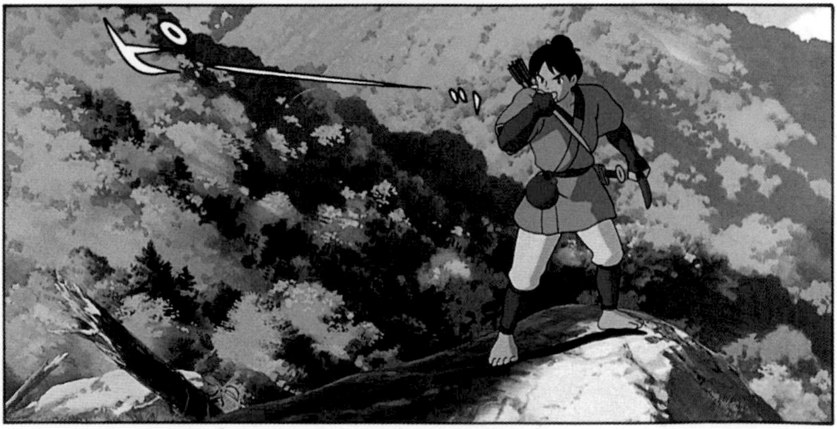

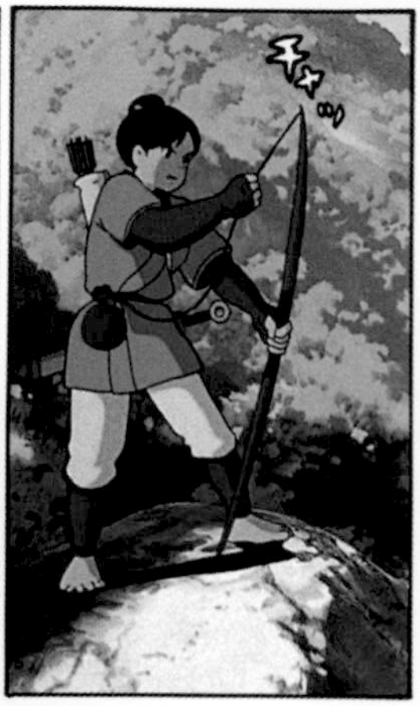
チャッ
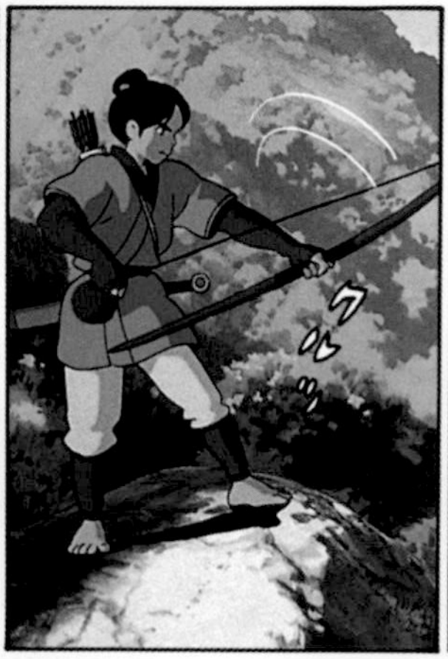
クルッ
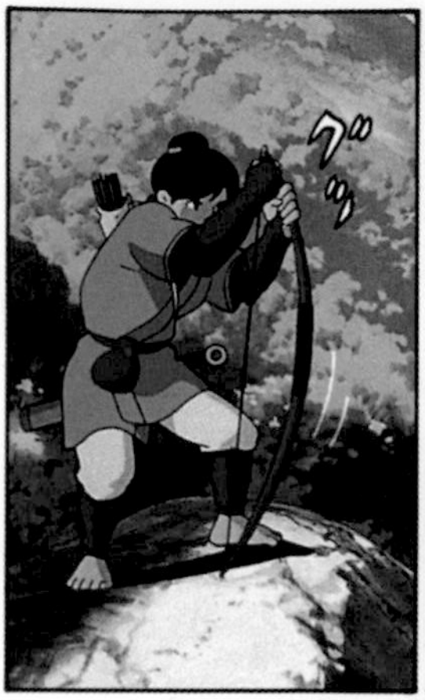
グッ
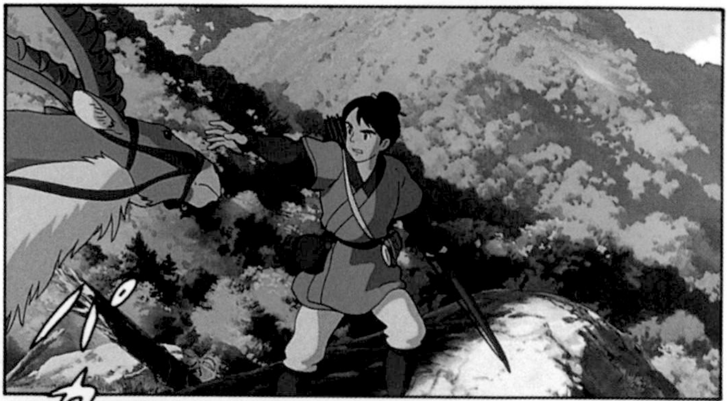
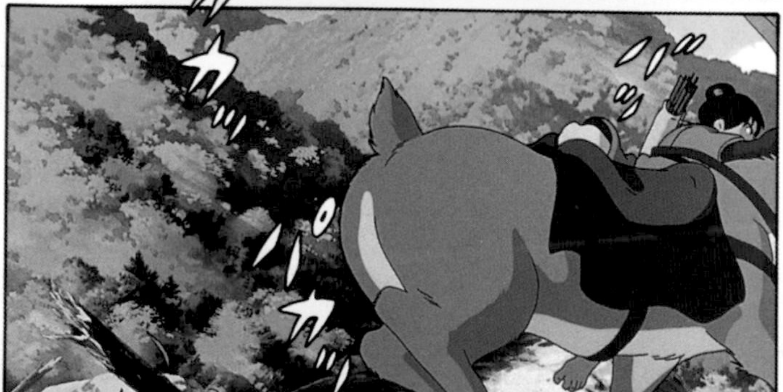

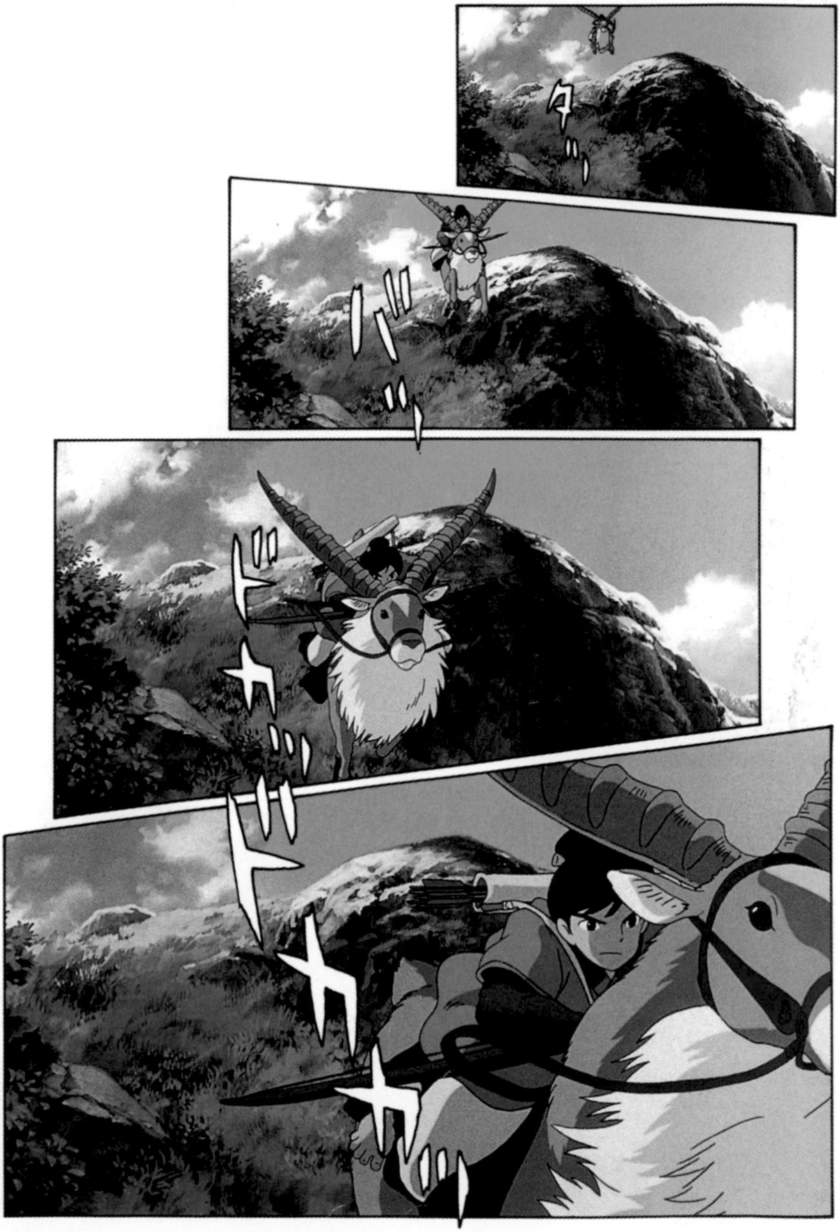
タッ
バッ
ドカッ
ドカカッ

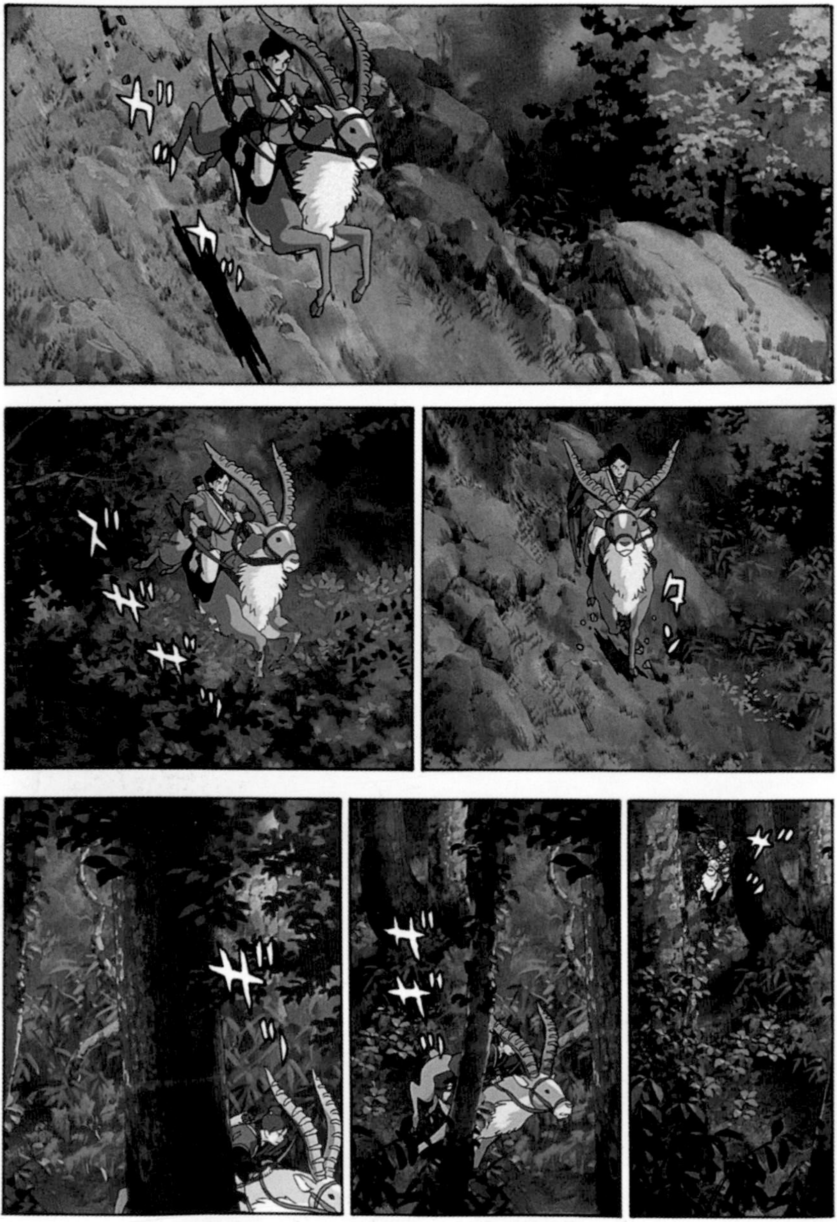
ガッ
ガッ
タッ
ズザザッ
ザッ
ザザッ
ザッ

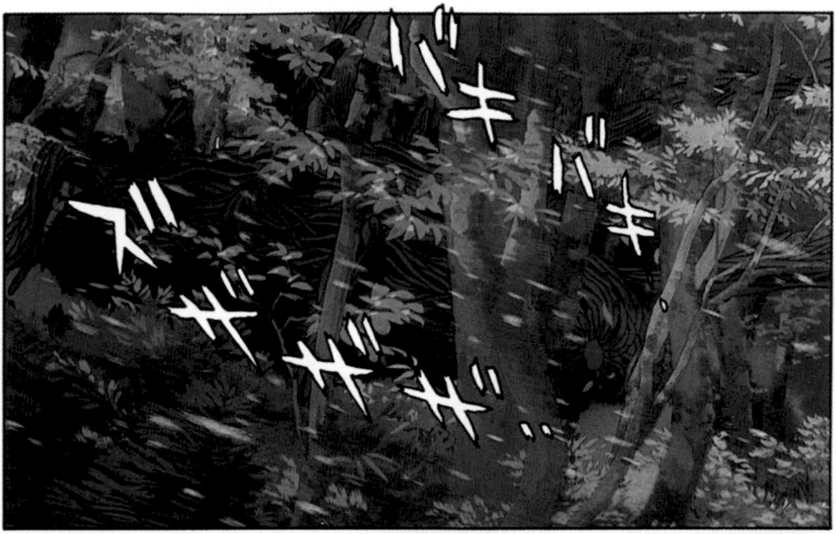
バキ
バキ
ズザザザ‥

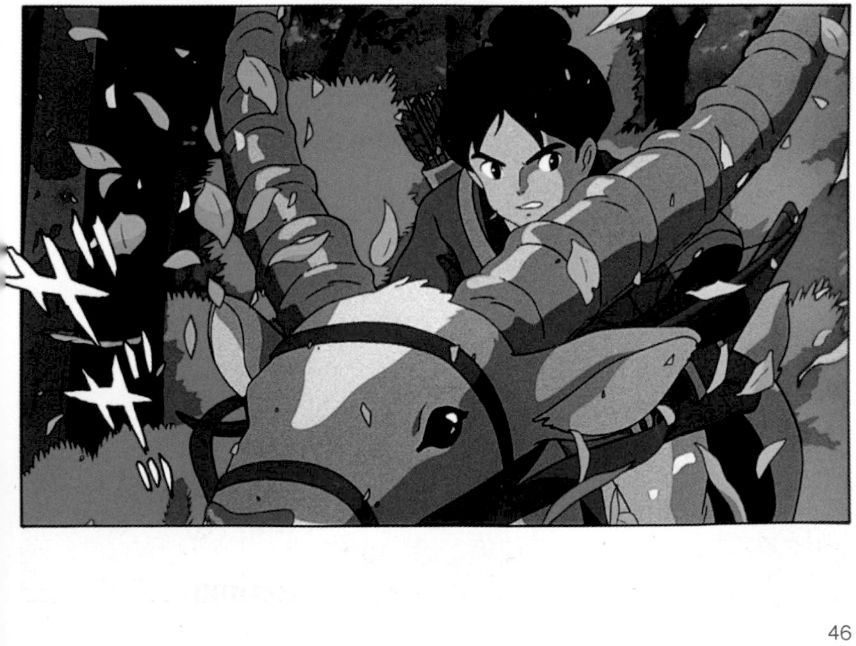
ザザ

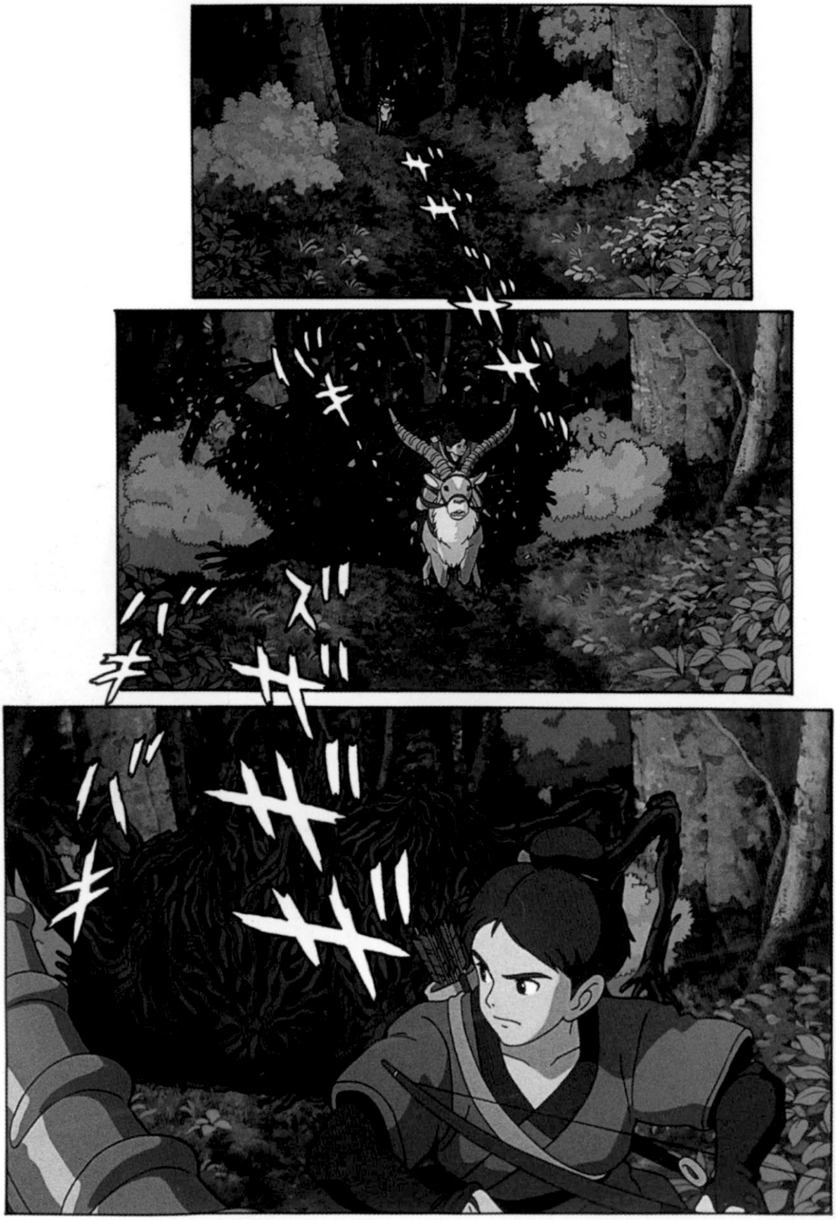
ザザザザ
ギ
バギ
ズザザ
バギ
ザザ

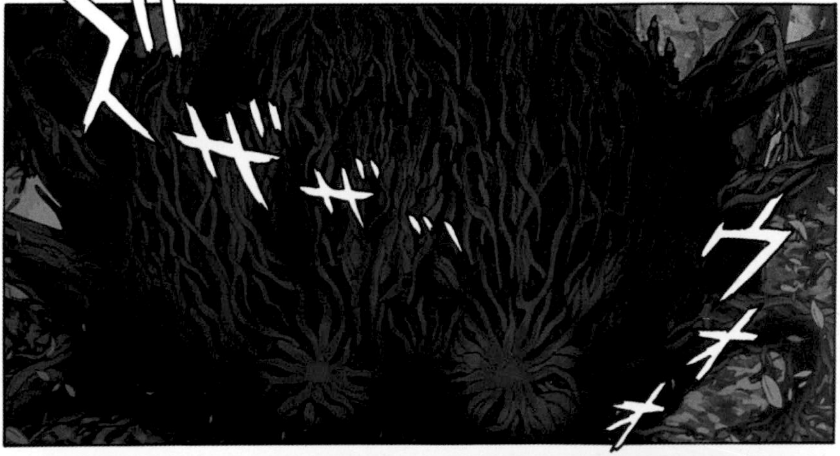

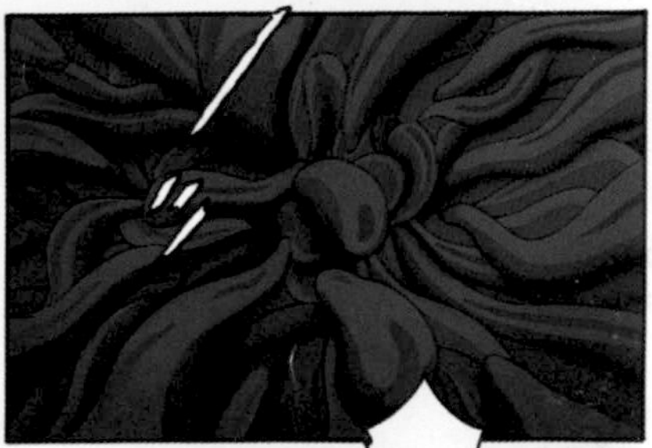

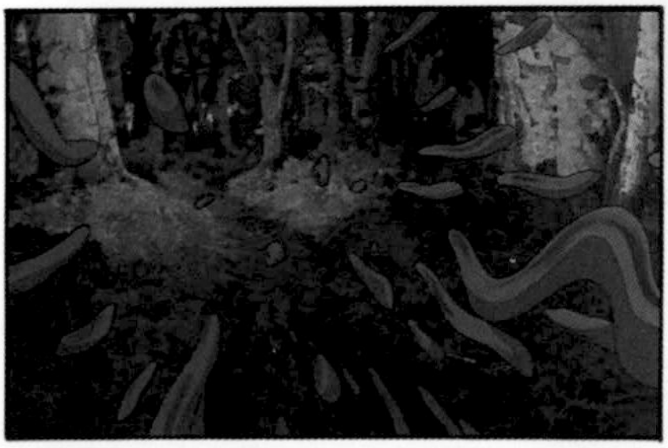

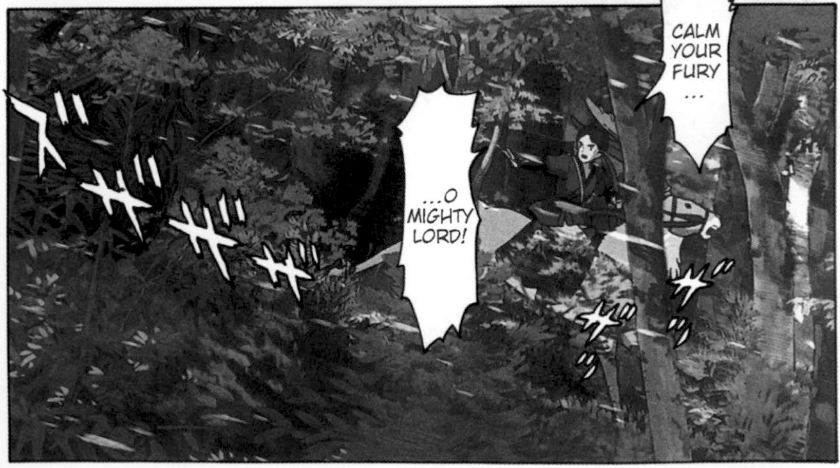
CALM YOUR FURY ...
...O MIGHTY LORD!

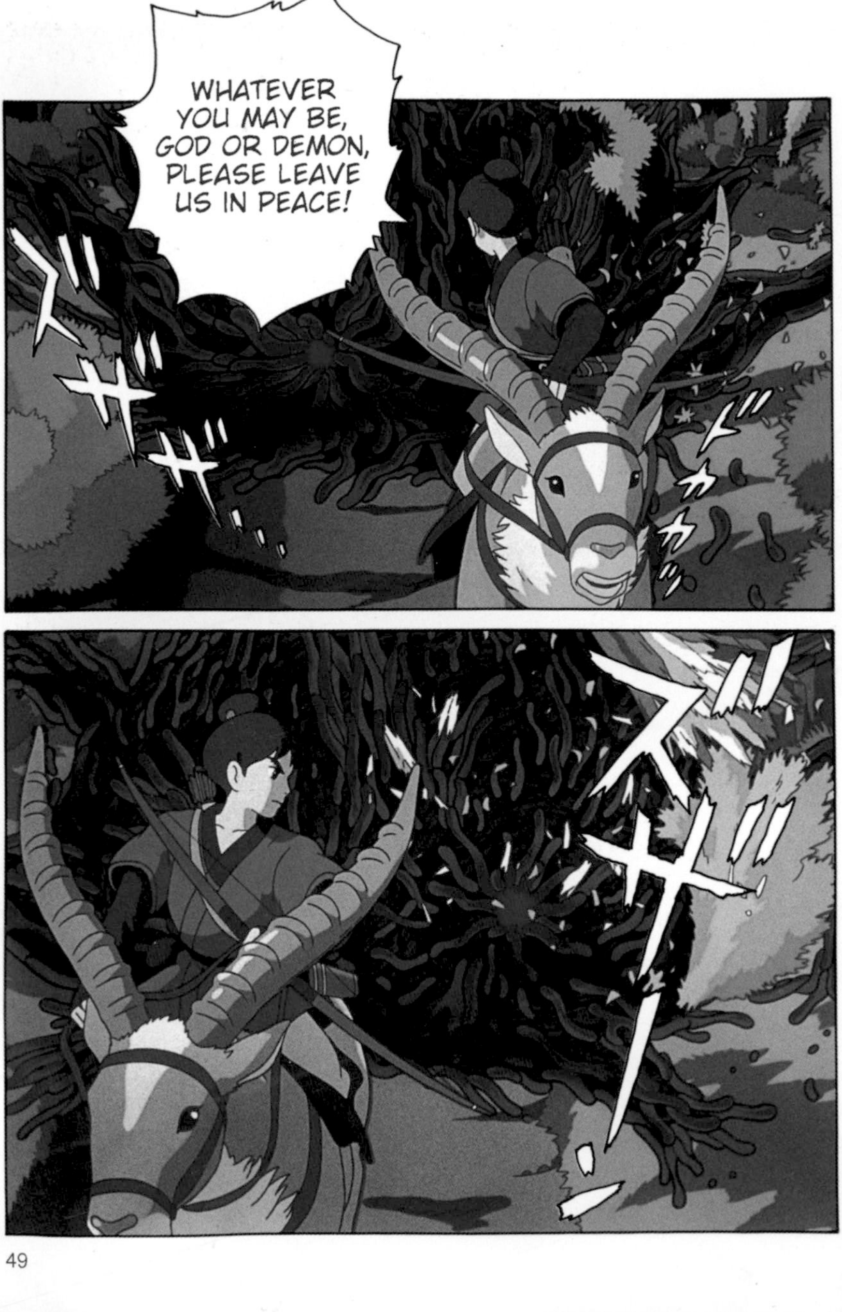
WHATEVER YOU MAY BE, GOD OR DEMON, PLEASE LEAVE US IN PEACE!

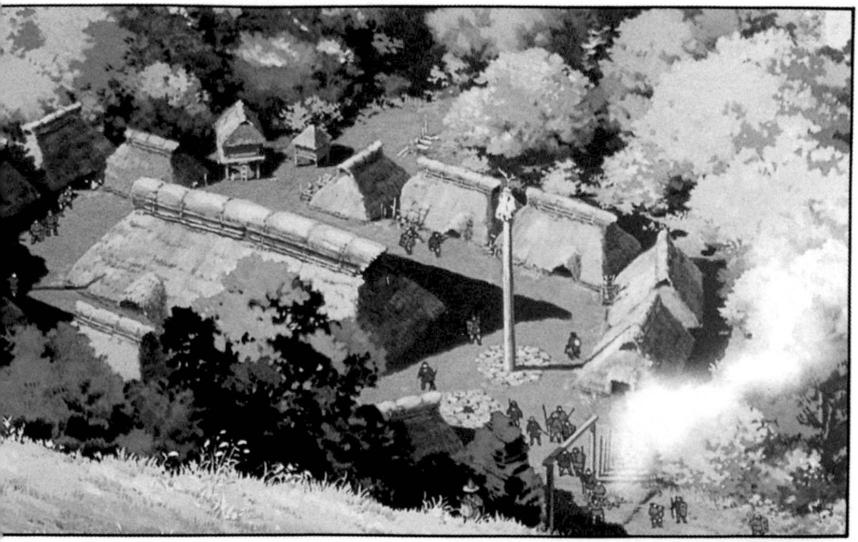
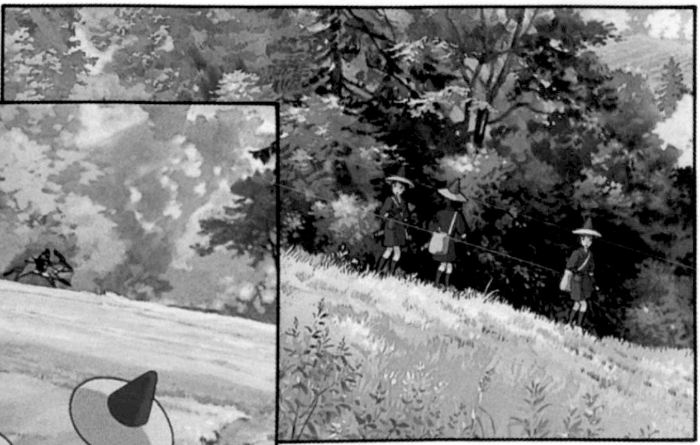
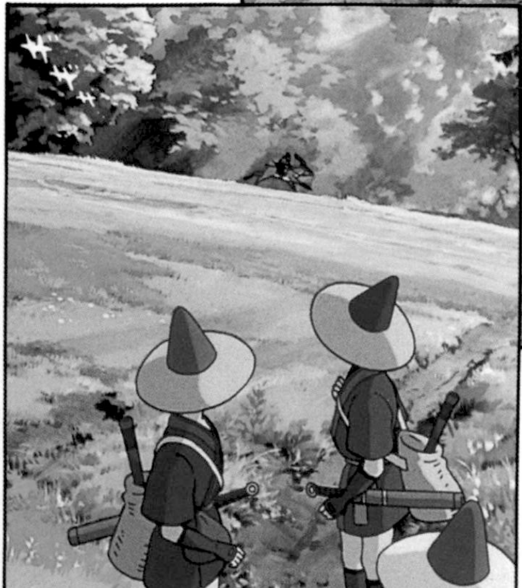

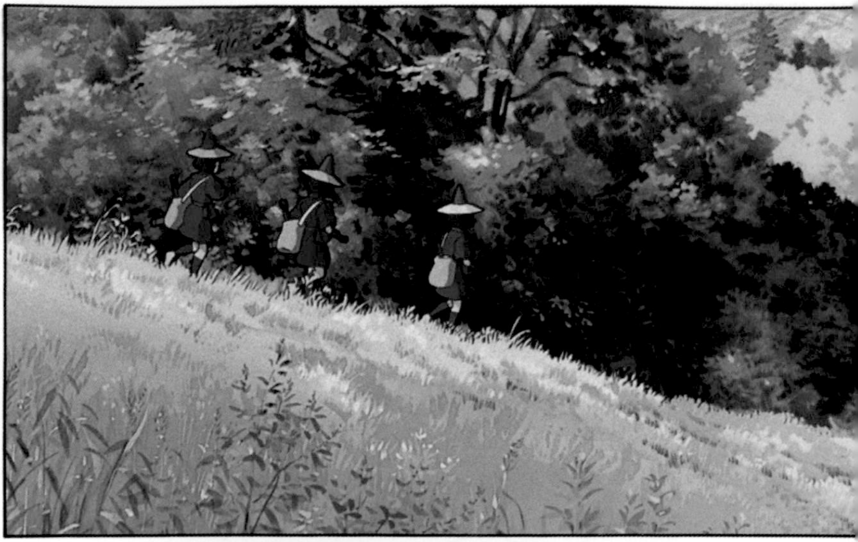
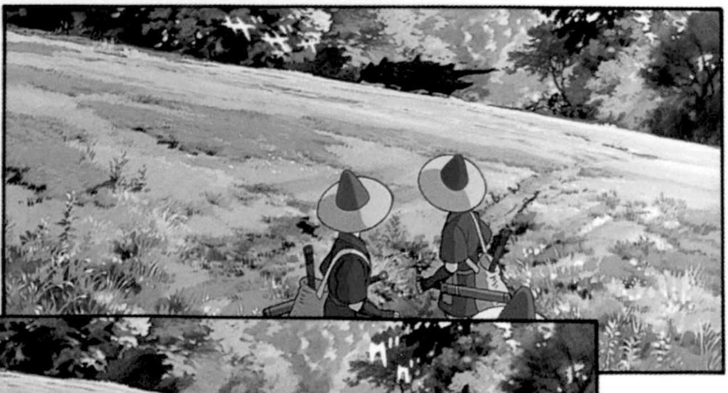
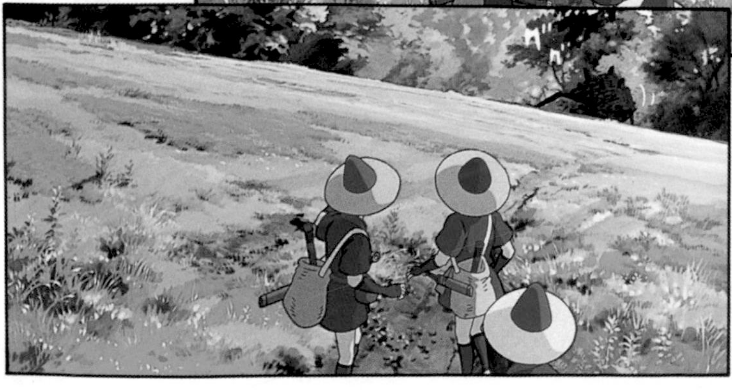

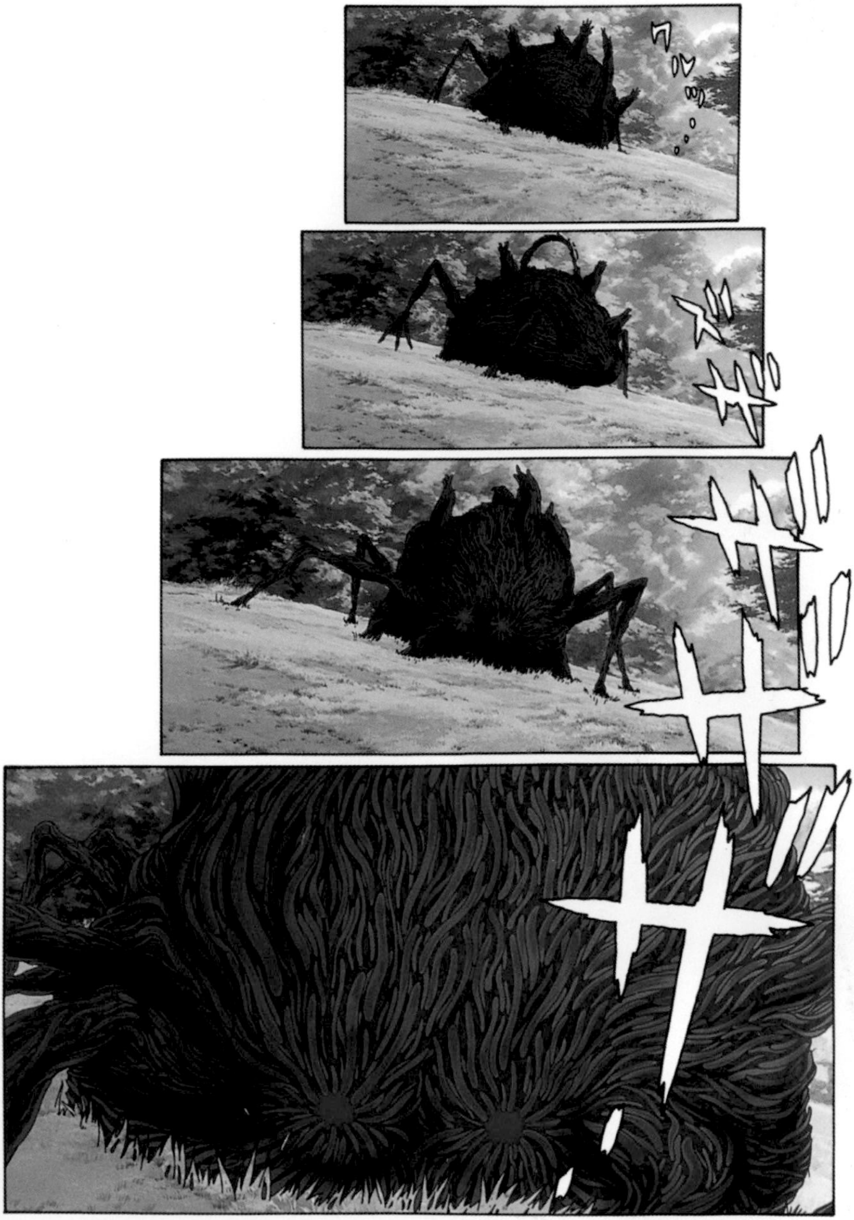
ズザ
ザザザ

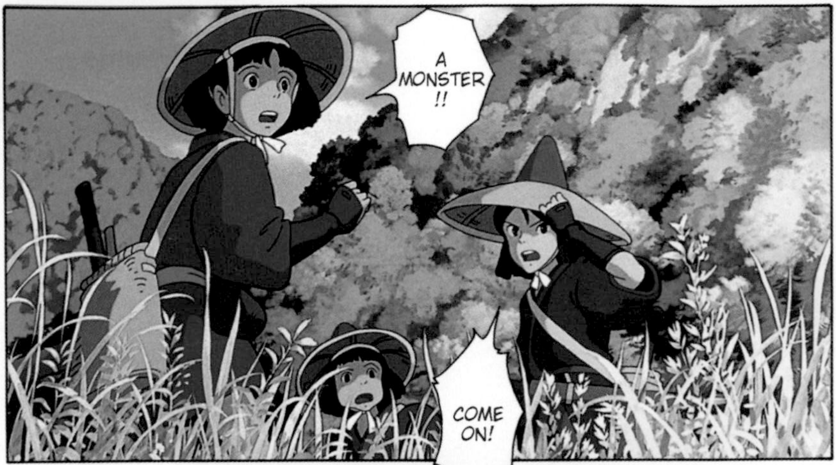
A MONSTER !!
COME ON!
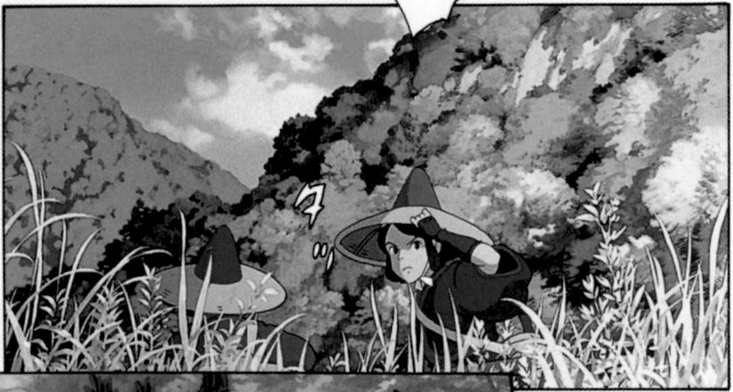
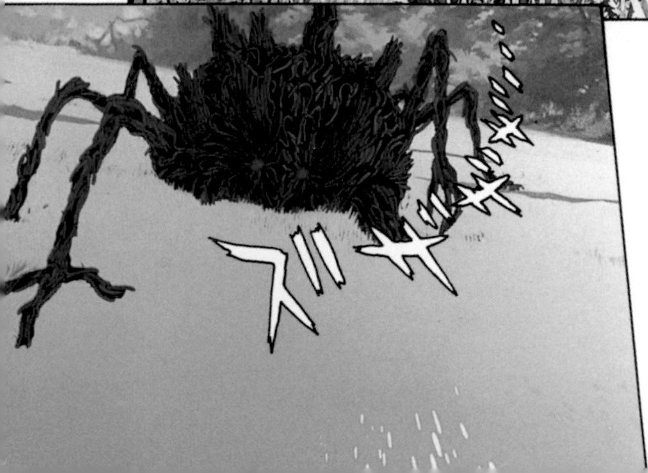

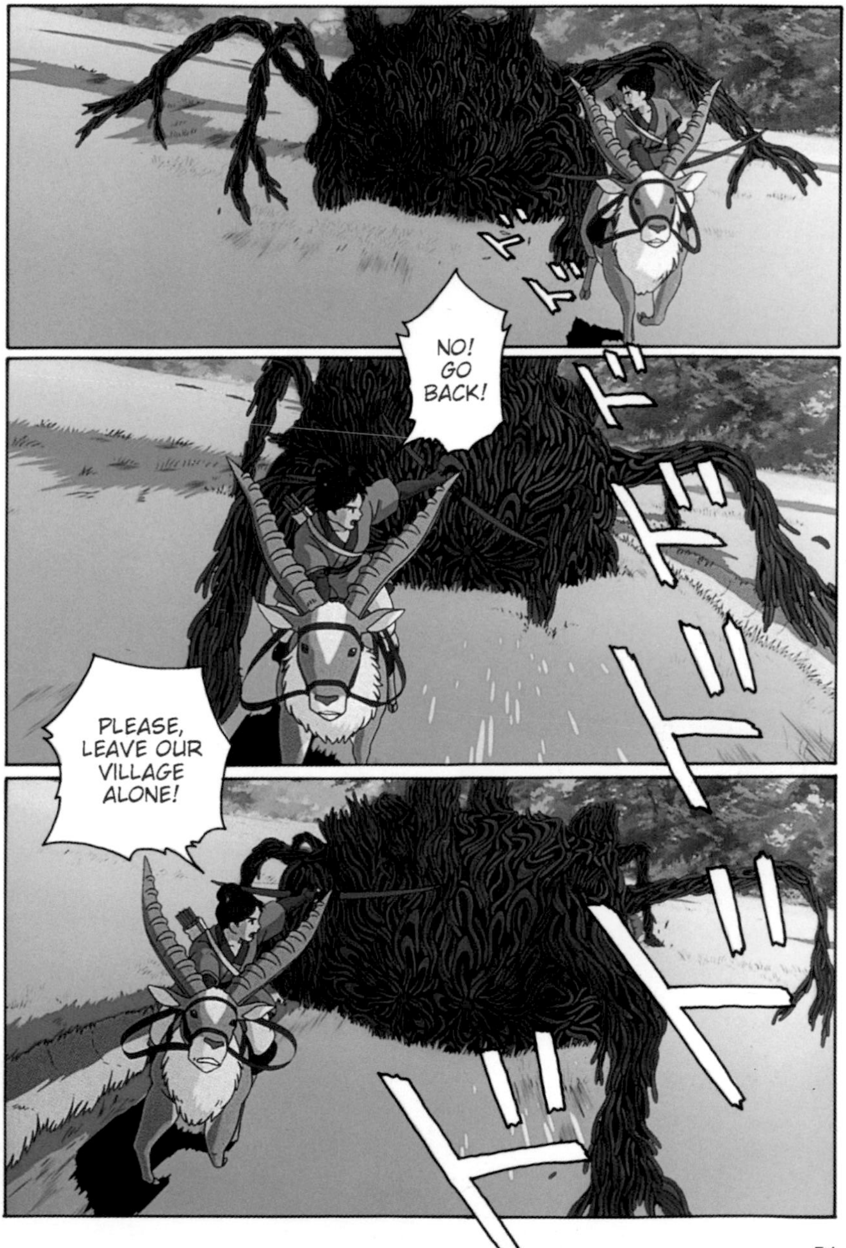
NO! GO BACK!
PLEASE, LEAVE OUR VILLAGE ALONE!

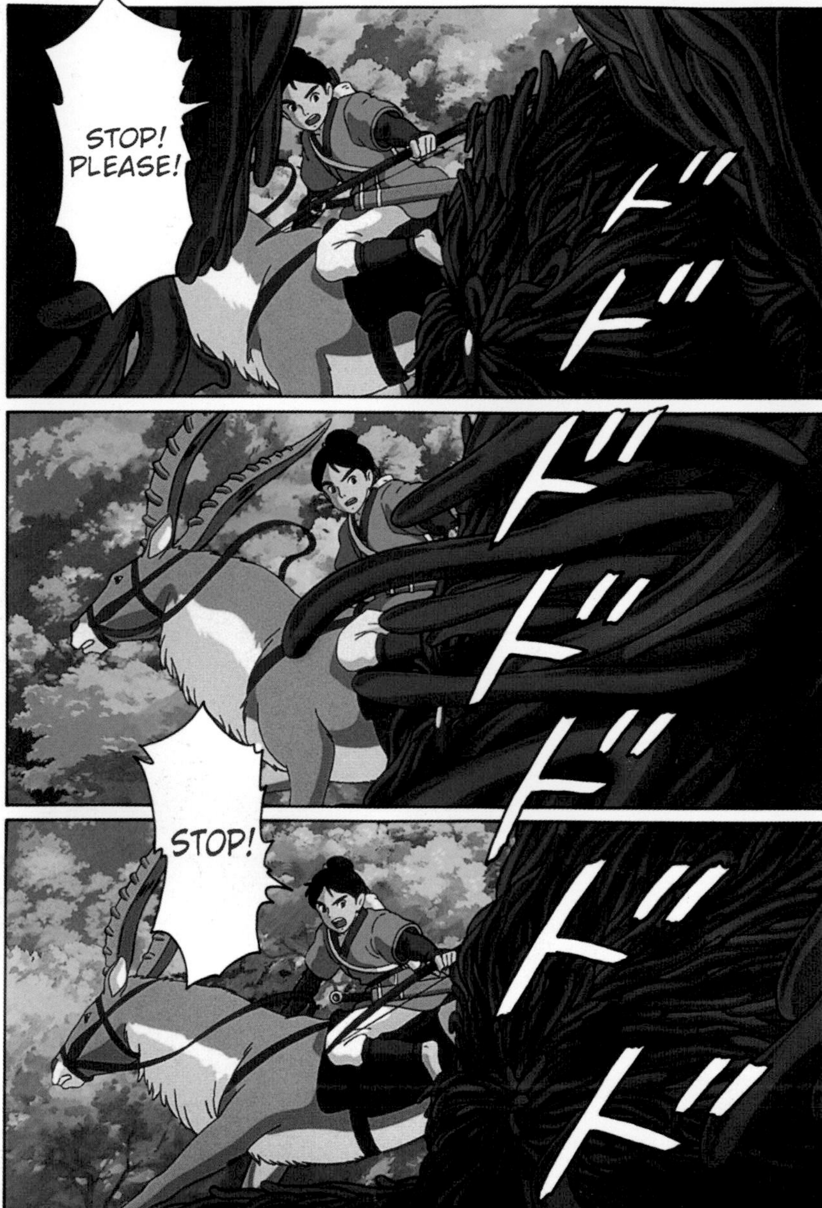
STOP! PLEASE!
ドドドドドドドド
STOP!

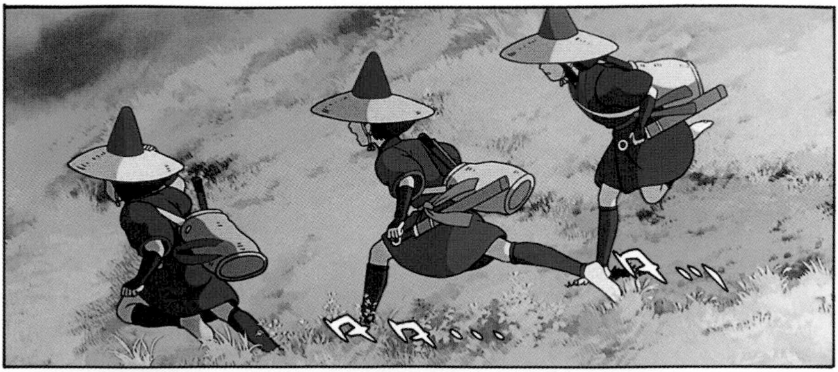

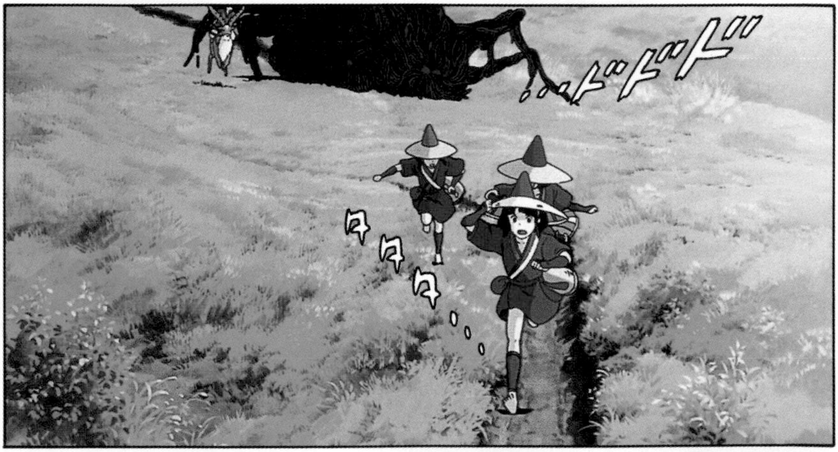

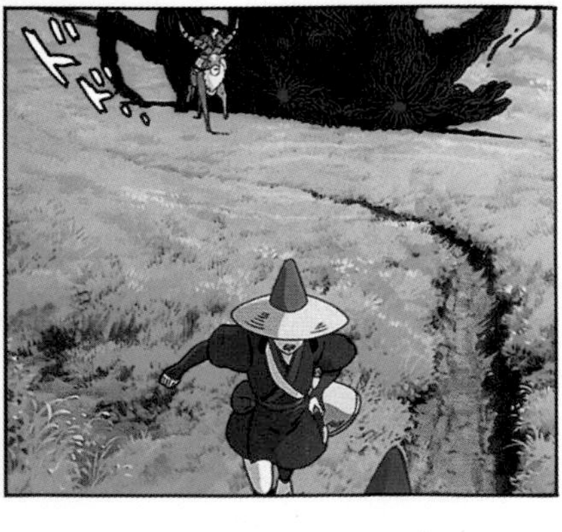

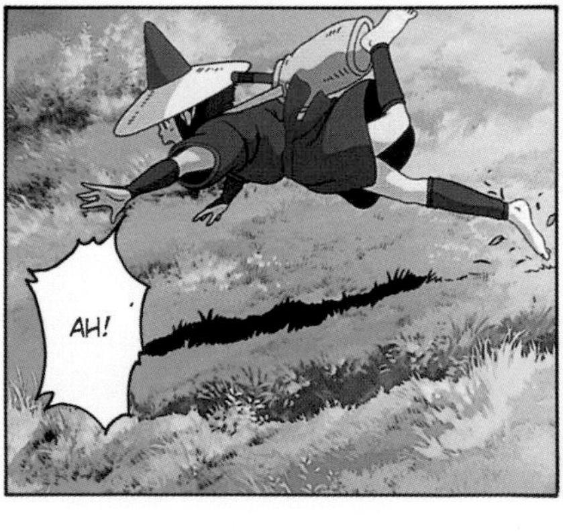
AH!

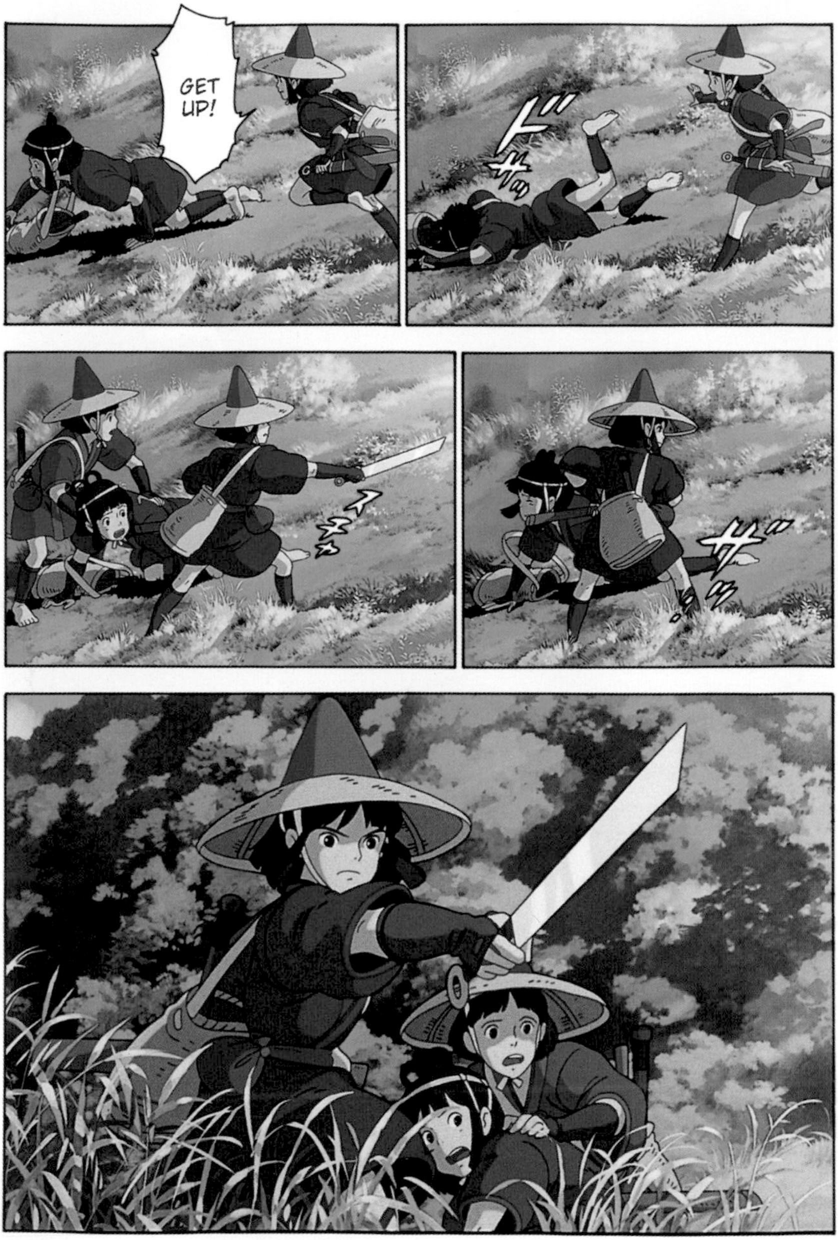
GET UP!

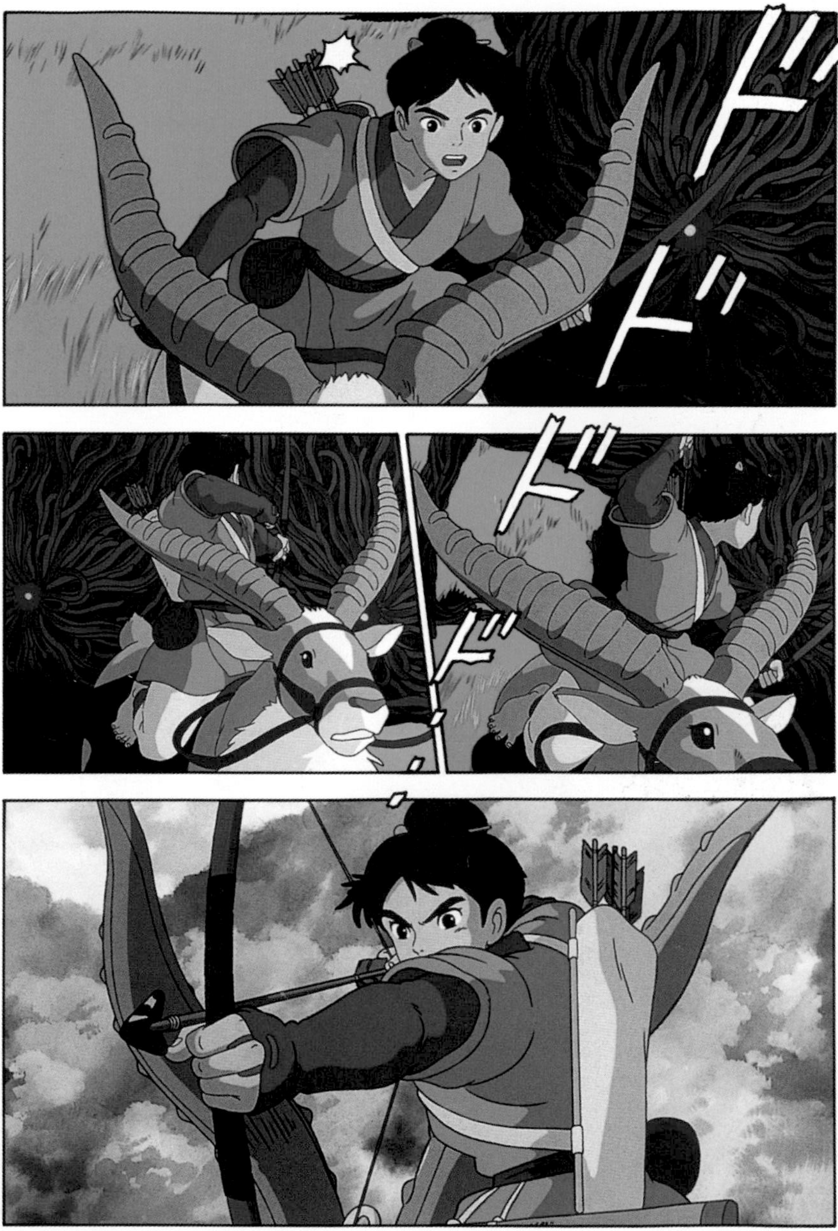
ド
ド
ド
ド

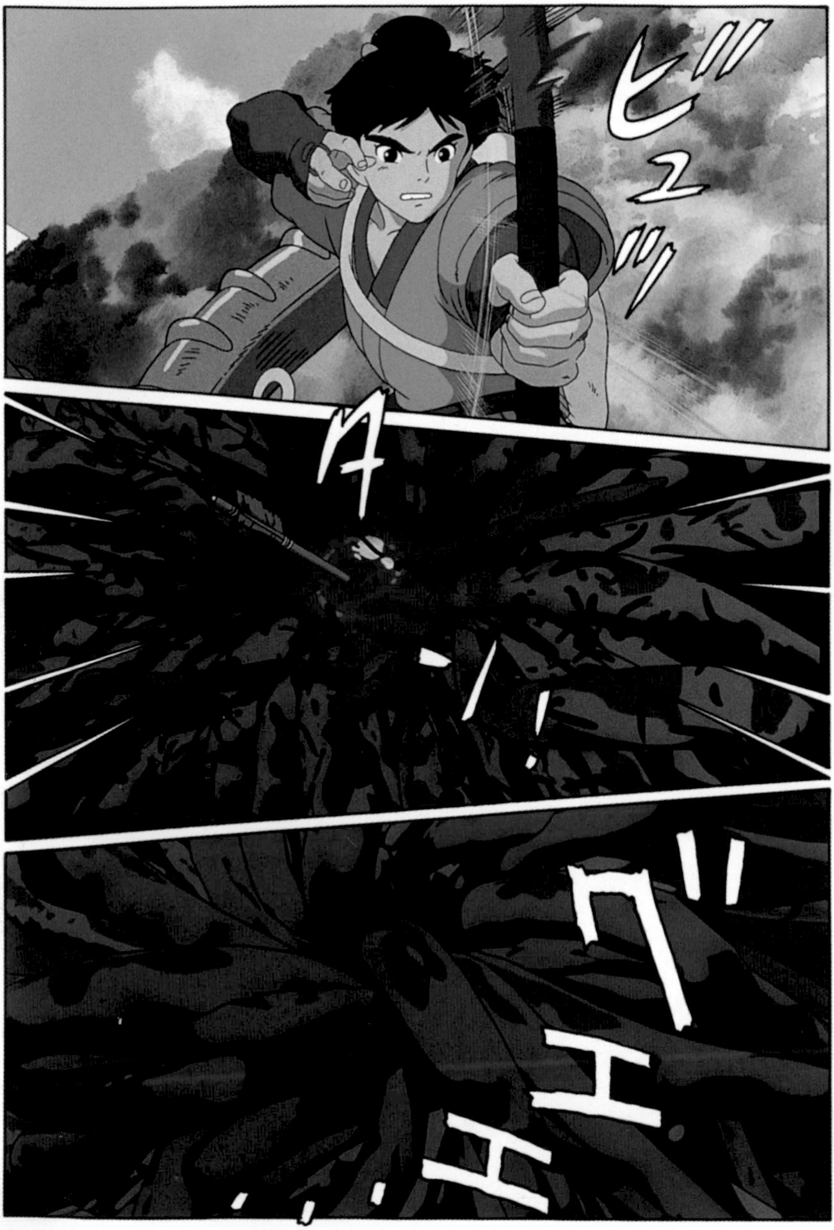
ビュッ
カッ!!
グエエ…

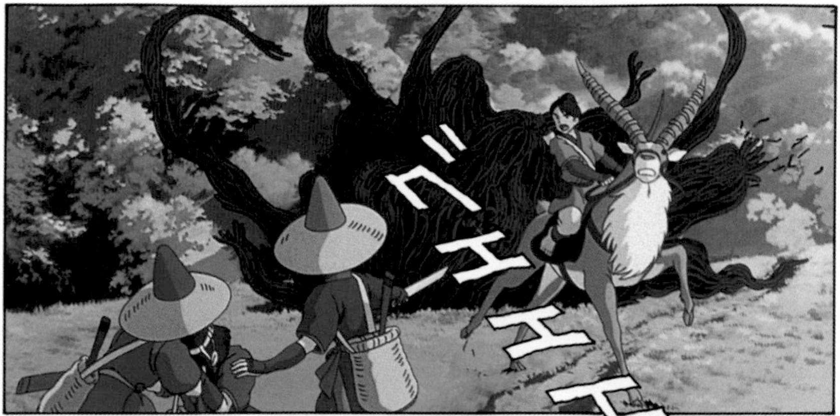

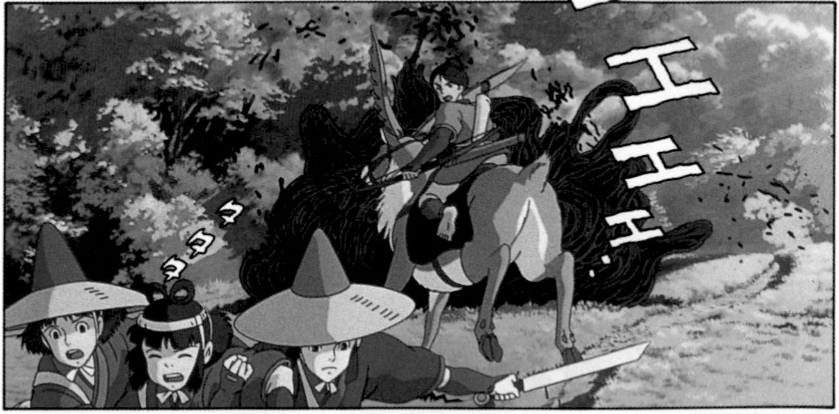

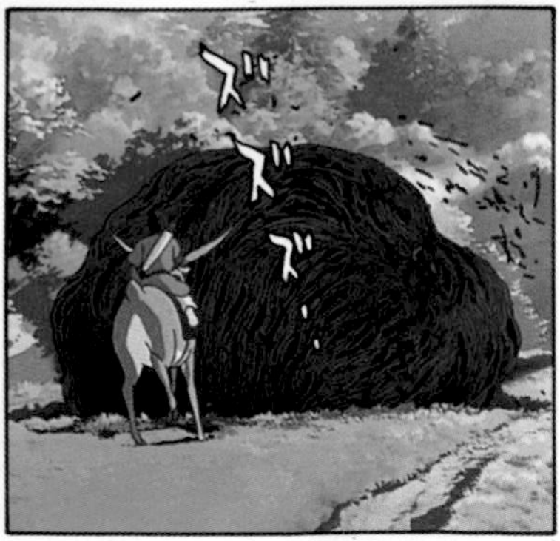
ズズズ

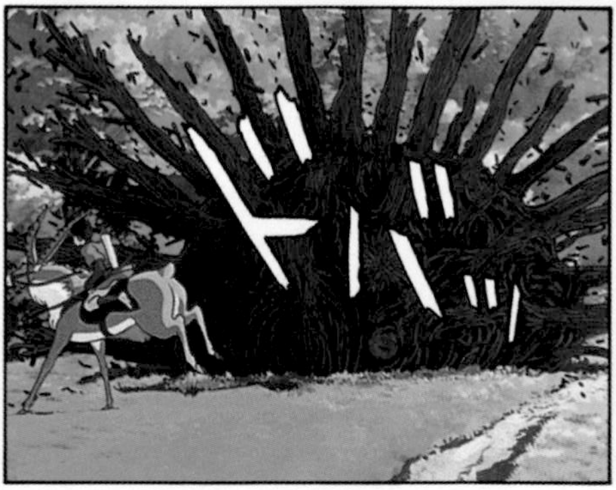

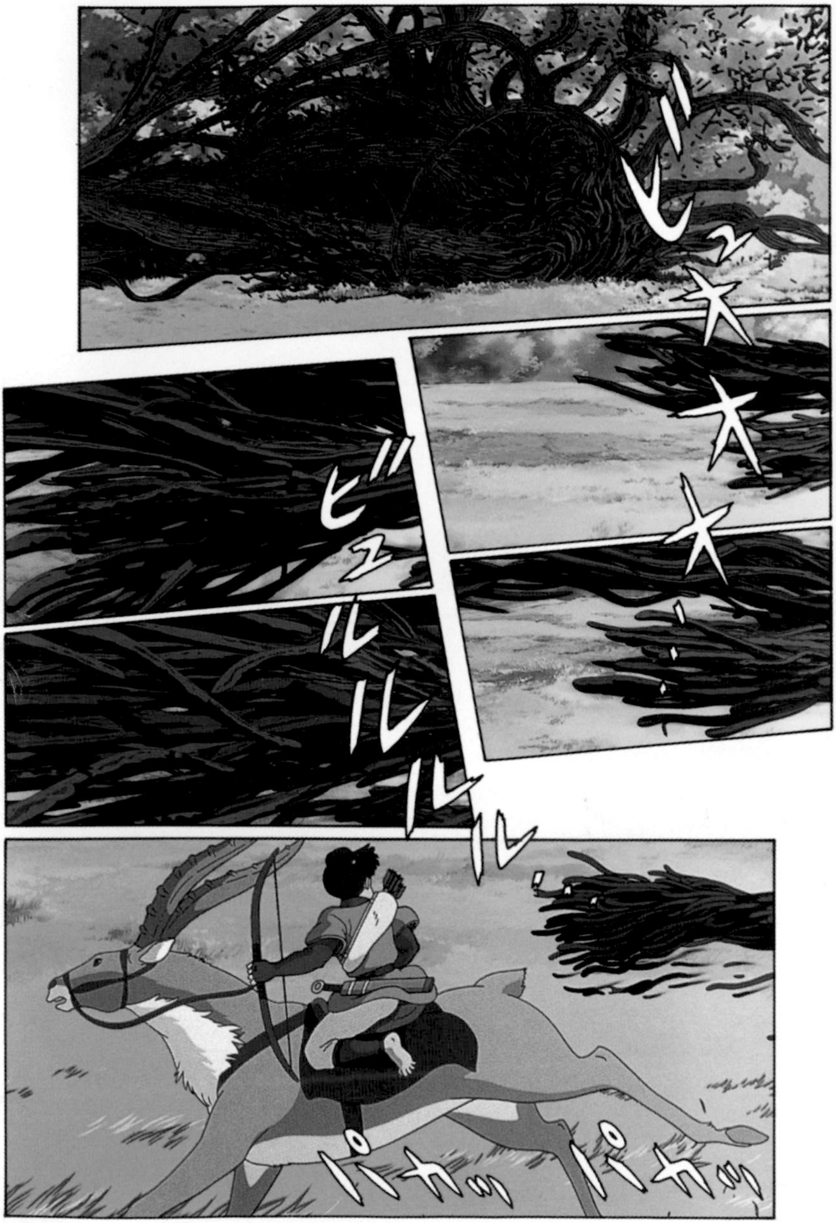
ビュススス……
ビュルルルル
パカッ パカッ

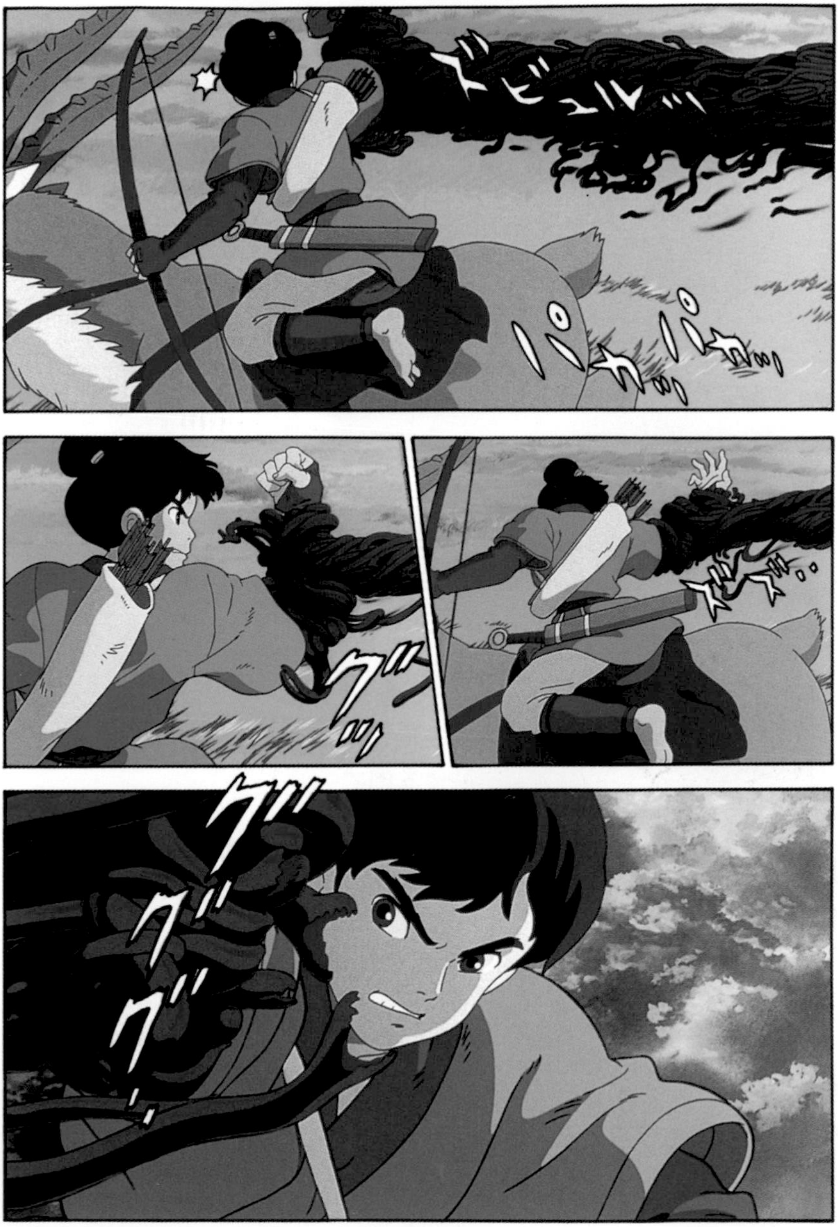
パパッ
グッ
ググググ

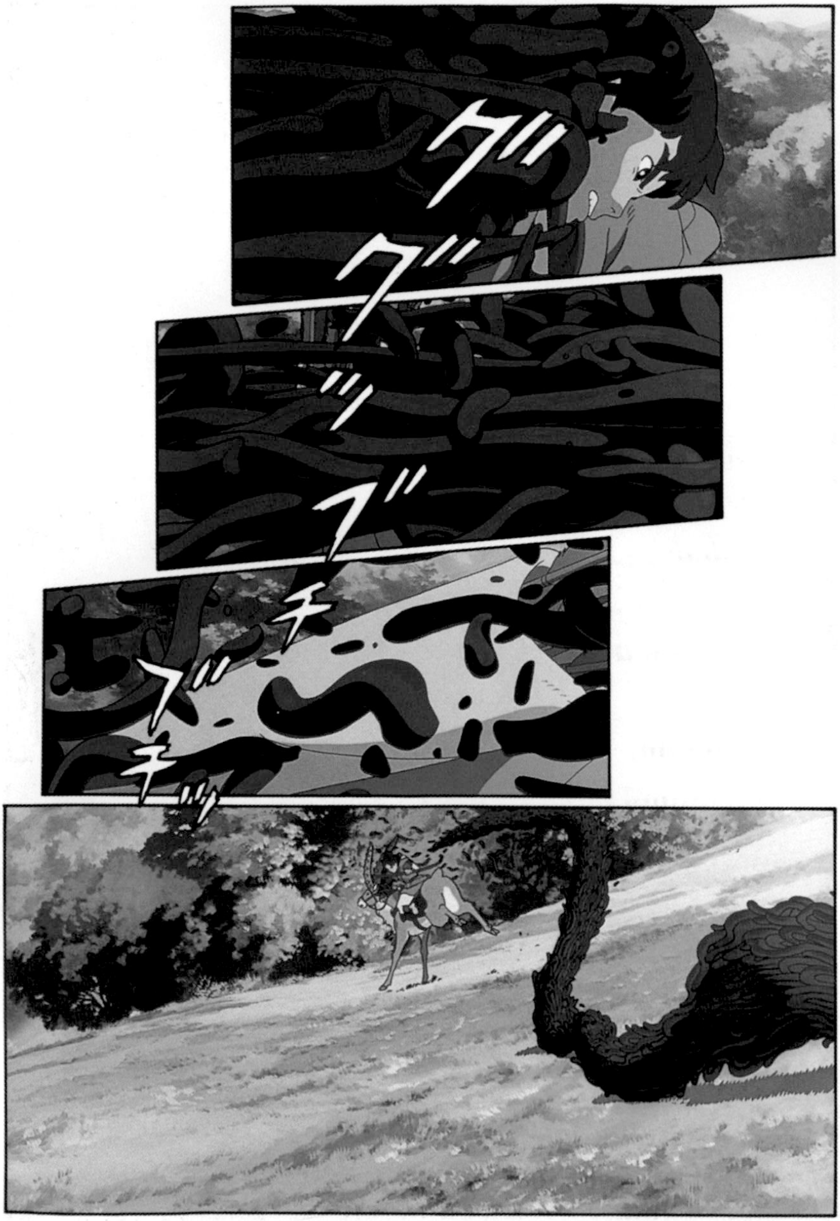
ググッ
ブチブチッ

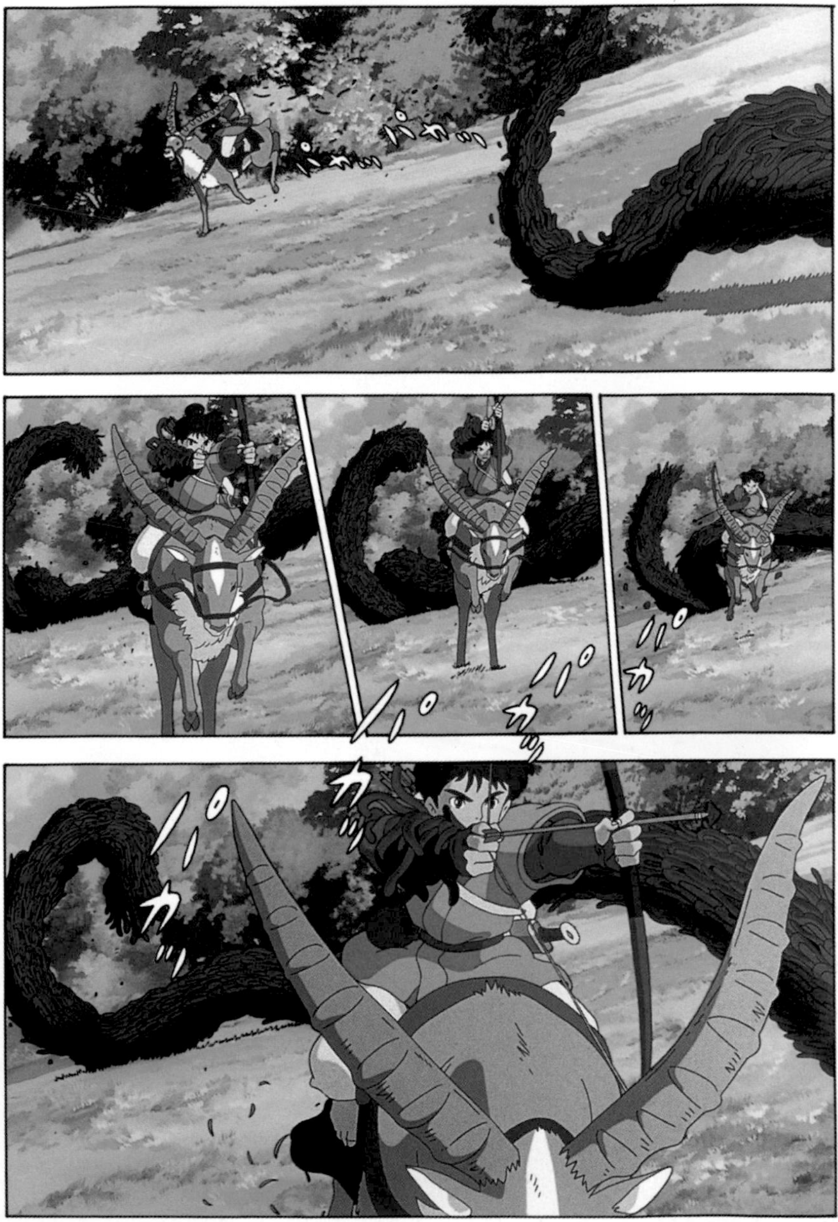
パカッ
パカッ
パカッ
パカッ
パカッ
パカッ

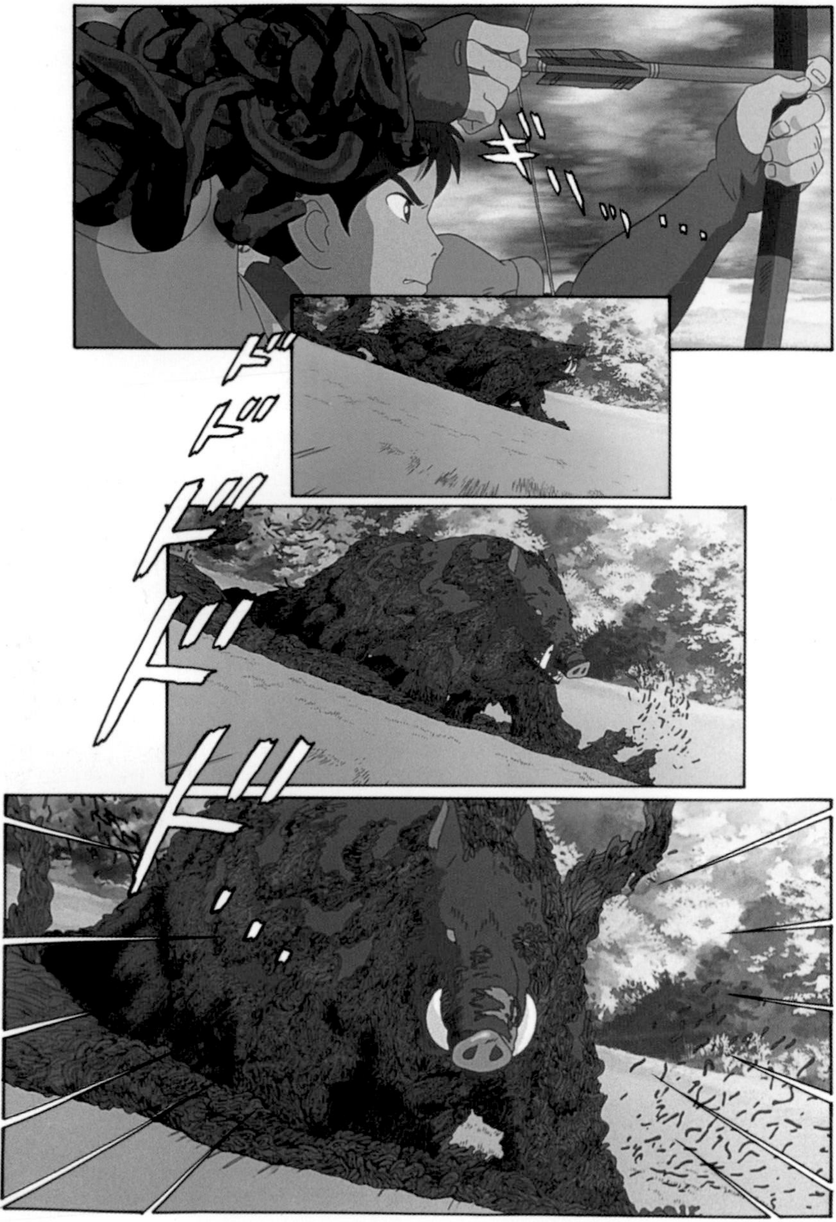
ギリリリ…
ドドドドド…

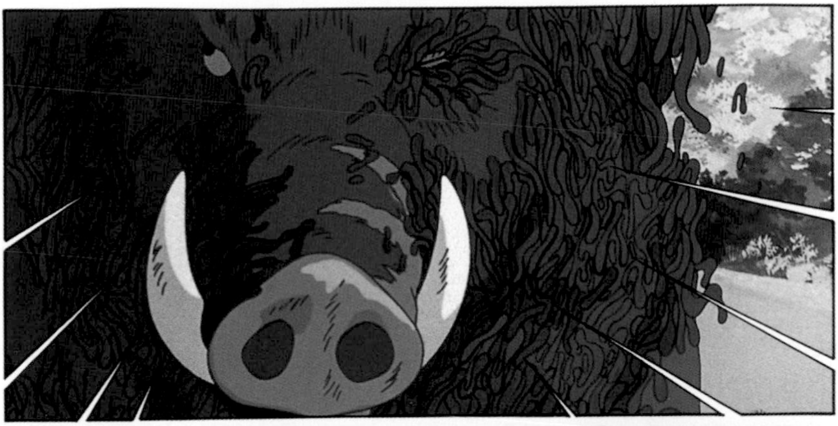
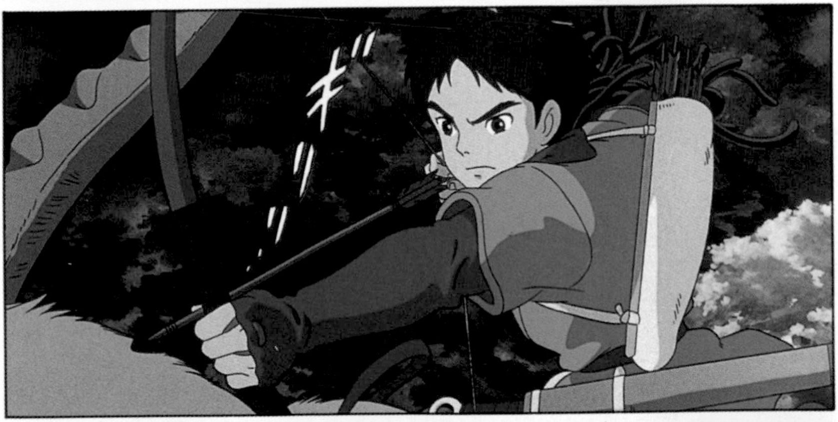
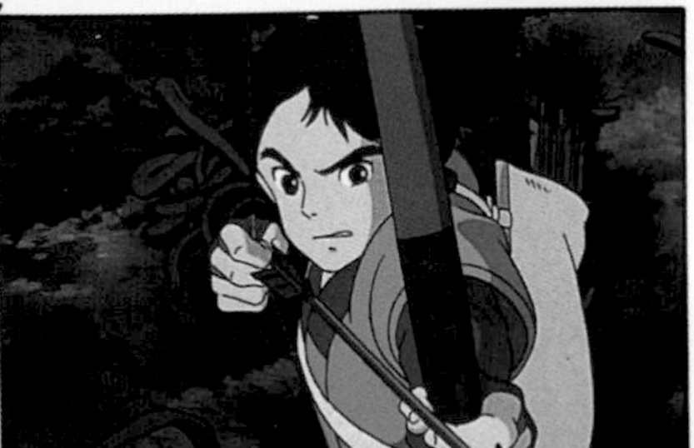
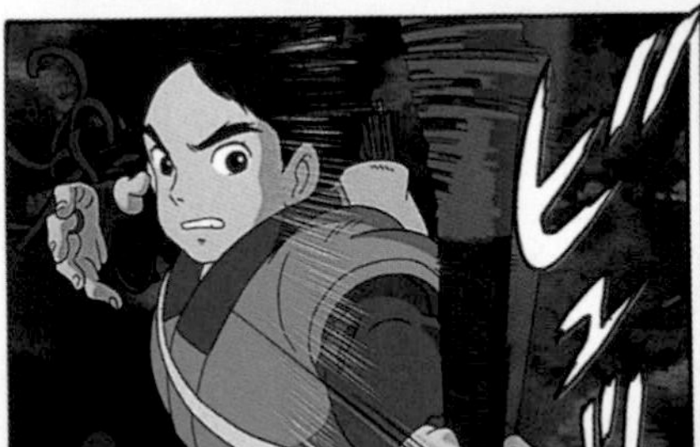

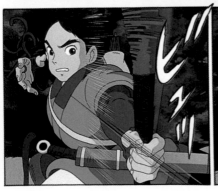

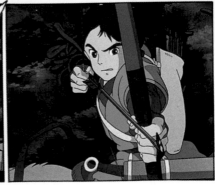

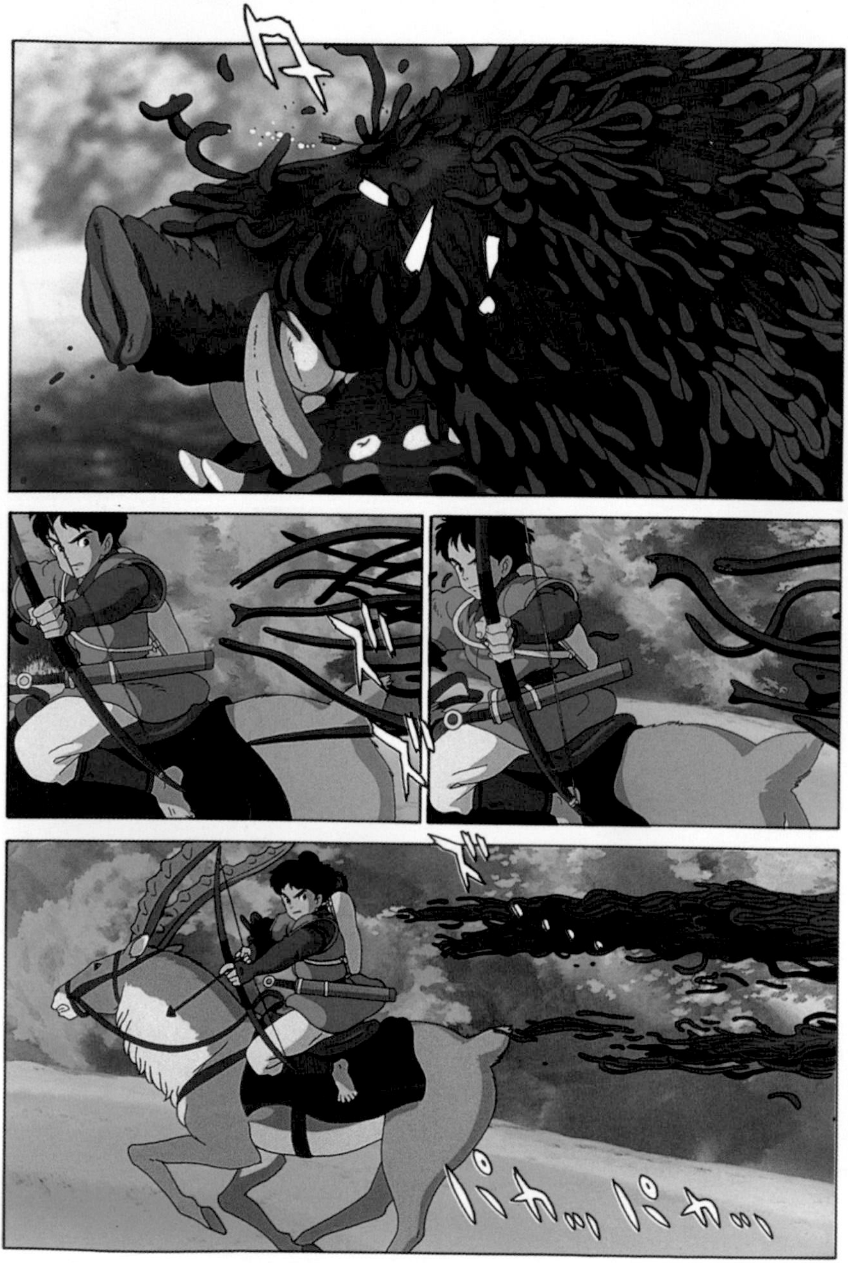
ズ
ズ
ズ
ぱか‥ぱか‥

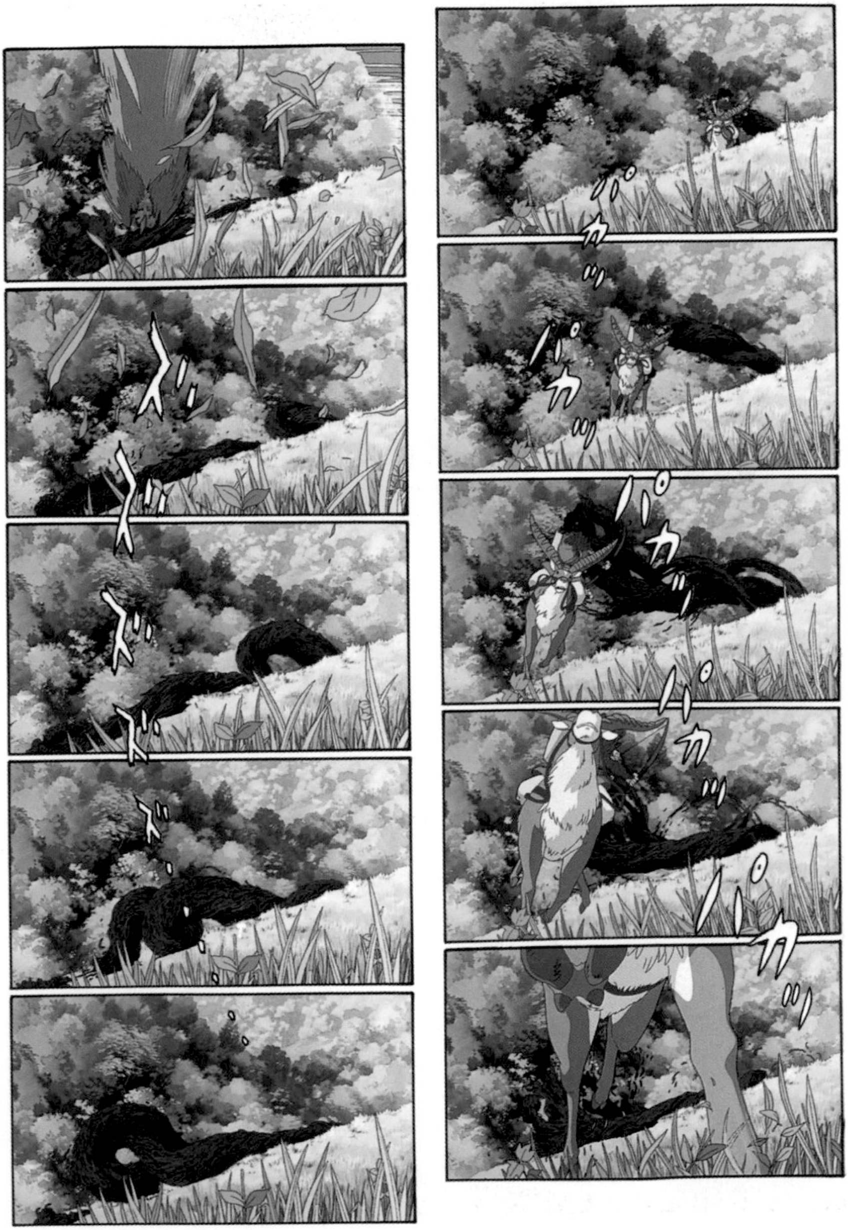

パカッ
パカッ
パカッ
パカッ
パカッ
ズ
ズ
ズ
ズ
ズ

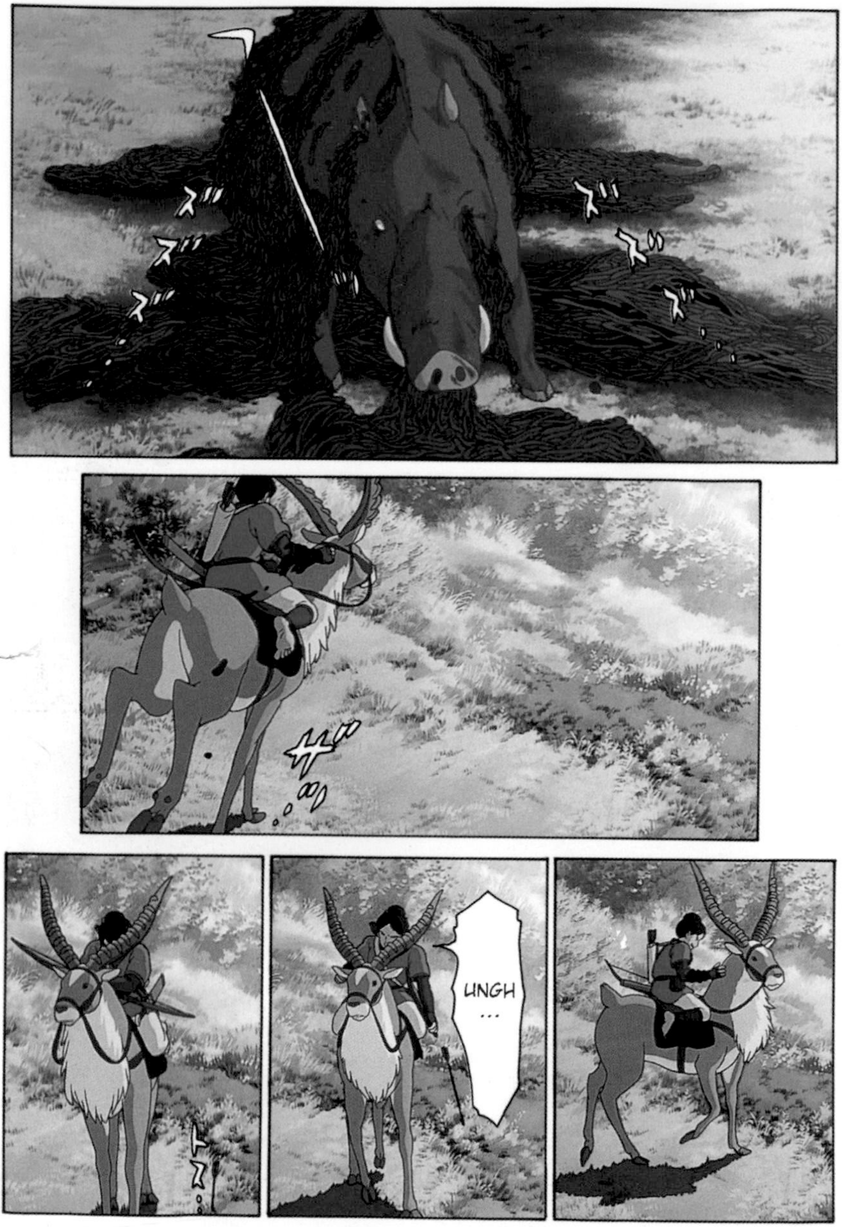
UNGH
...

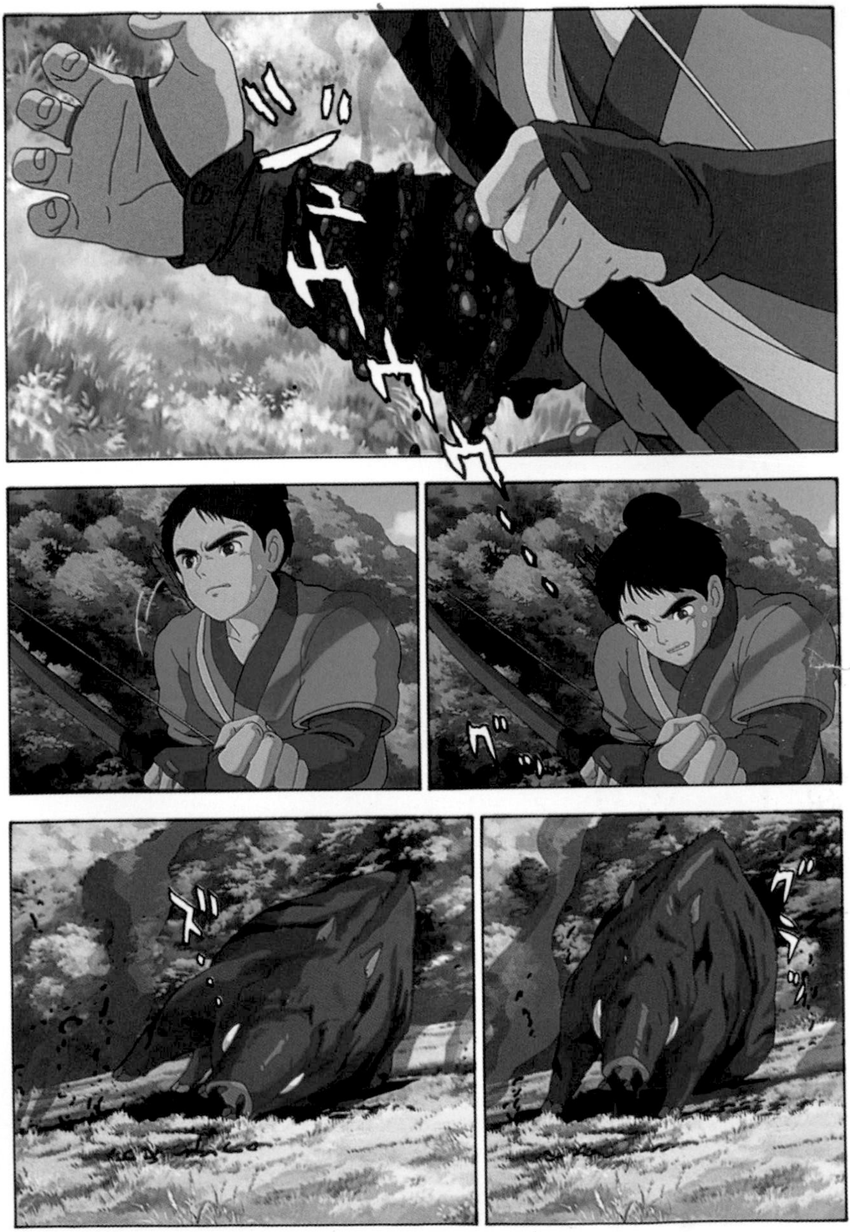

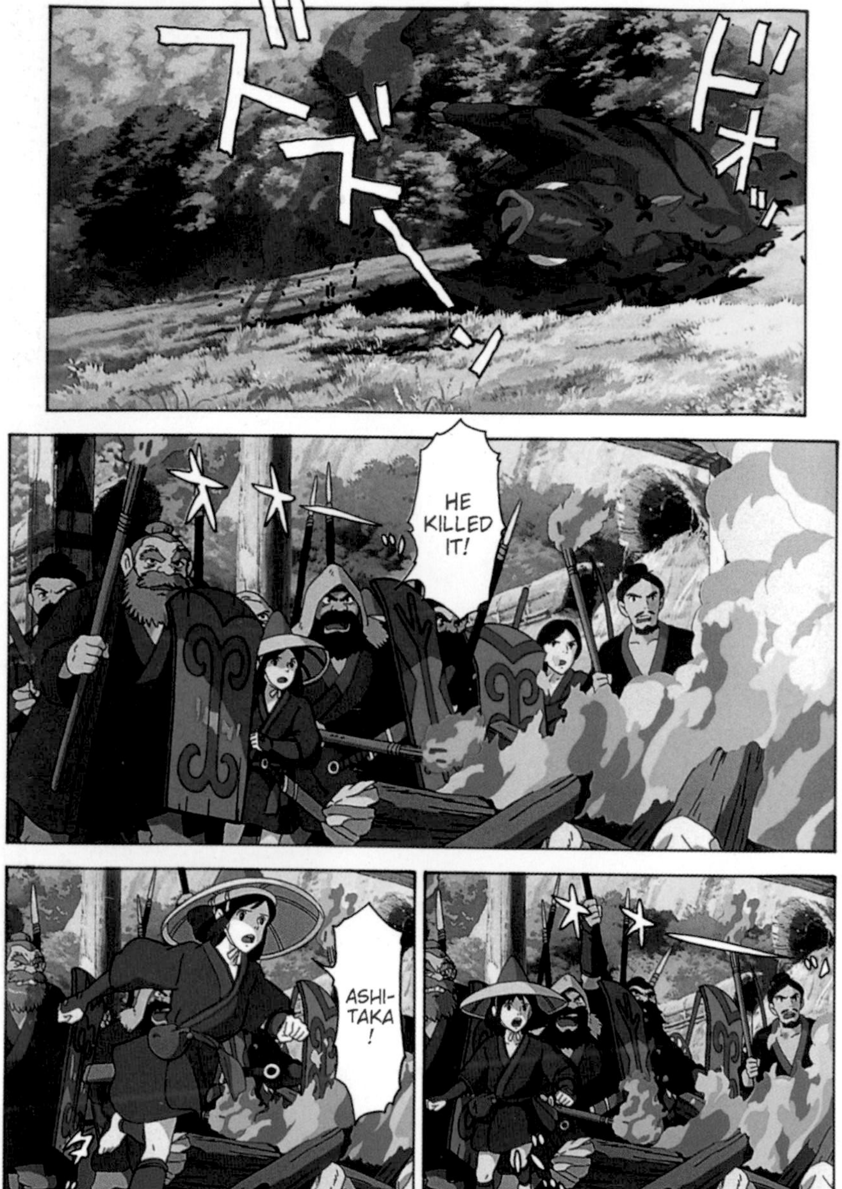
HE KILLED IT!
ASHI-TAKA!

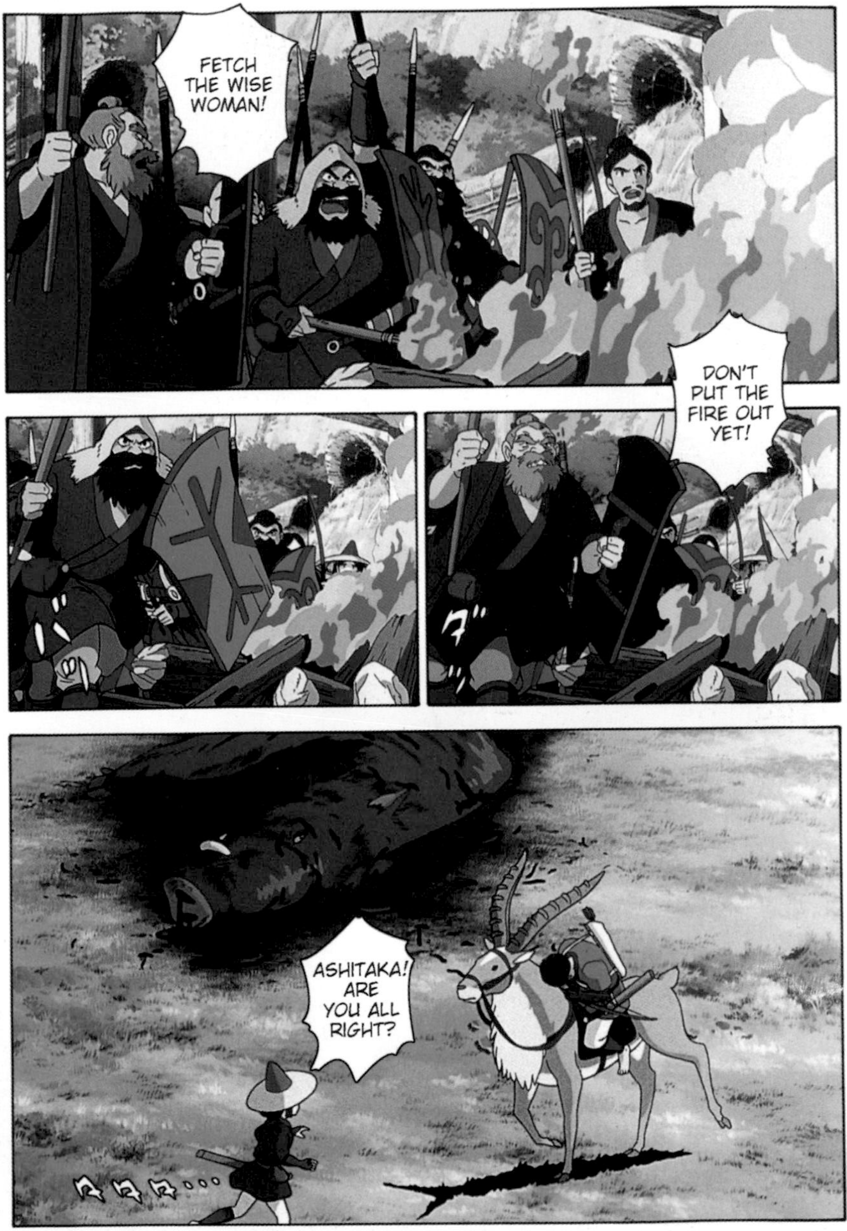
FETCH THE WISE WOMAN!
DON'T PUT THE FIRE OUT YET!
ASHITAKA! ARE YOU ALL RIGHT?

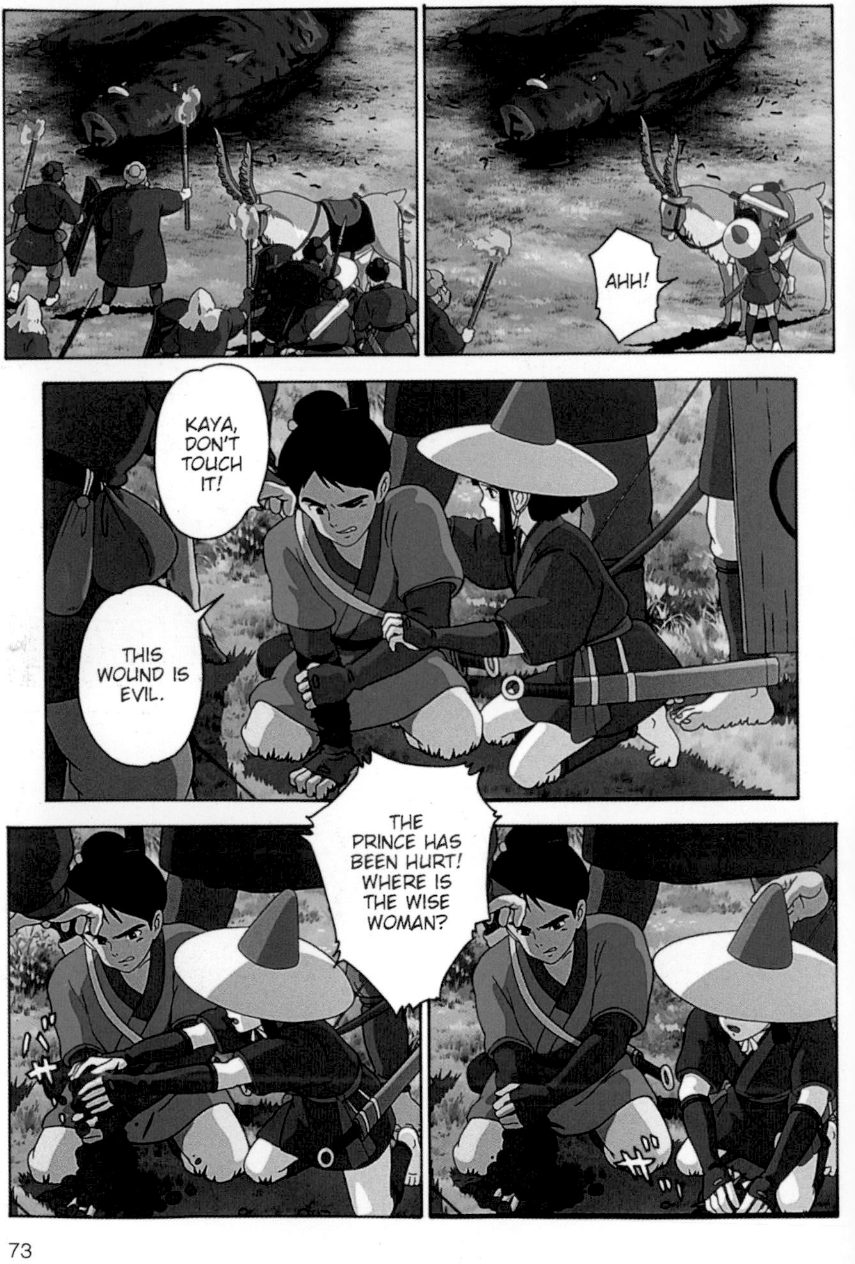
AHH!
KAYA, DON'T TOUCH IT!
THIS WOUND IS EVIL.
THE PRINCE HAS BEEN HURT! WHERE IS THE WISE WOMAN?

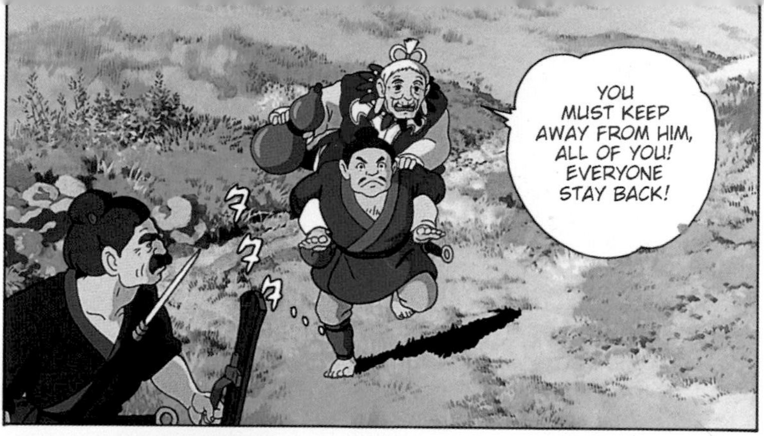
YOU MUST KEEP AWAY FROM HIM, ALL OF YOU! EVERYONE STAY BACK!

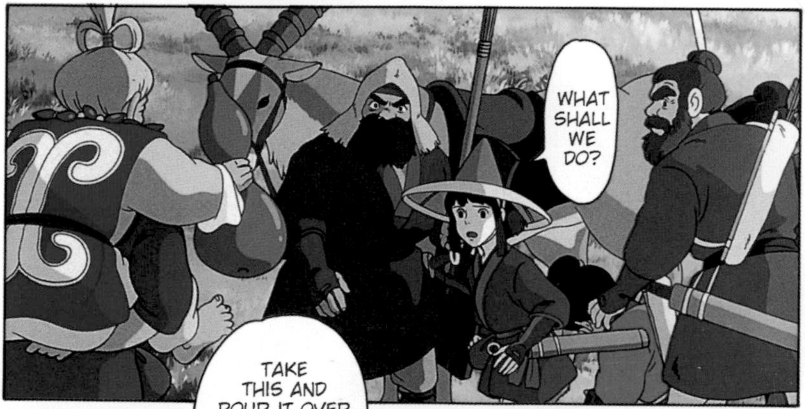
WHAT SHALL WE DO?
TAKE THIS AND POUR IT OVER HIS WOUND. BUT BE CAREFUL!

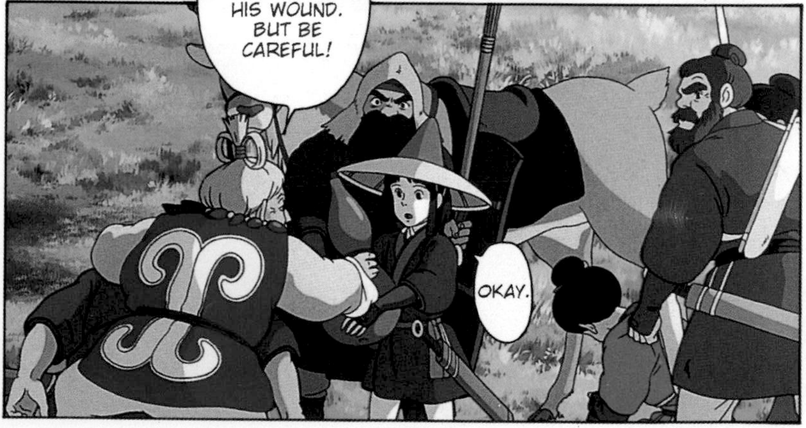
OKAY.

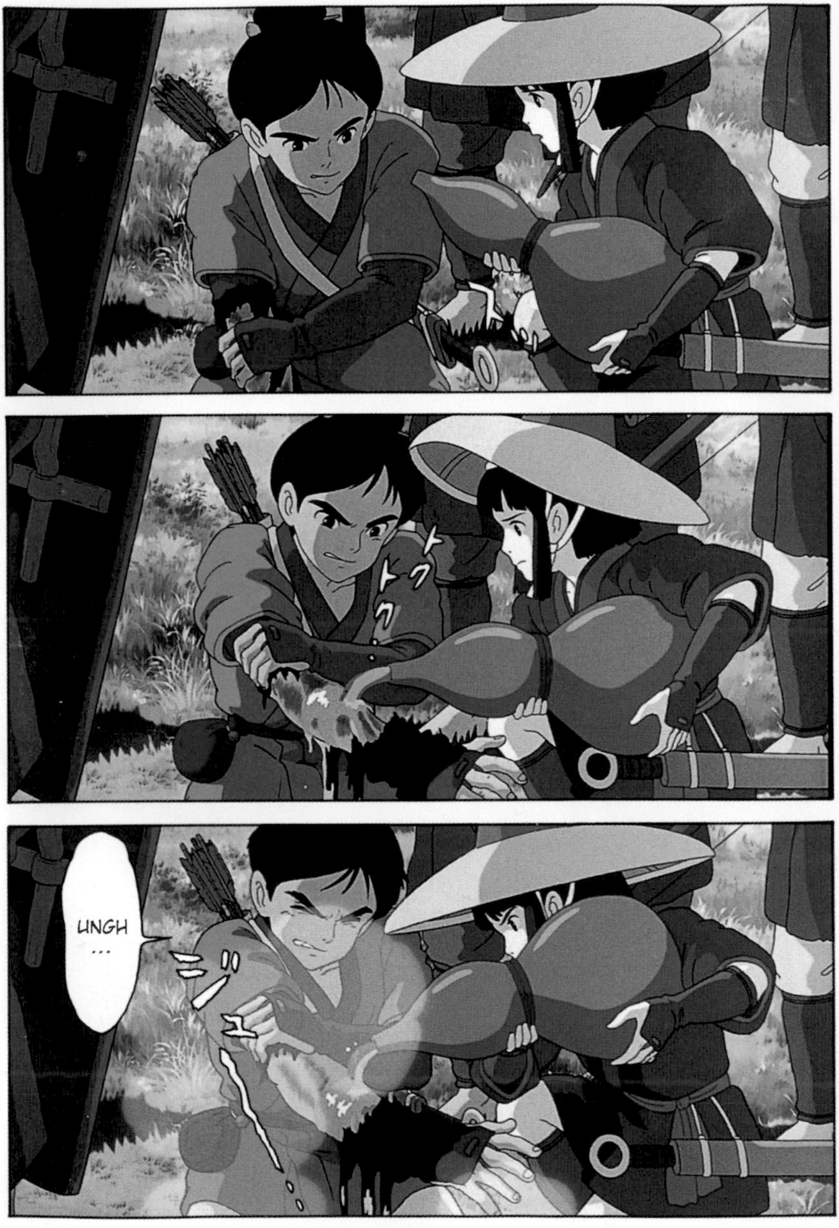
トクトク
UNGH ...

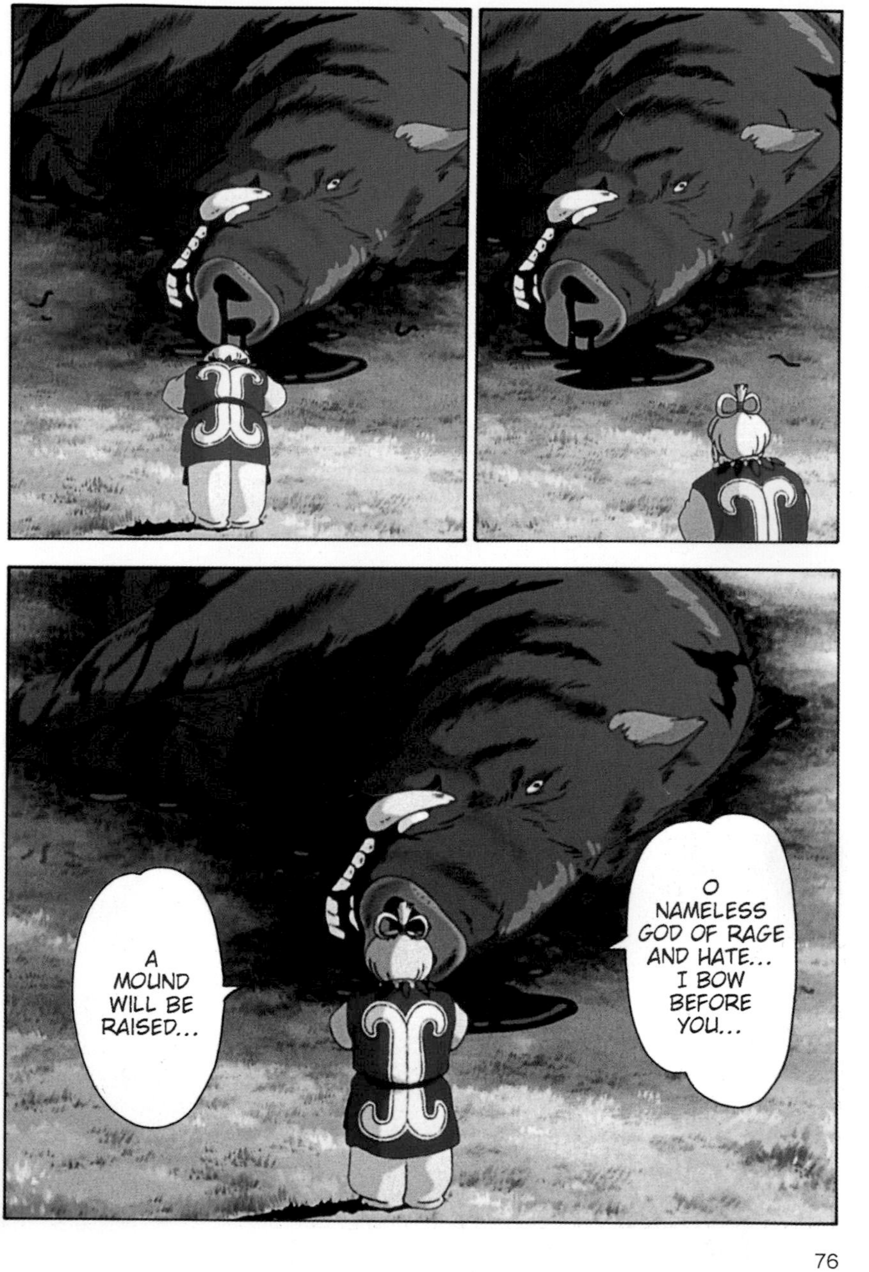
O NAMELESS GOD OF RAGE AND HATE... I BOW BEFORE YOU...
A MOUND WILL BE RAISED...

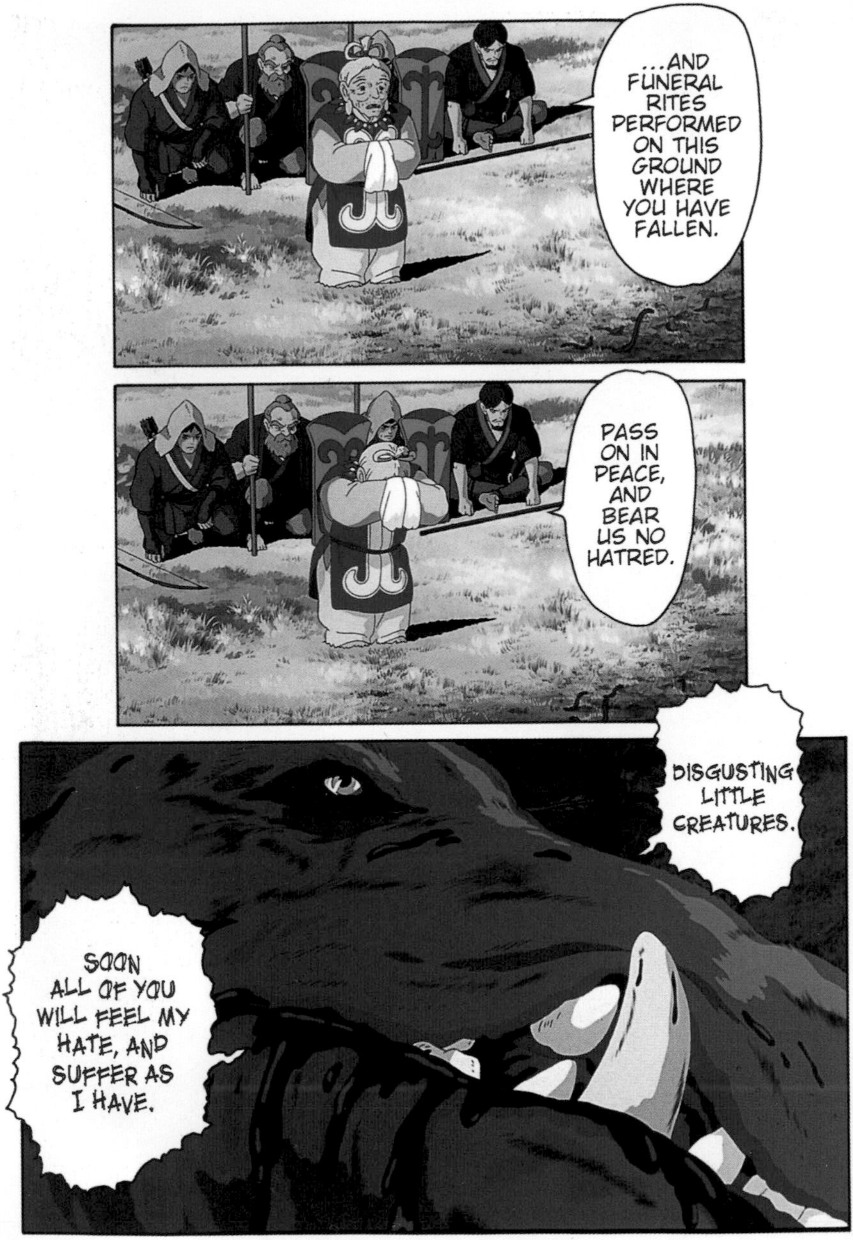
...AND FUNERAL RITES PERFORMED ON THIS GROUND WHERE YOU HAVE FALLEN.
PASS ON IN PEACE, AND BEAR US NO HATRED.
DISGUSTING LITTLE CREATURES.
SOON ALL OF YOU WILL FEEL MY HATE, AND SUFFER AS I HAVE.

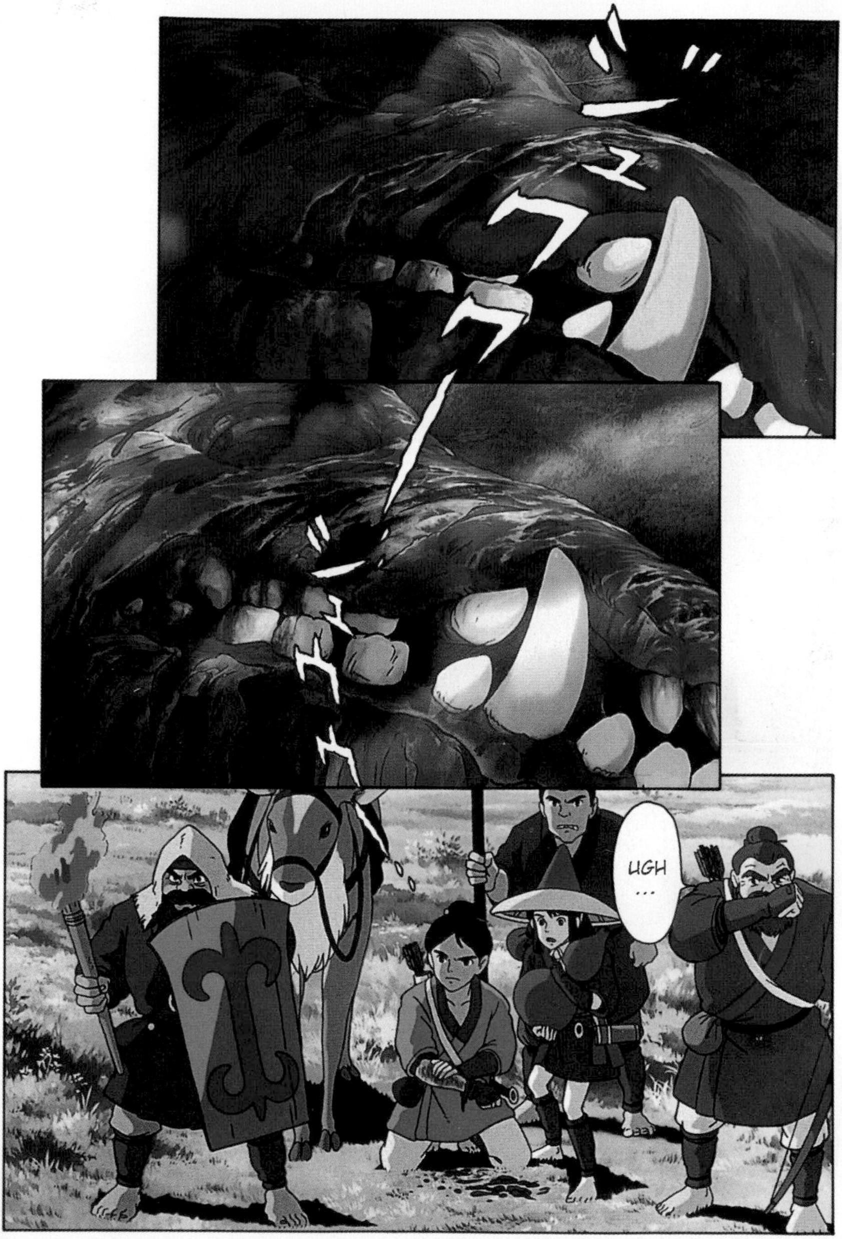
UGH ...

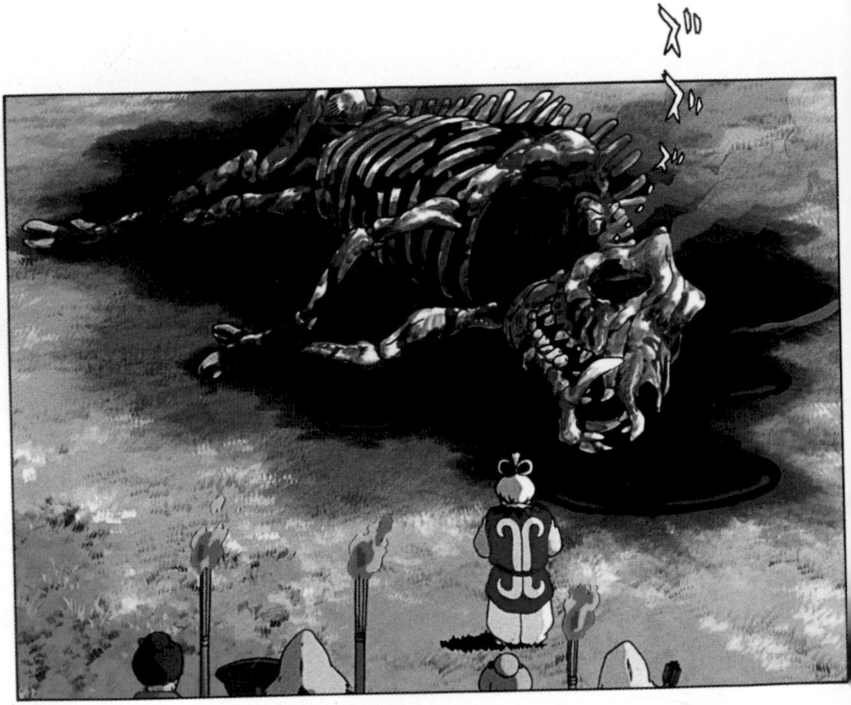
ズズズ

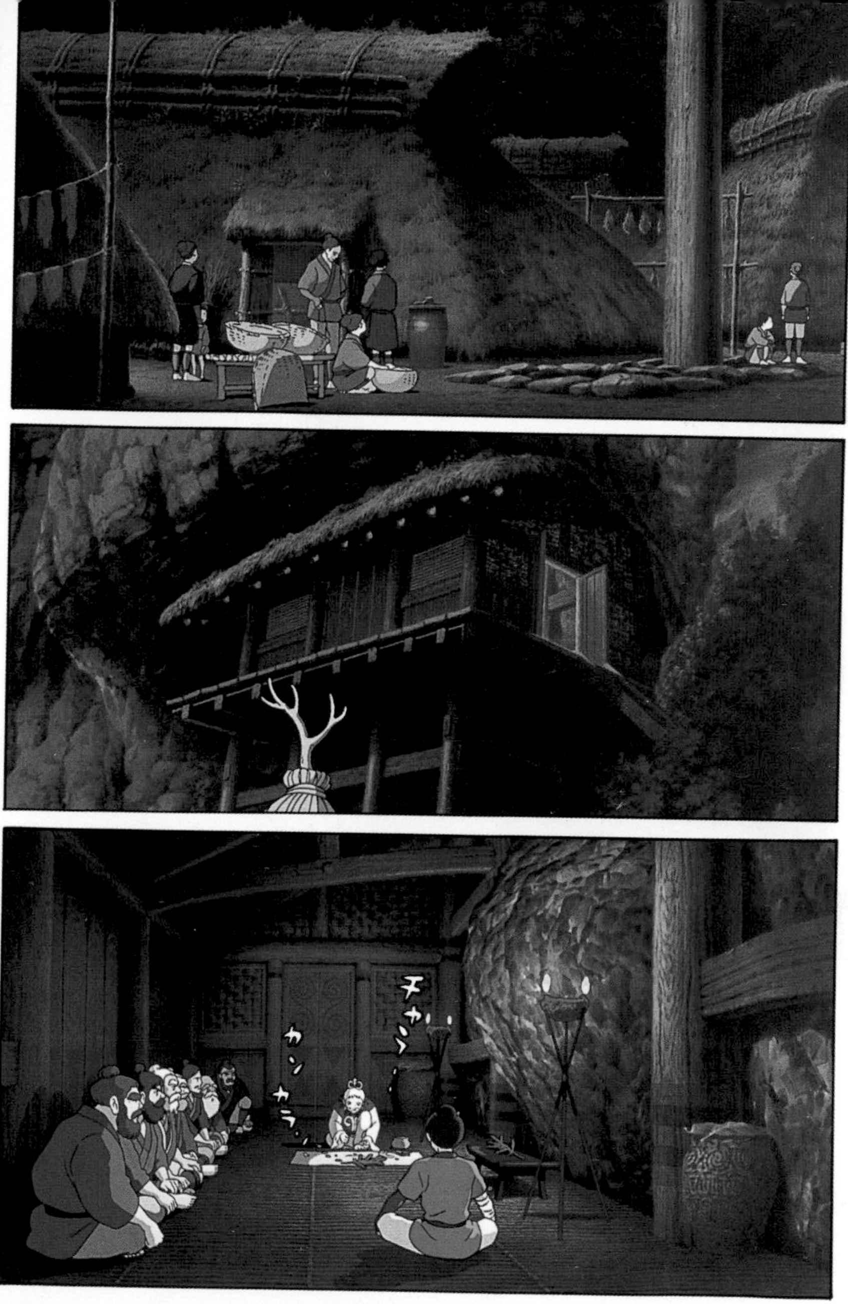
チャン…
カン
カラ…

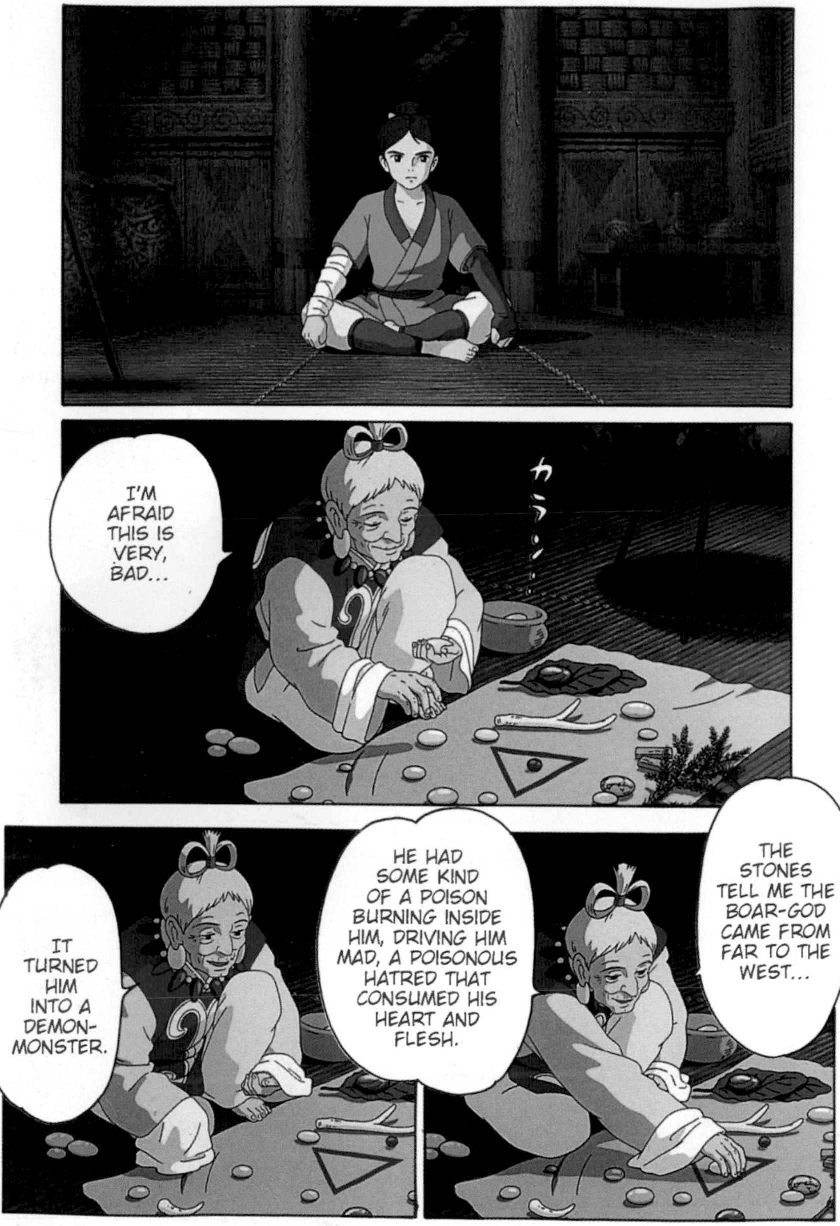
I'M AFRAID THIS IS VERY, BAD...
カラ…
THE STONES TELL ME THE BOAR-GOD CAME FROM FAR TO THE WEST...
HE HAD SOME KIND OF A POISON BURNING INSIDE HIM, DRIVING HIM MAD, A POISONOUS HATRED THAT CONSUMED HIS HEART AND FLESH.
IT TURNED HIM INTO A DEMON-MONSTER.

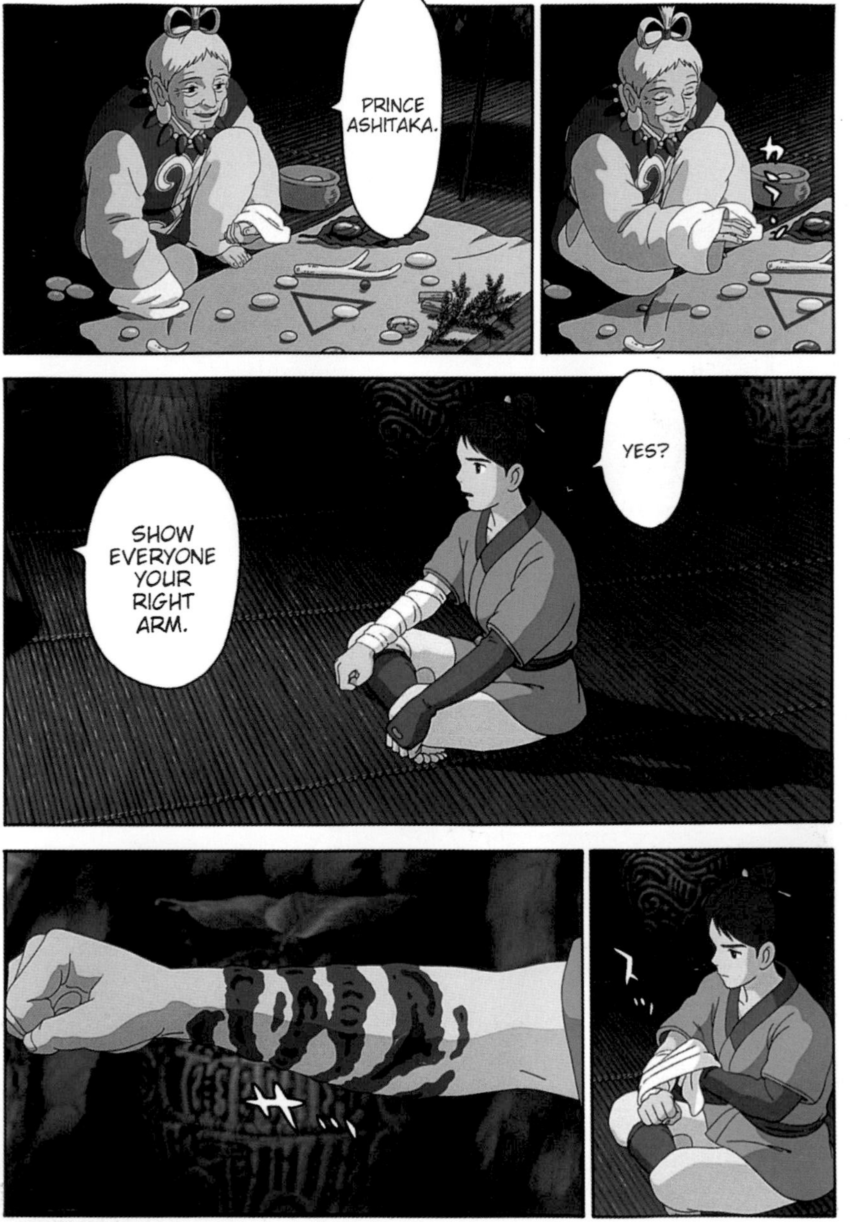
PRINCE ASHITAKA.
YES?
SHOW EVERYONE YOUR RIGHT ARM.

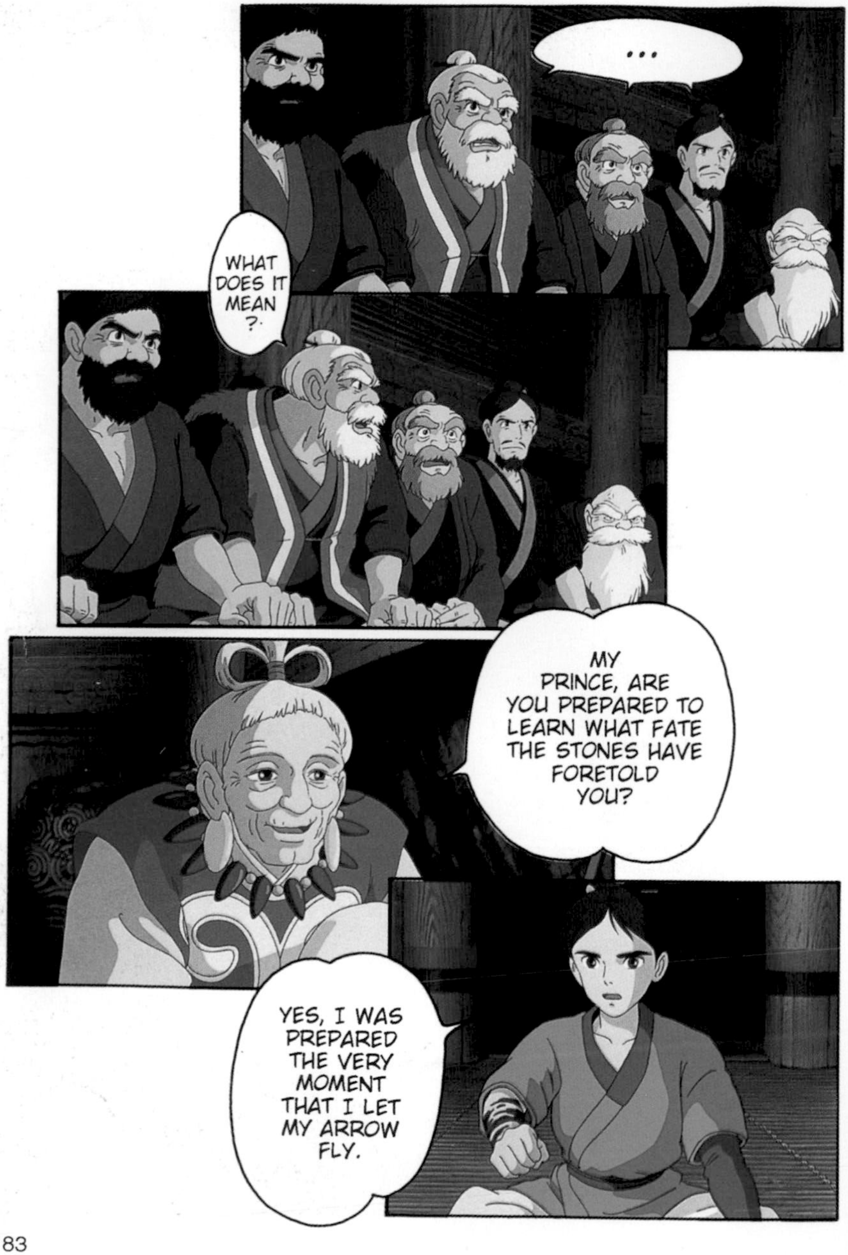
...
WHAT DOES IT MEAN?
MY PRINCE, ARE YOU PREPARED TO LEARN WHAT FATE THE STONES HAVE FORETOLD YOU?
YES, I WAS PREPARED THE VERY MOMENT THAT I LET MY ARROW FLY.

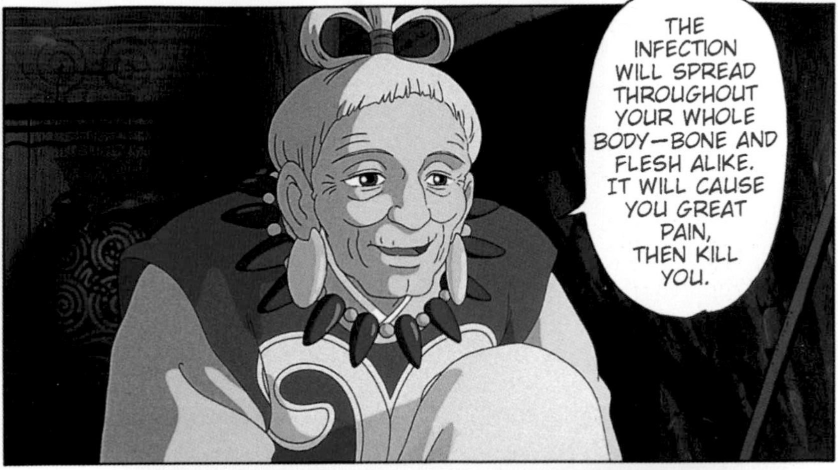
THE INFECTION WILL SPREAD THROUGHOUT YOUR WHOLE BODY—BONE AND FLESH ALIKE. IT WILL CAUSE YOU GREAT PAIN, THEN KILL YOU.

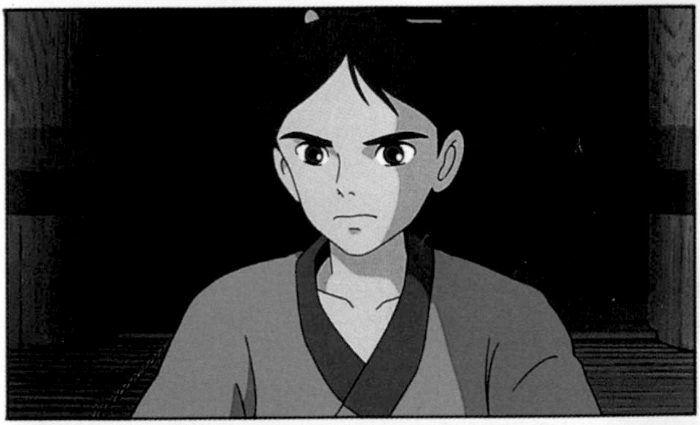

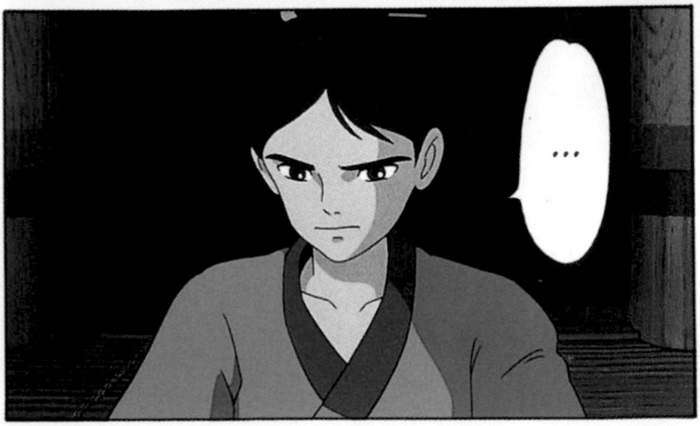
...

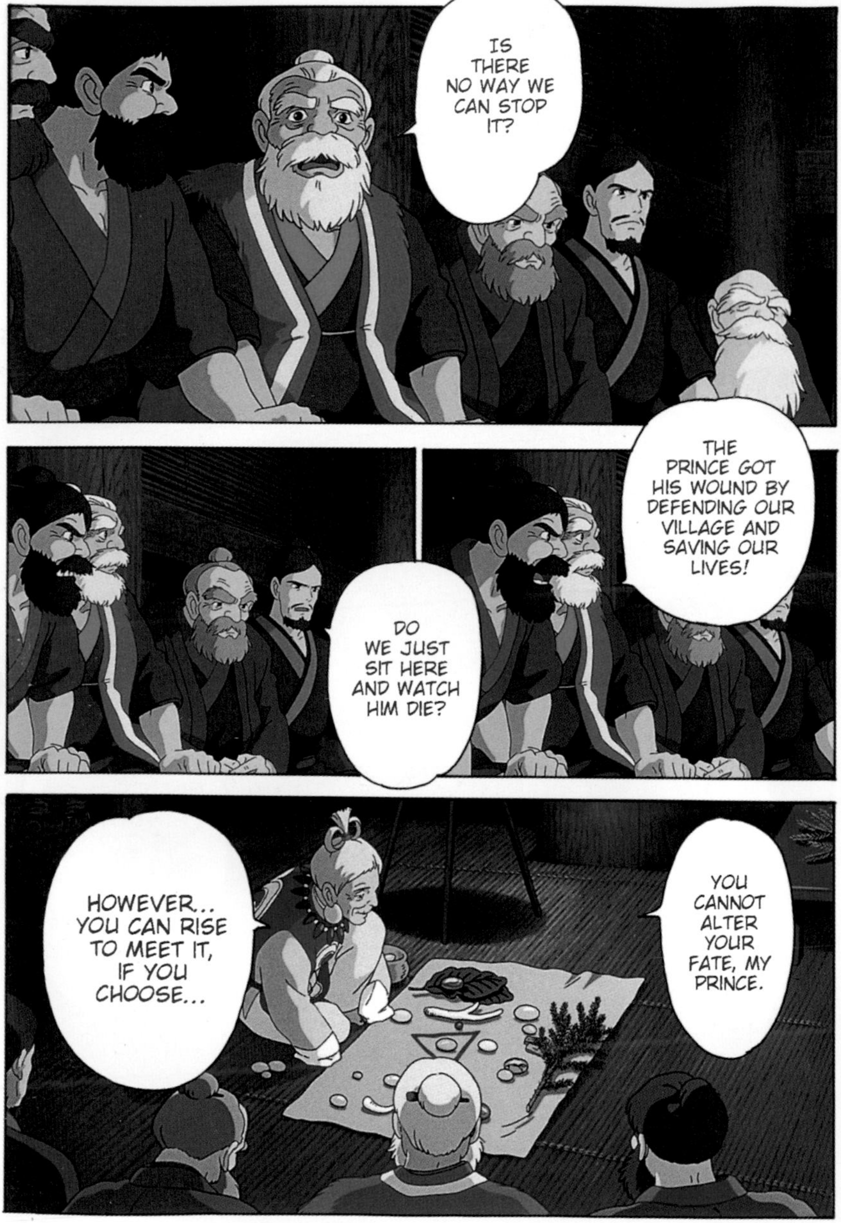
IS THERE NO WAY WE CAN STOP IT?
THE PRINCE GOT HIS WOUND BY DEFENDING OUR VILLAGE AND SAVING OUR LIVES!
DO WE JUST SIT HERE AND WATCH HIM DIE?
YOU CANNOT ALTER YOUR FATE, MY PRINCE.
HOWEVER... YOU CAN RISE TO MEET IT, IF YOU CHOOSE...

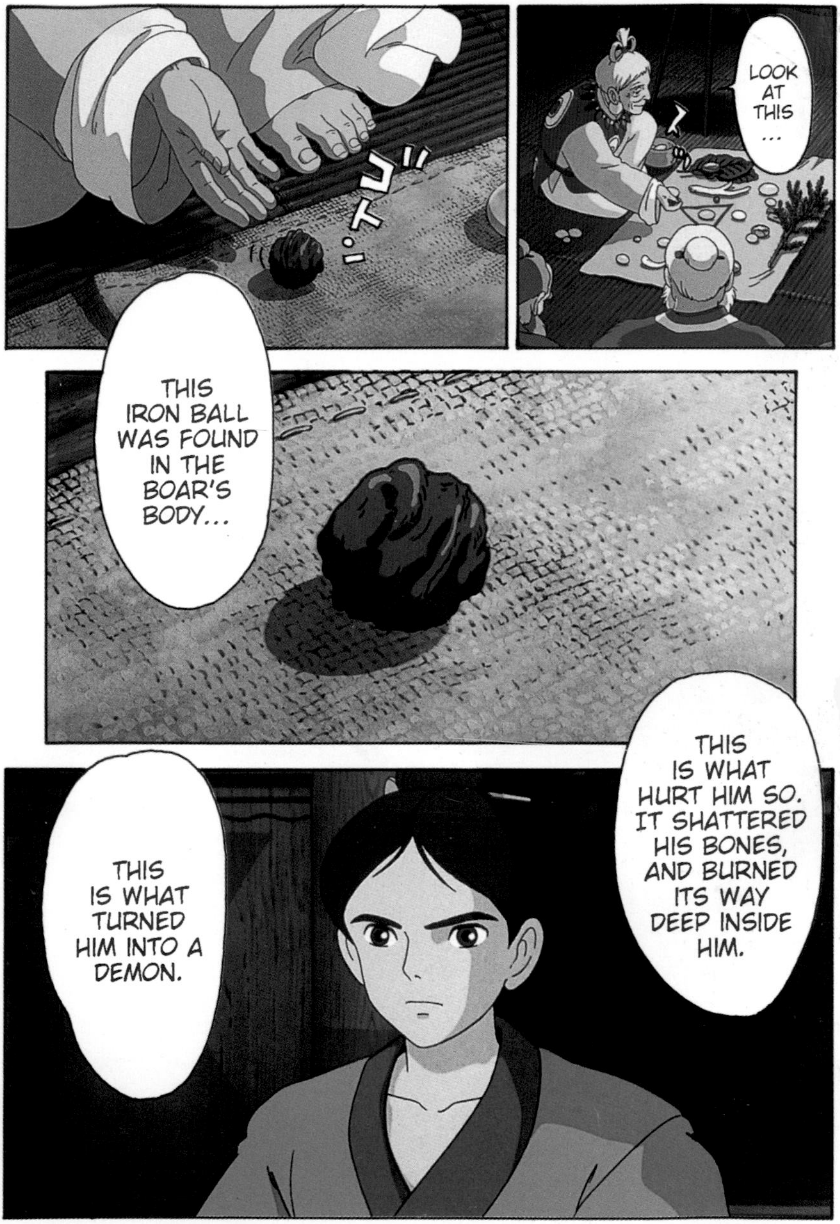
LOOK AT THIS ...
THIS IRON BALL WAS FOUND IN THE BOAR'S BODY...
THIS IS WHAT HURT HIM SO. IT SHATTERED HIS BONES, AND BURNED ITS WAY DEEP INSIDE HIM.
THIS IS WHAT TURNED HIM INTO A DEMON.

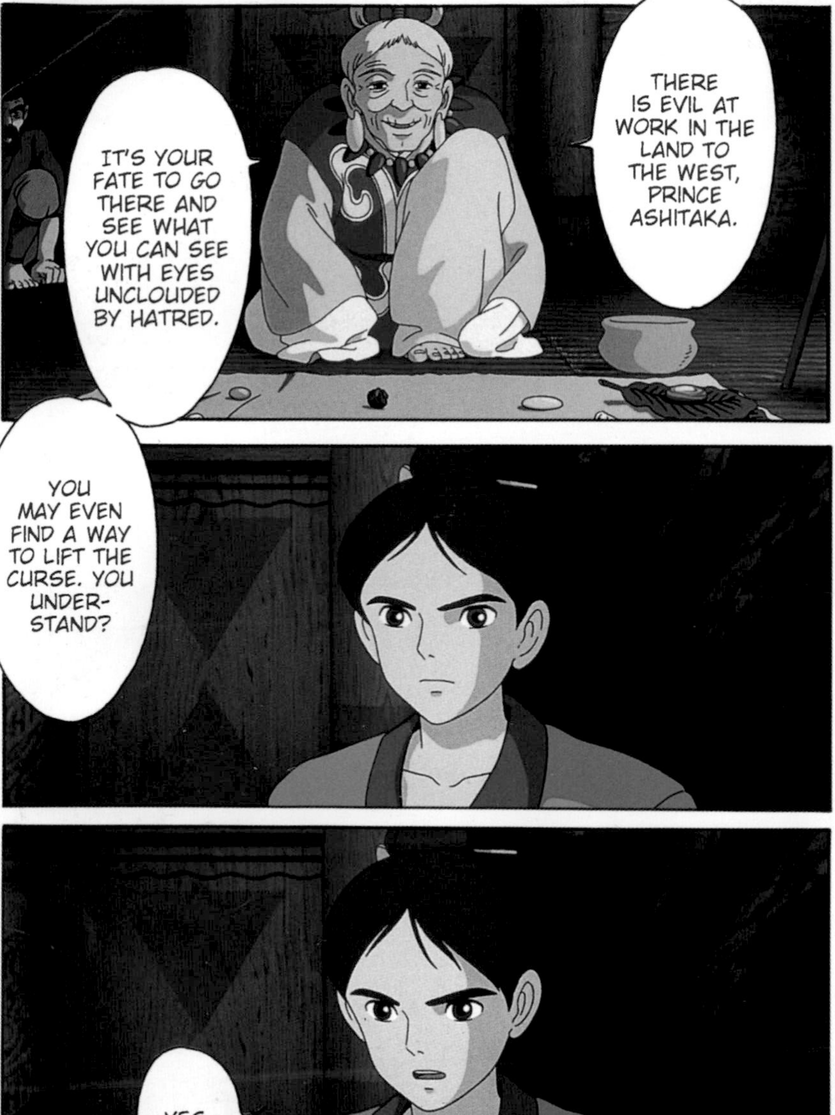
THERE IS EVIL AT WORK IN THE LAND TO THE WEST, PRINCE ASHITAKA.
IT'S YOUR FATE TO GO THERE AND SEE WHAT YOU CAN SEE WITH EYES UNCLOUDED BY HATRED.
YOU MAY EVEN FIND A WAY TO LIFT THE CURSE. YOU UNDER-STAND?
YES.

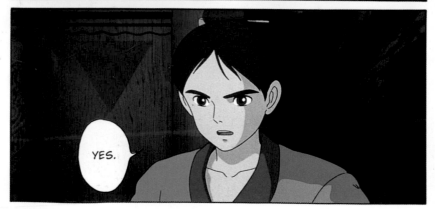

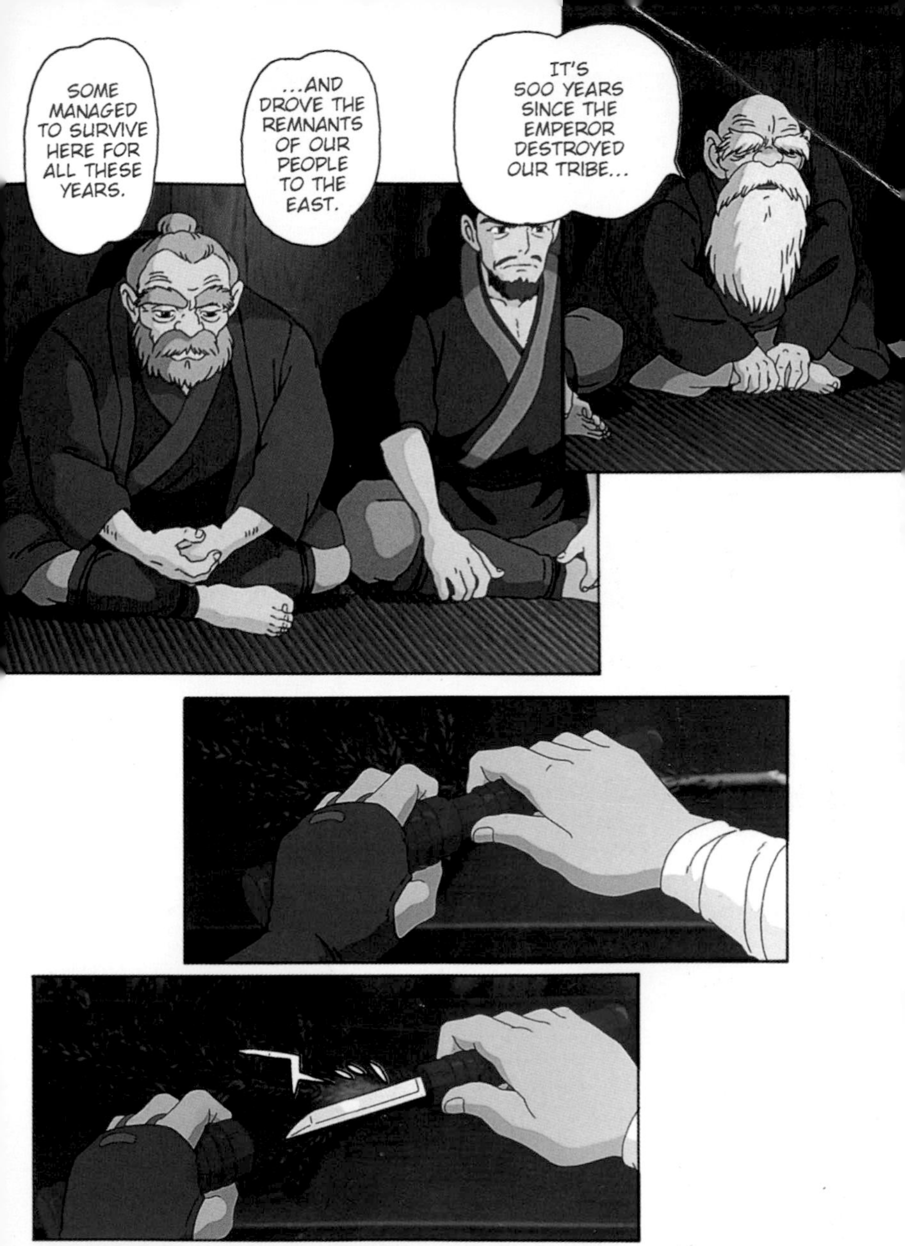
IT'S 500 YEARS SINCE THE EMPEROR DESTROYED OUR TRIBE...
...AND DROVE THE REMNANTS OF OUR PEOPLE TO THE EAST.
SOME MANAGED TO SURVIVE HERE FOR ALL THESE YEARS.

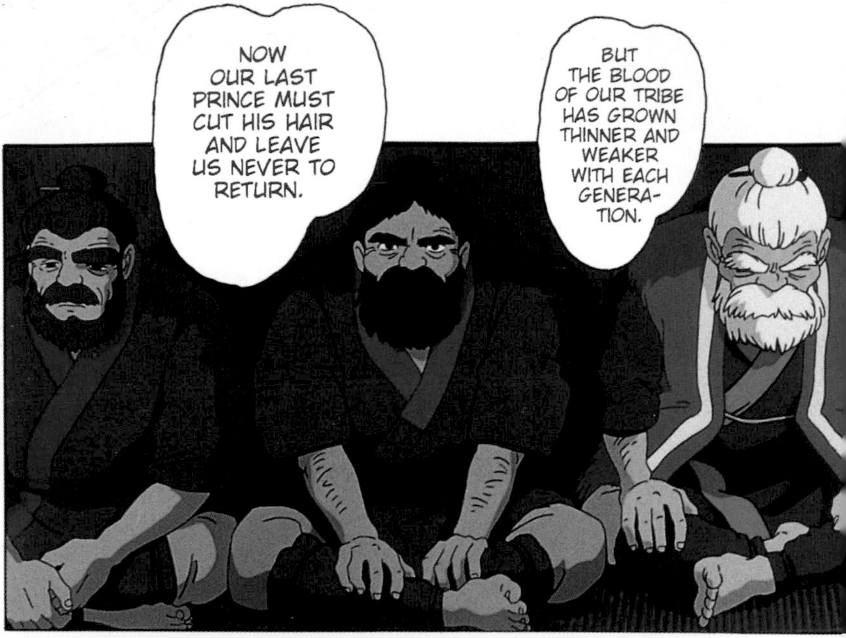
BUT THE BLOOD OF OUR TRIBE HAS GROWN THINNER AND WEAKER WITH EACH GENERATION.
NOW OUR LAST PRINCE MUST CUT HIS HAIR AND LEAVE US NEVER TO RETURN.

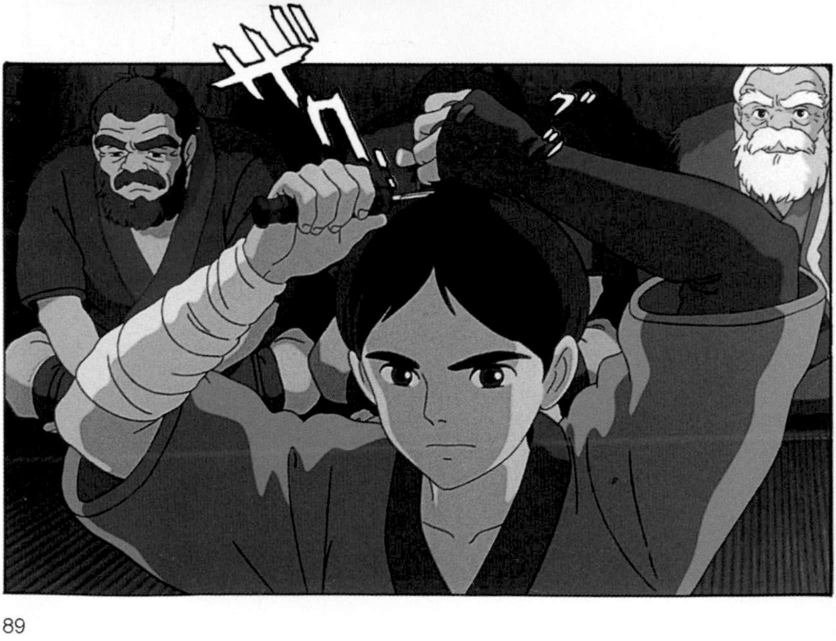

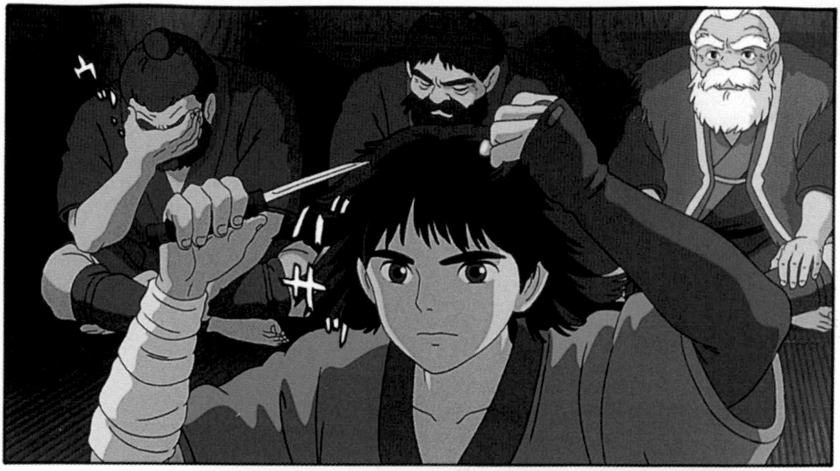
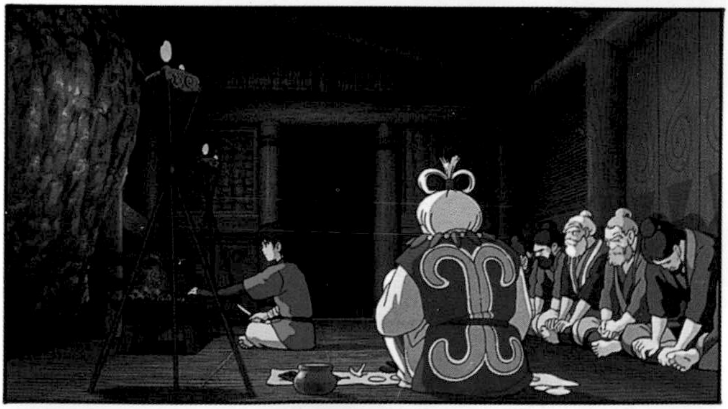
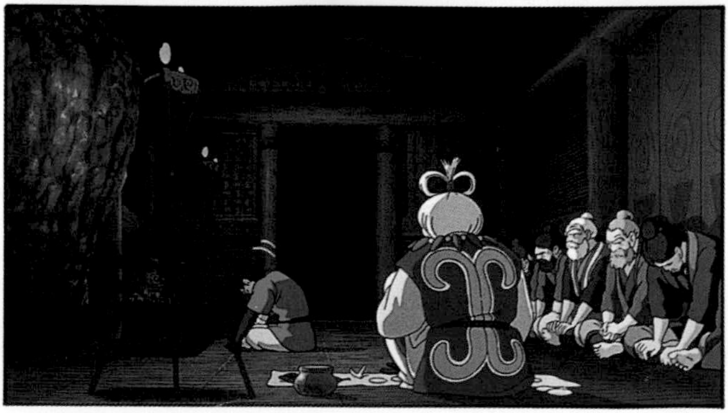

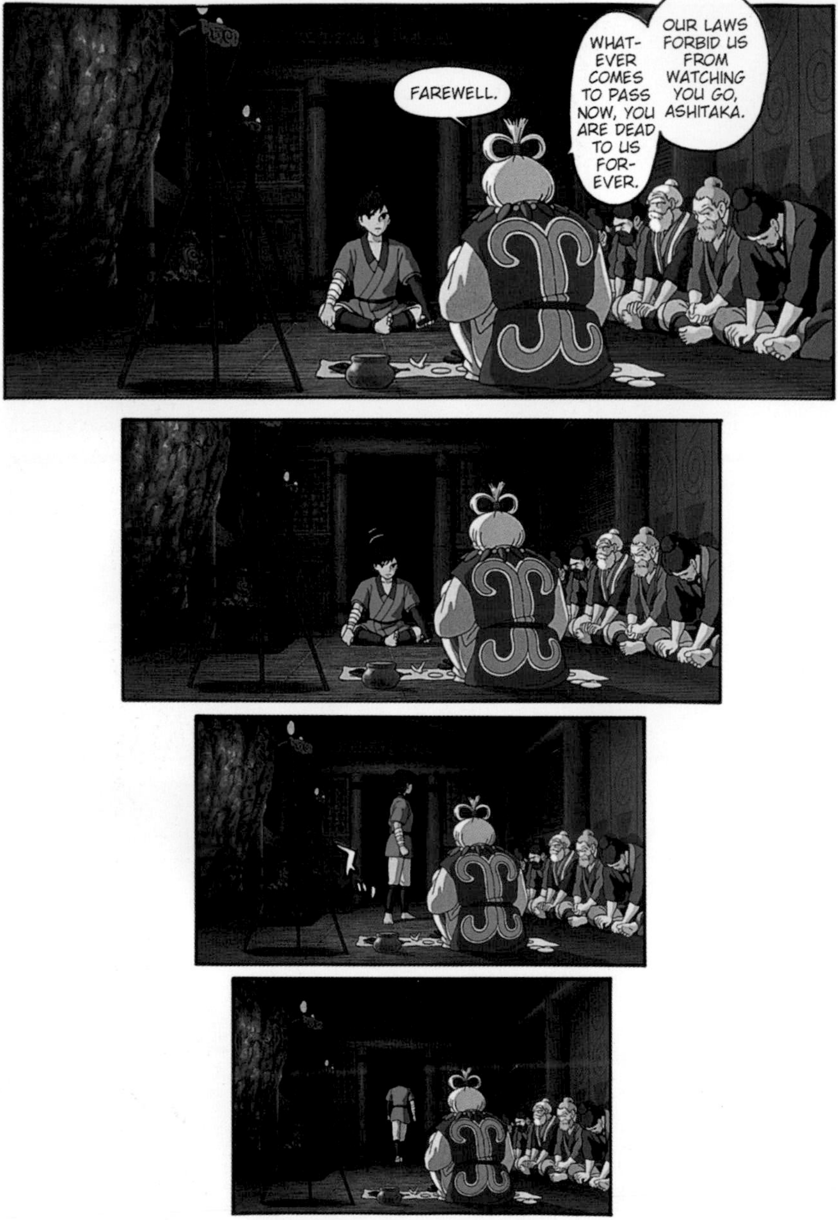
OUR LAWS FORBID US FROM WATCHING YOU GO, ASHITAKA.
WHATEVER COMES TO PASS NOW, YOU ARE DEAD TO US FOREVER.
FAREWELL.

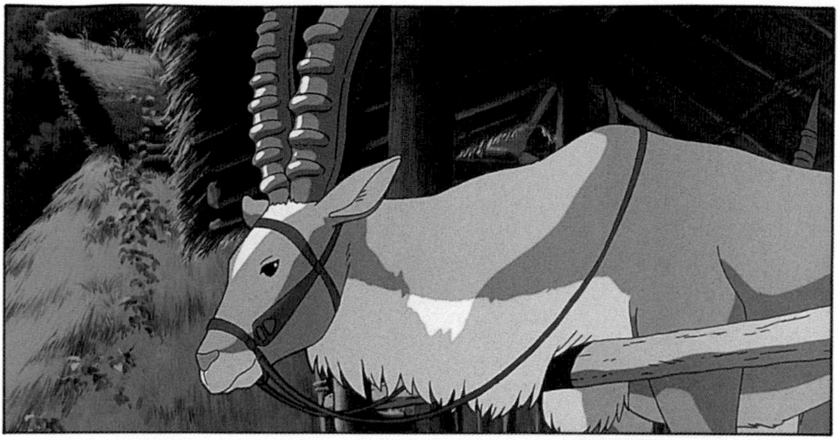

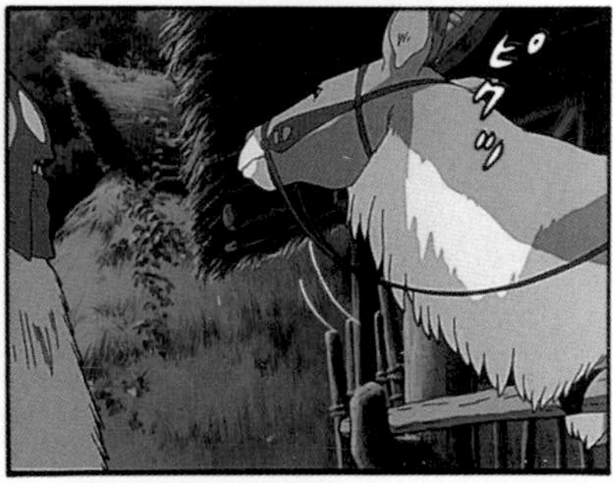
ピクッ

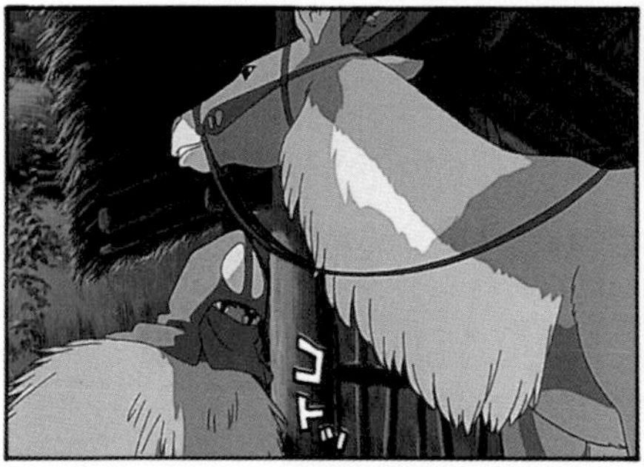
コトッ

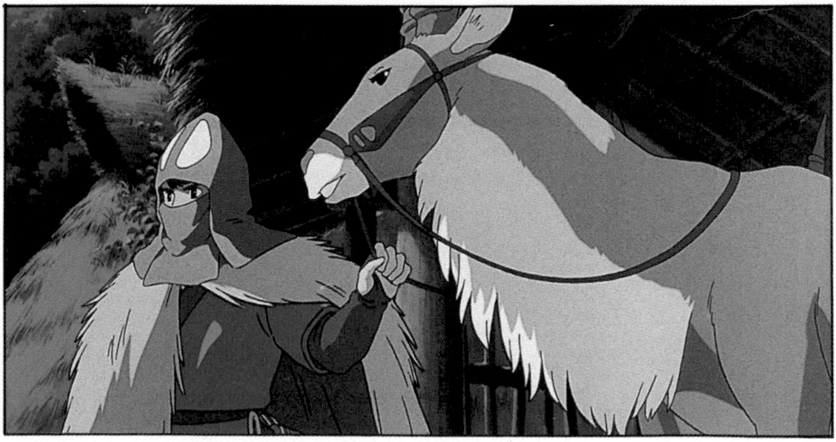

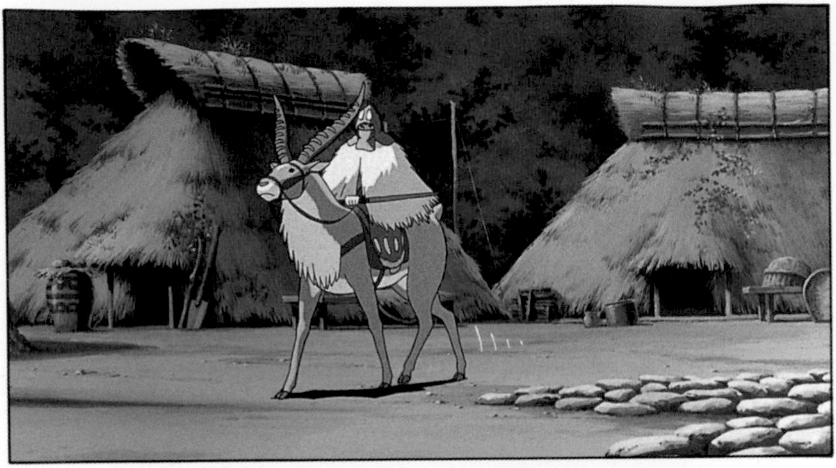

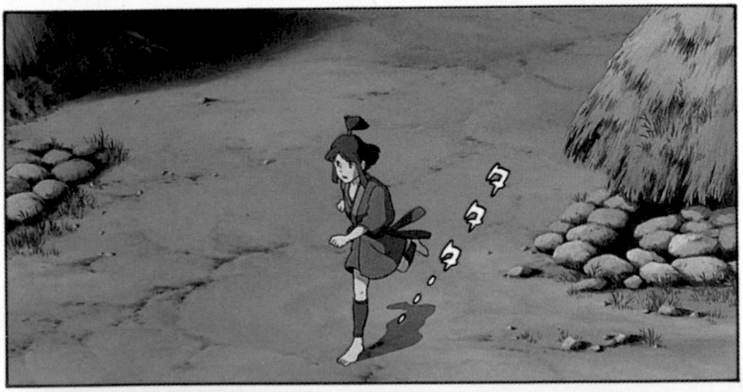

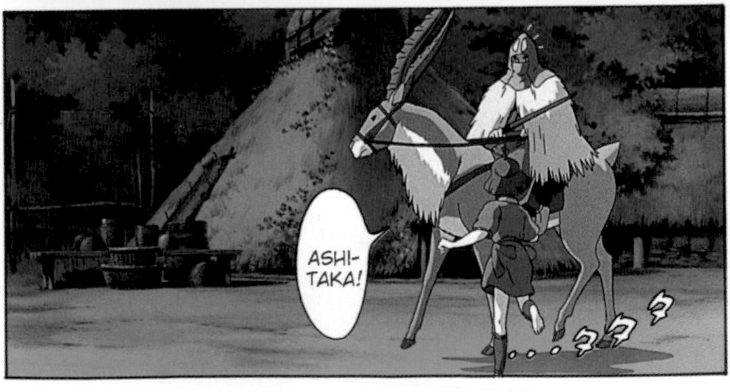
ASHI-
TAKA!

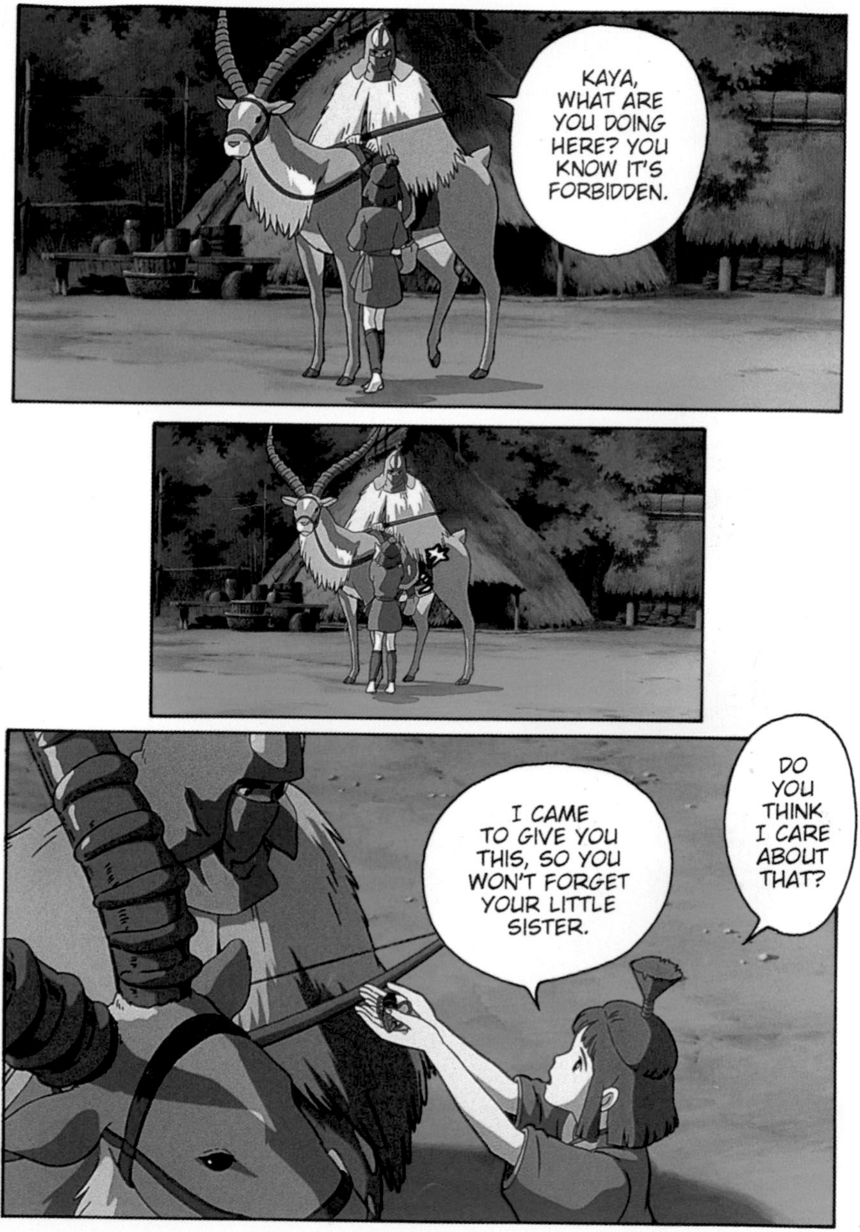
KAYA, WHAT ARE YOU DOING HERE? YOU KNOW IT'S FORBIDDEN.
DO YOU THINK I CARE ABOUT THAT?
I CAME TO GIVE YOU THIS, SO YOU WON'T FORGET YOUR LITTLE SISTER.

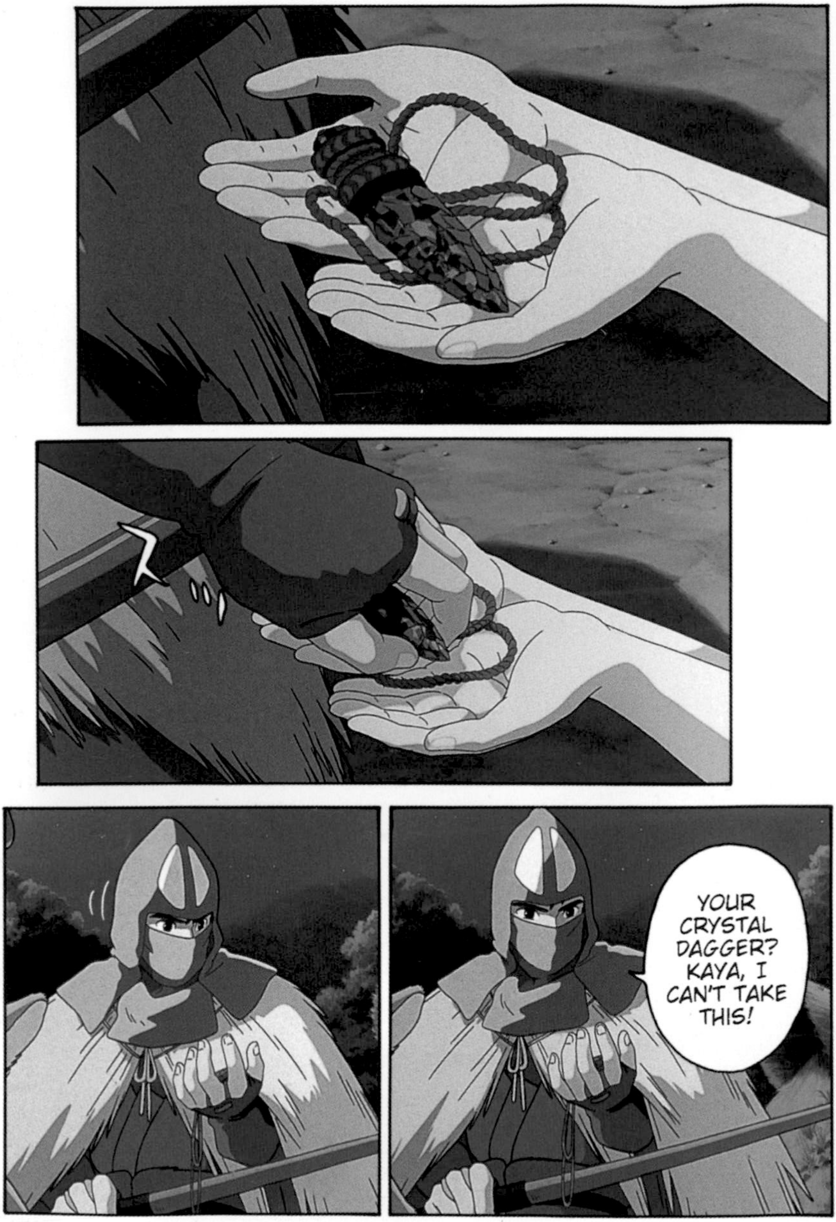
YOUR CRYSTAL DAGGER? KAYA, I CAN'T TAKE THIS!

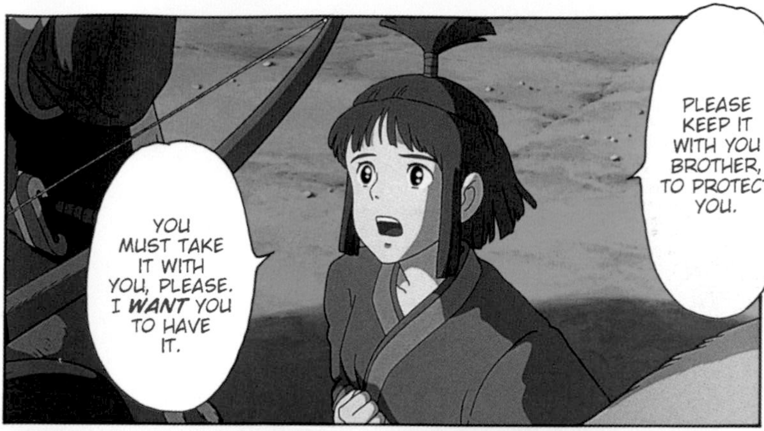
PLEASE KEEP IT WITH YOU BROTHER, TO PROTECT YOU.
YOU MUST TAKE IT WITH YOU, PLEASE. I *WANT* YOU TO HAVE IT.

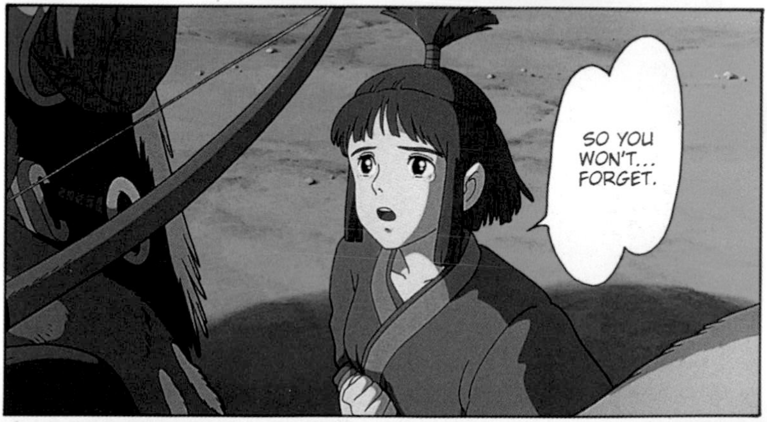
SO YOU WON'T... FORGET.

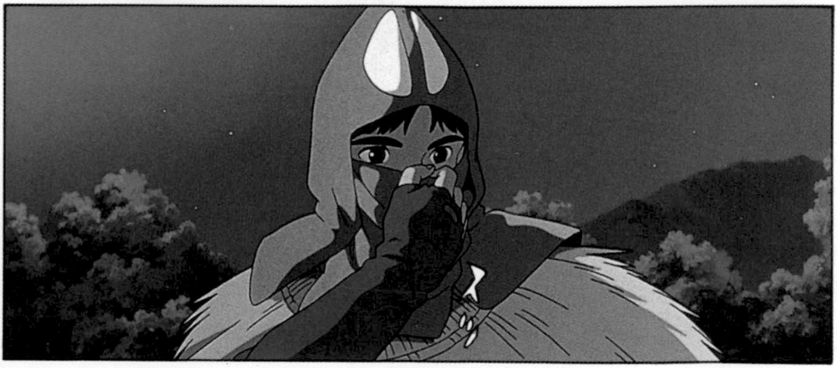

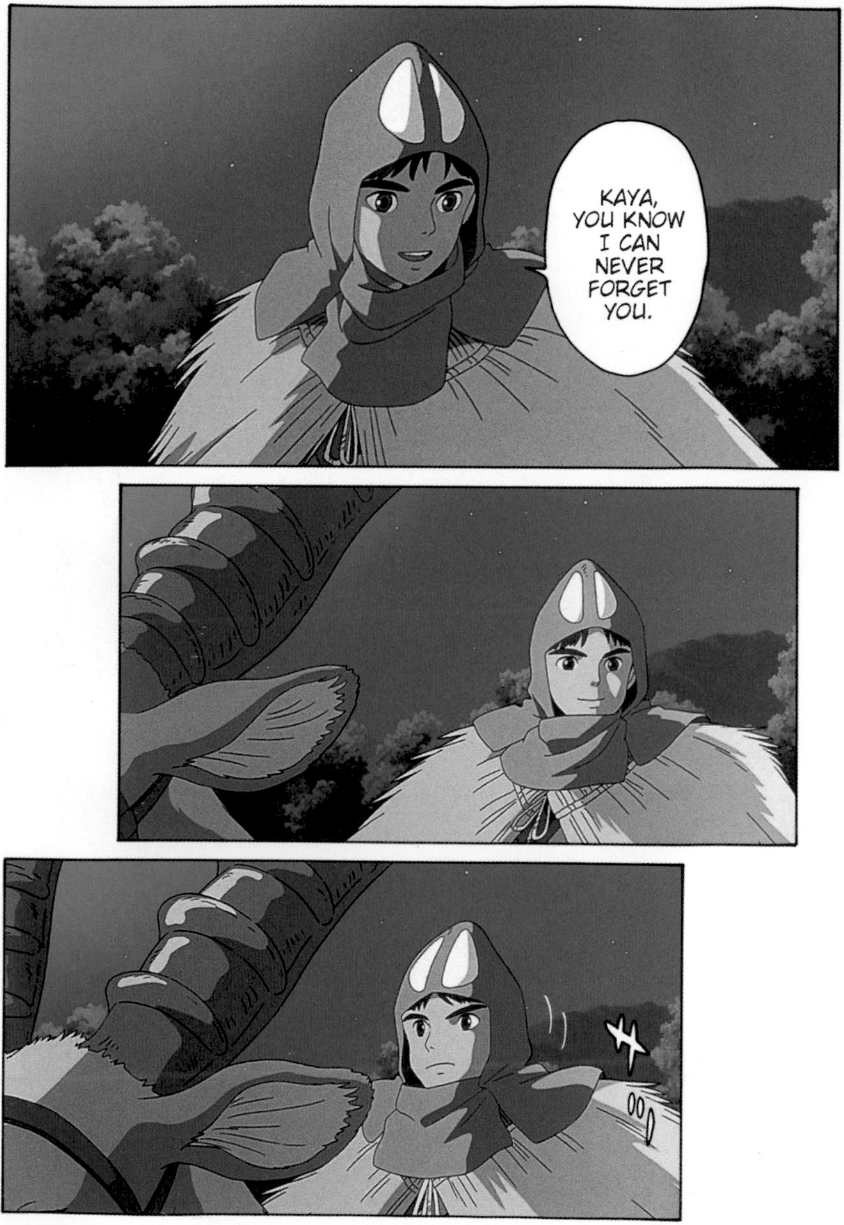
KAYA, YOU KNOW I CAN NEVER FORGET YOU.

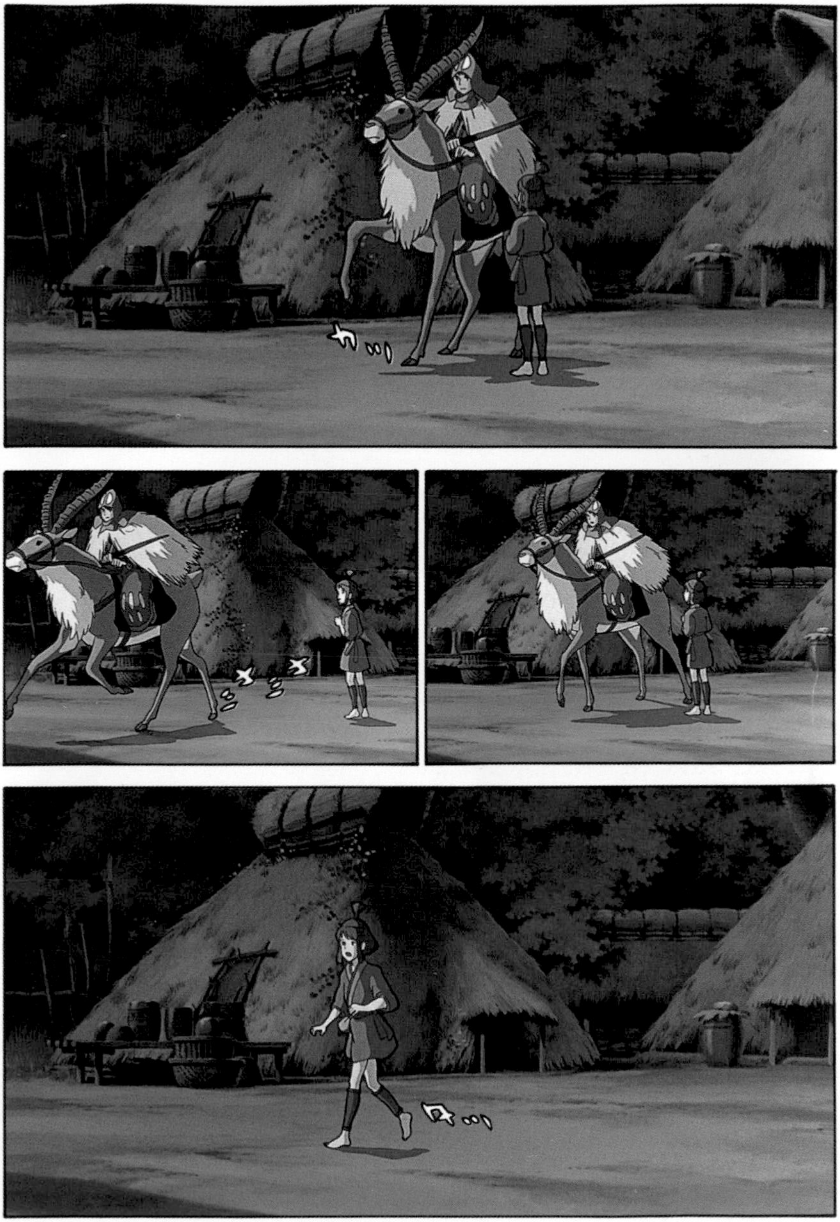

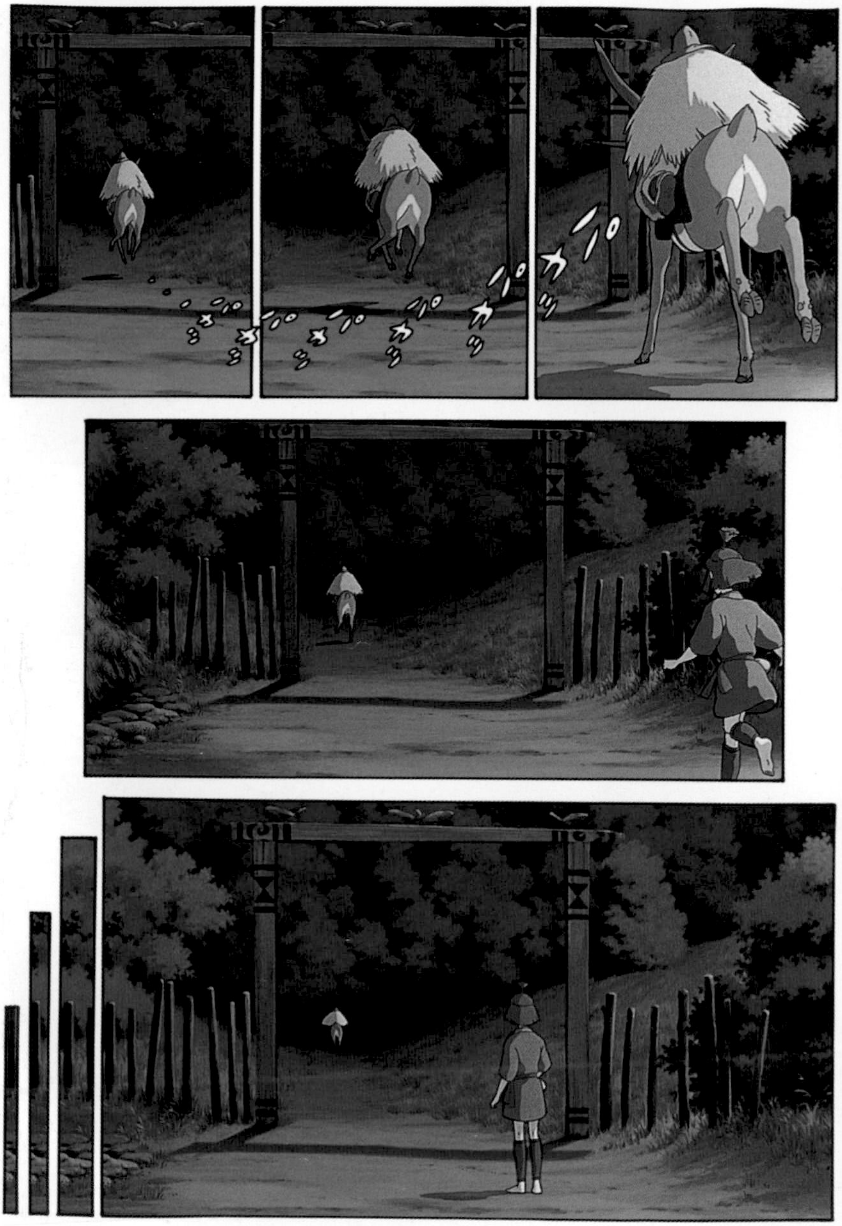
パカッ
パカッ
パカッ
パカッ

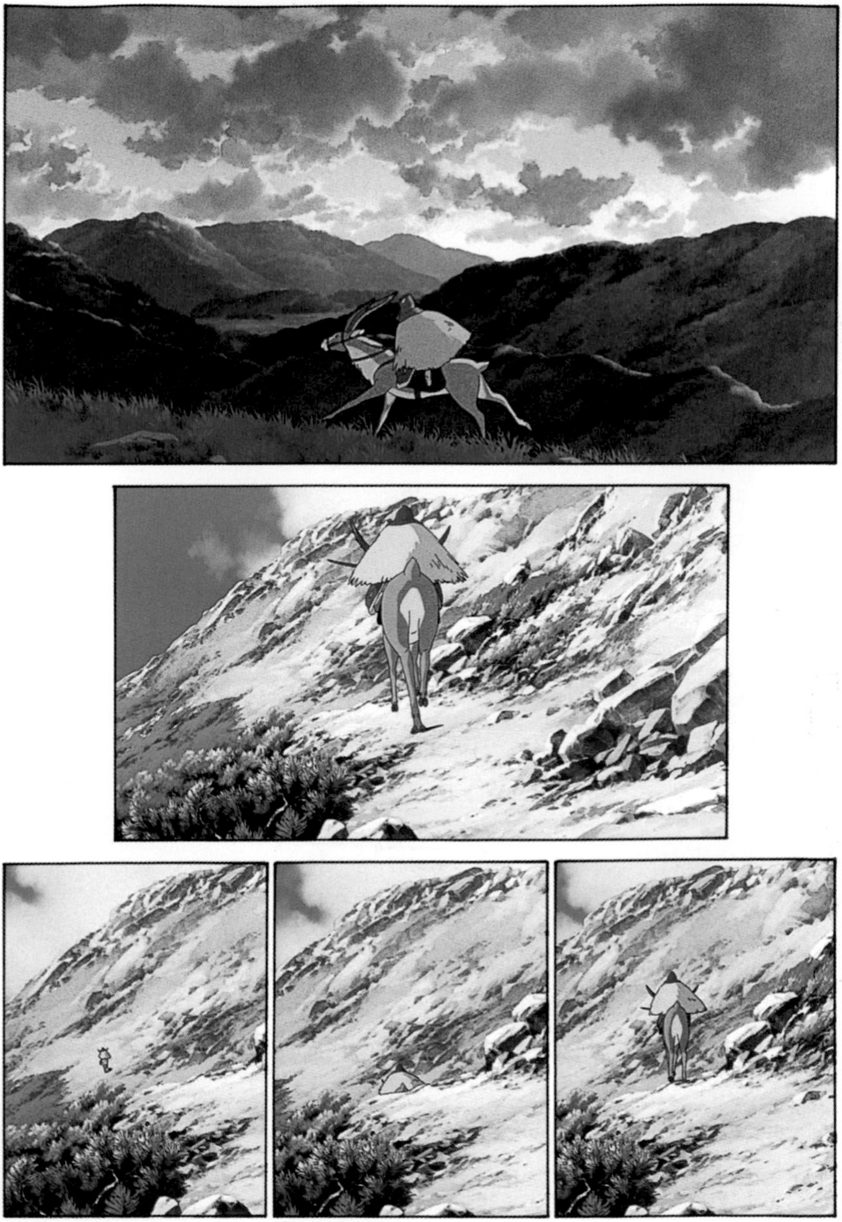

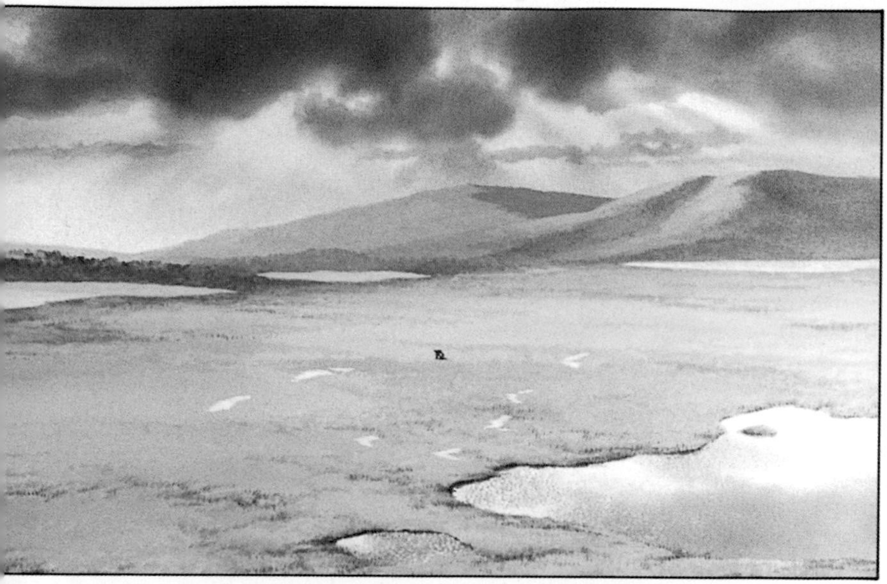

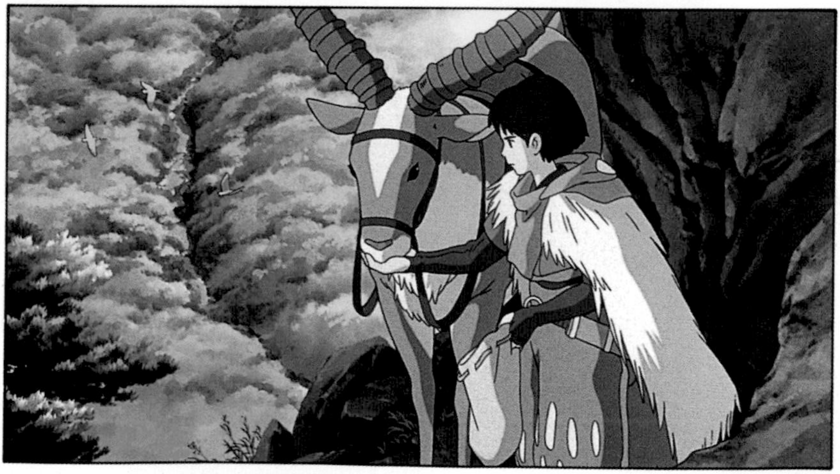

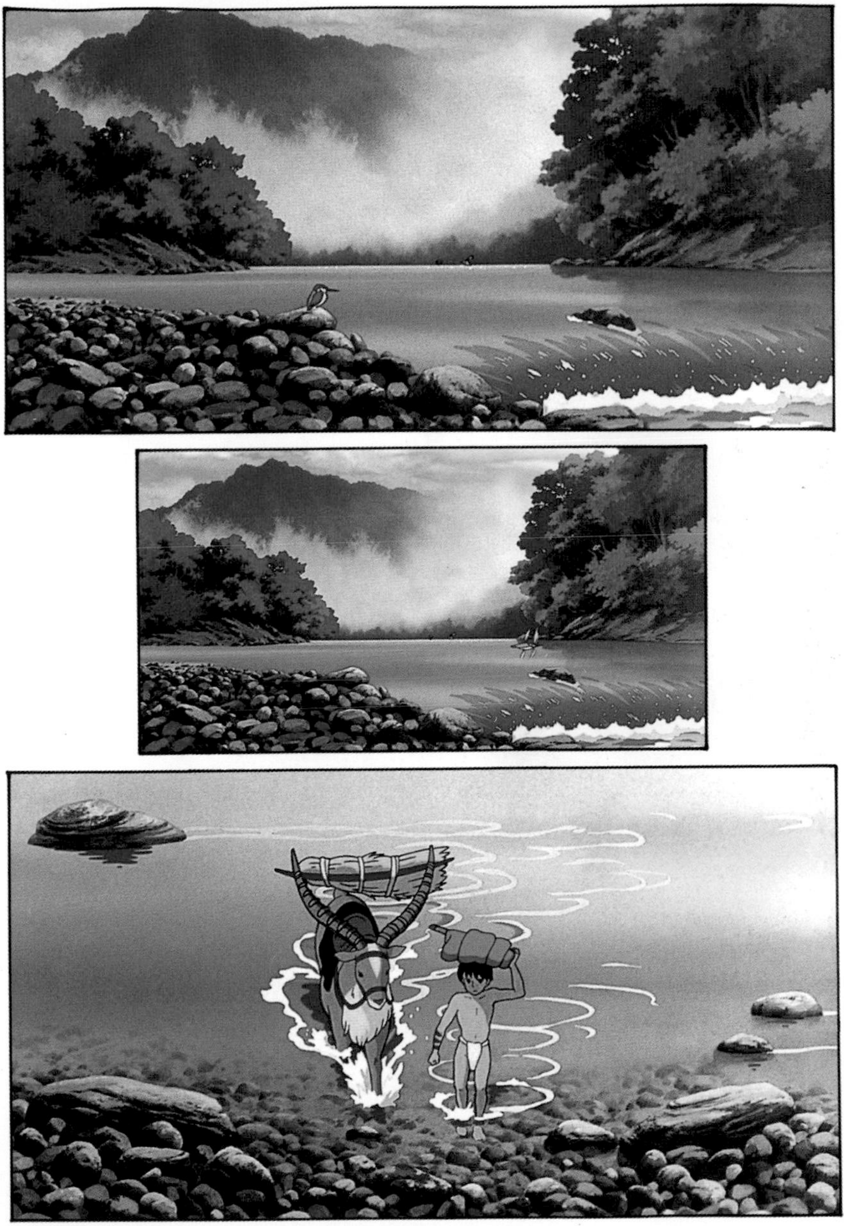

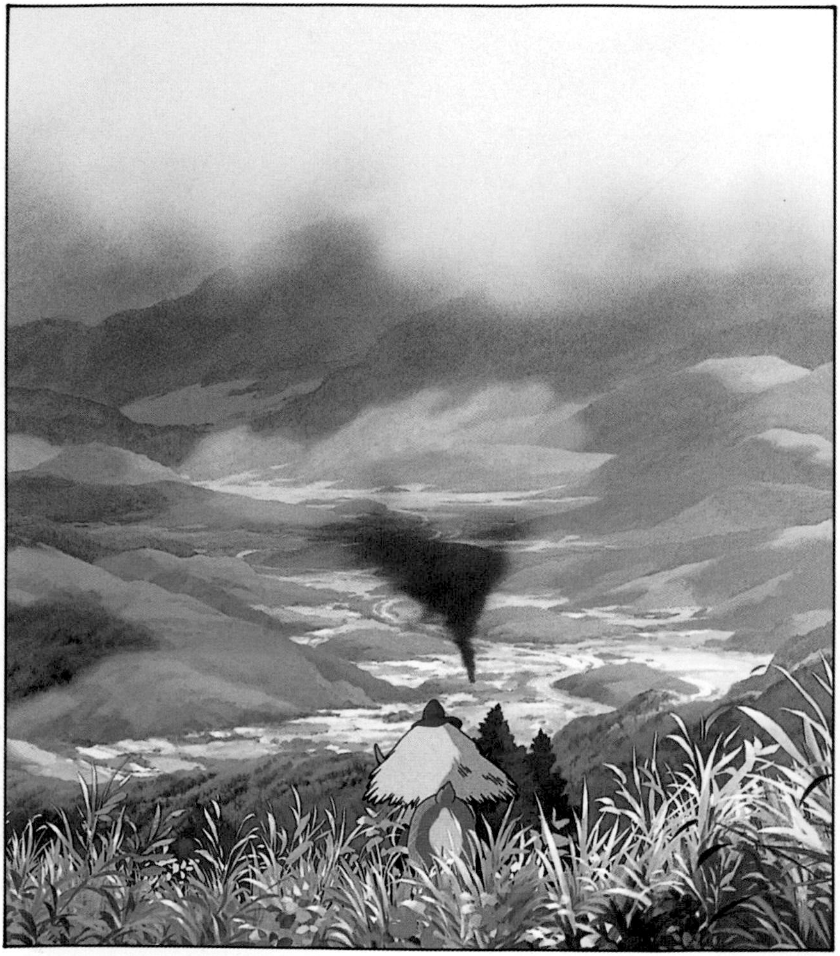

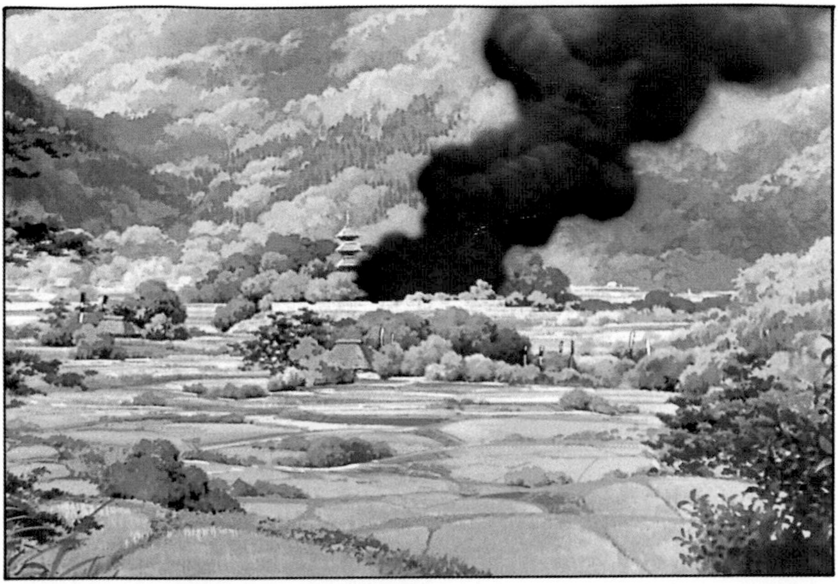

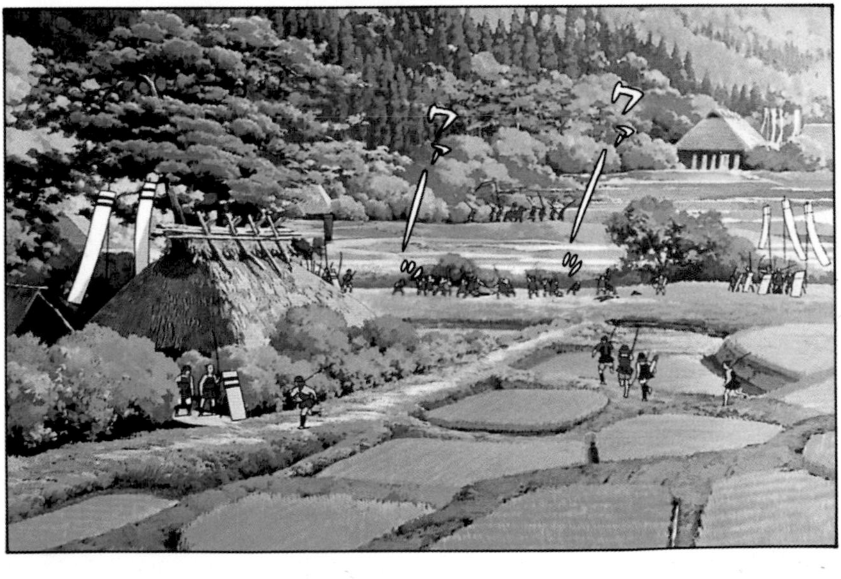
ワァーッ
ワァーッ

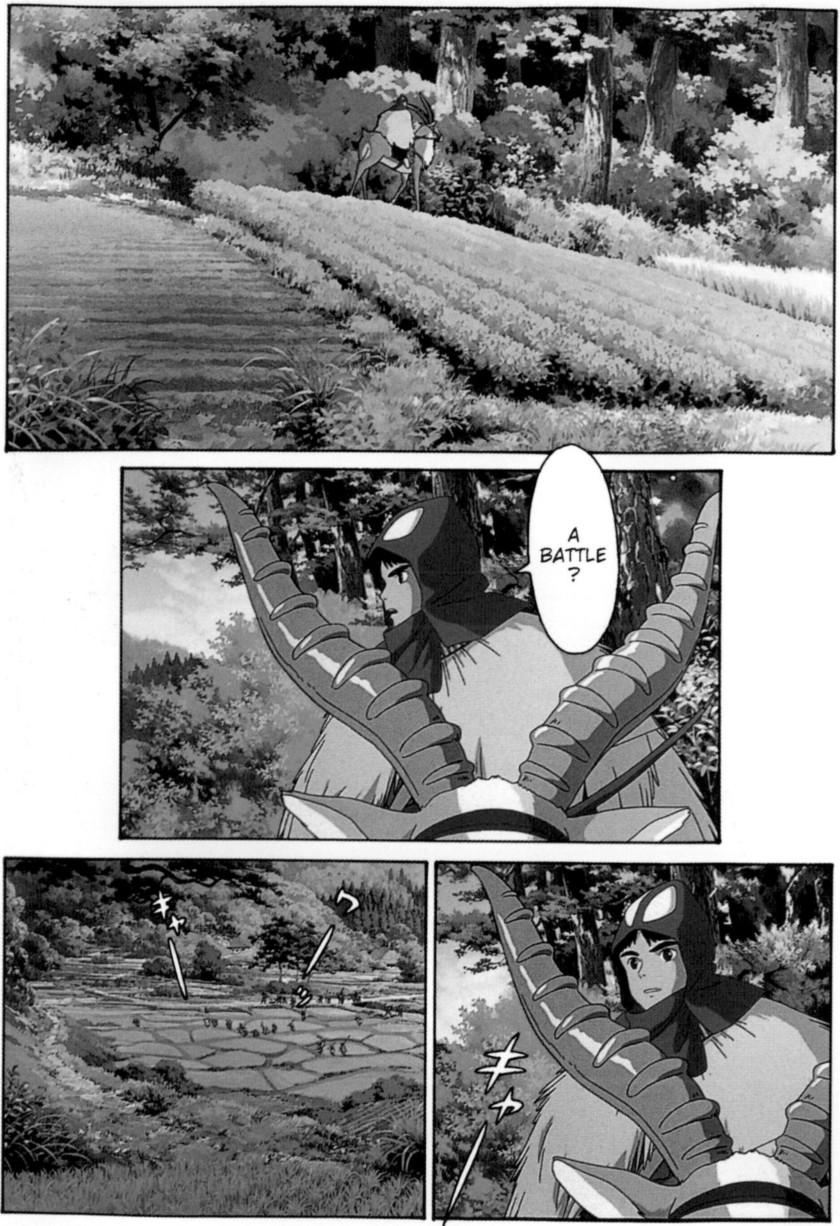
A BATTLE ?

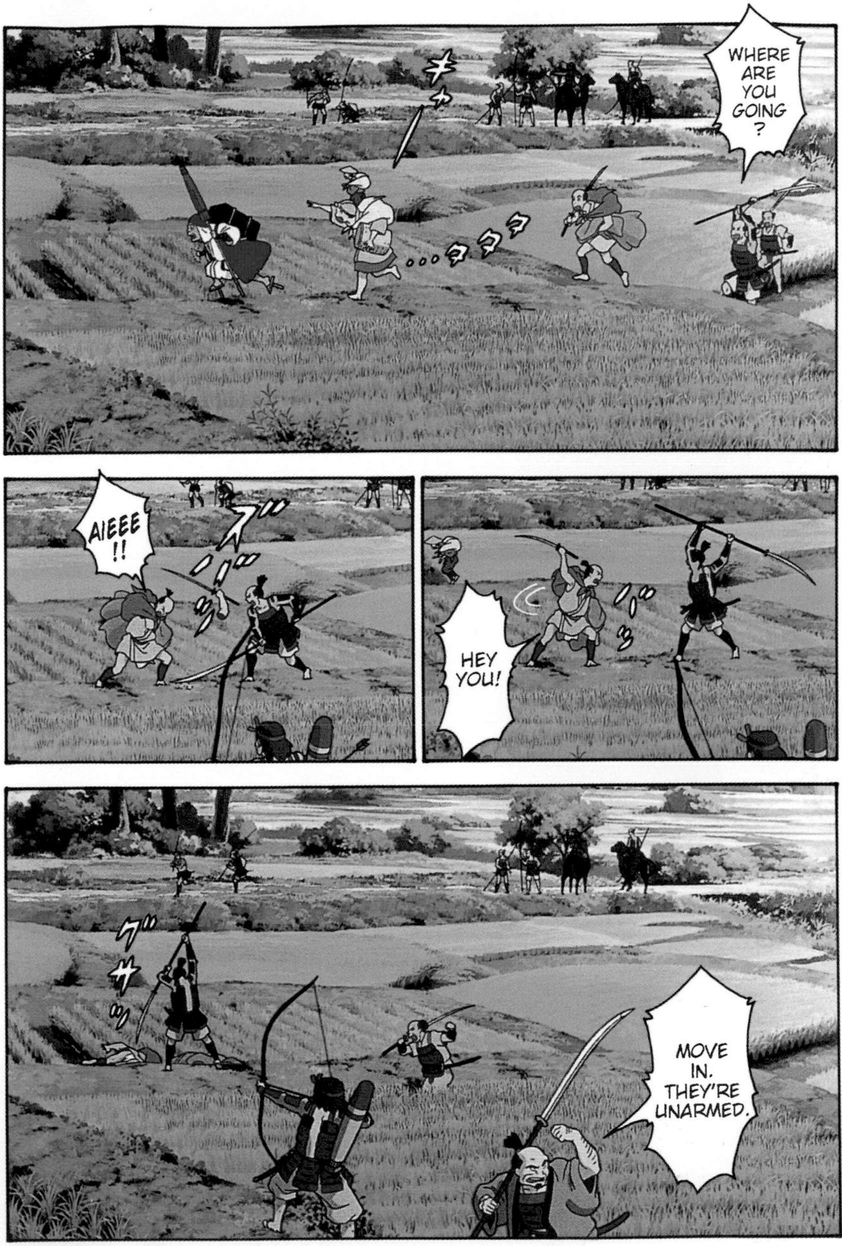
WHERE ARE YOU GOING?
HEY YOU!
AIEEE!!
MOVE IN. THEY'RE UNARMED.

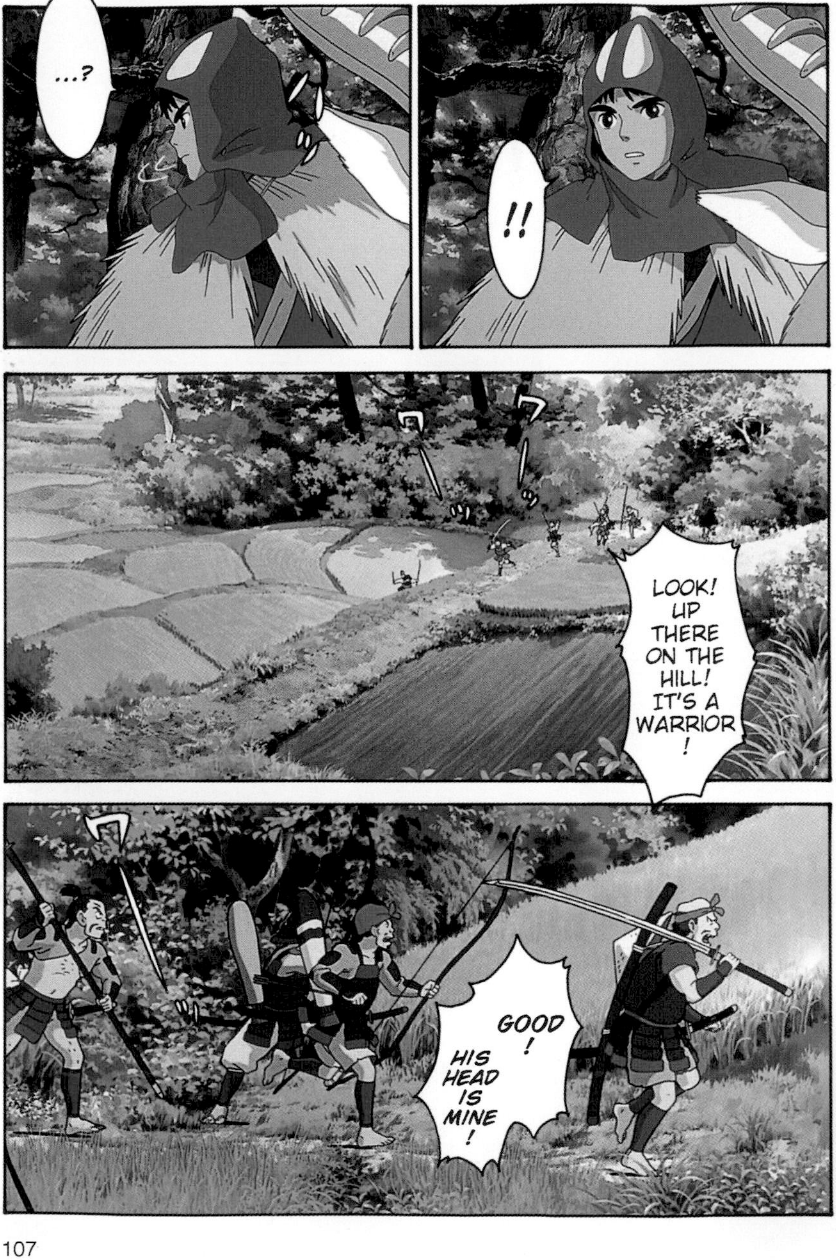
...?
!!
LOOK! UP THERE ON THE HILL! IT'S A WARRIOR!
GOOD! HIS HEAD IS MINE!

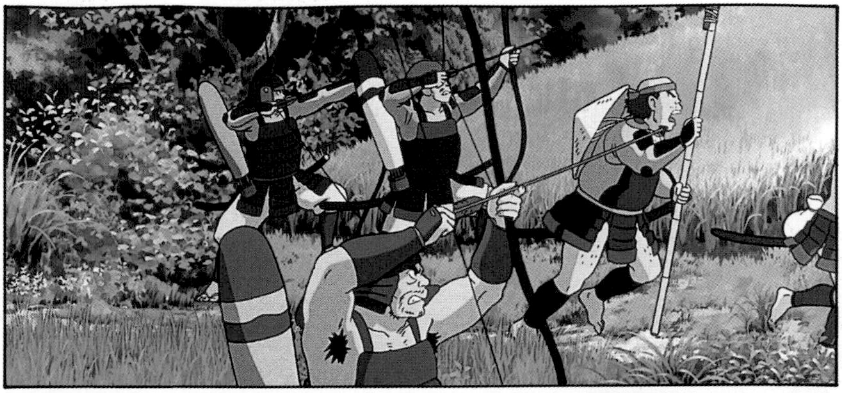
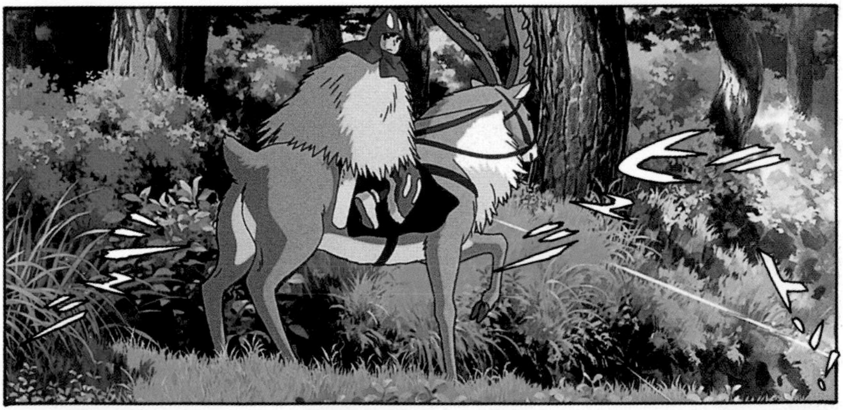
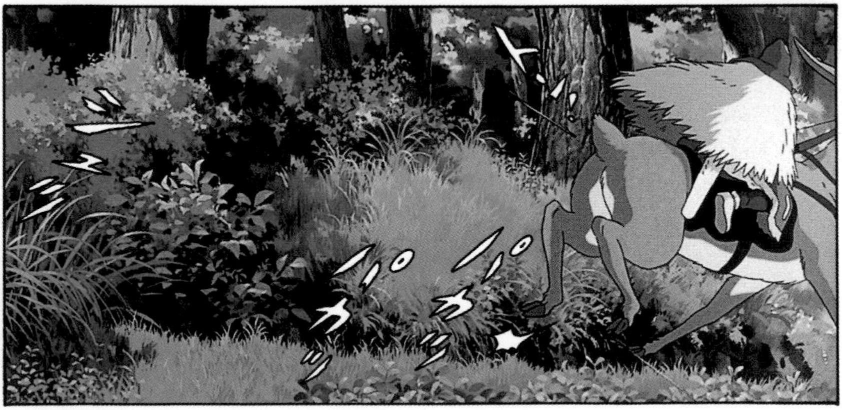

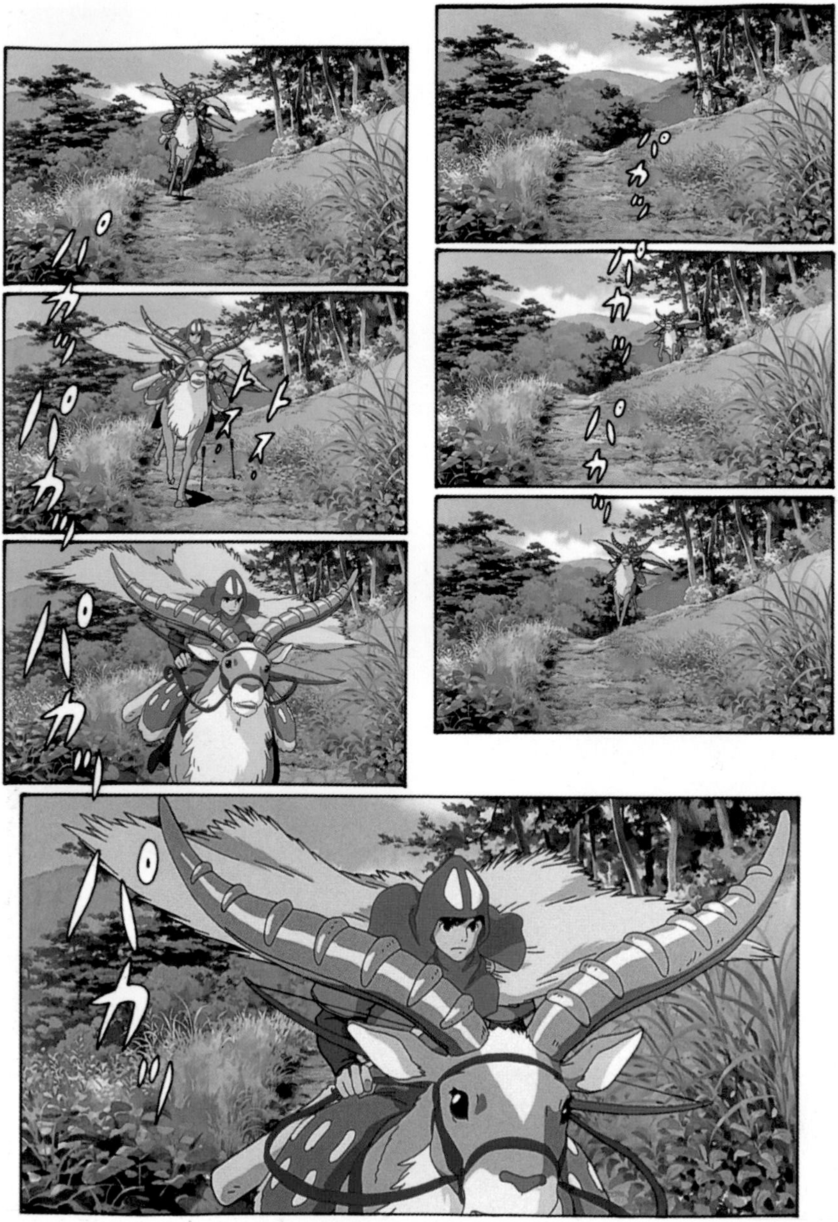
パカッ
パカッ
パカッ
パカッ
ドス
ドス
パカッ
パカッ
パカッ

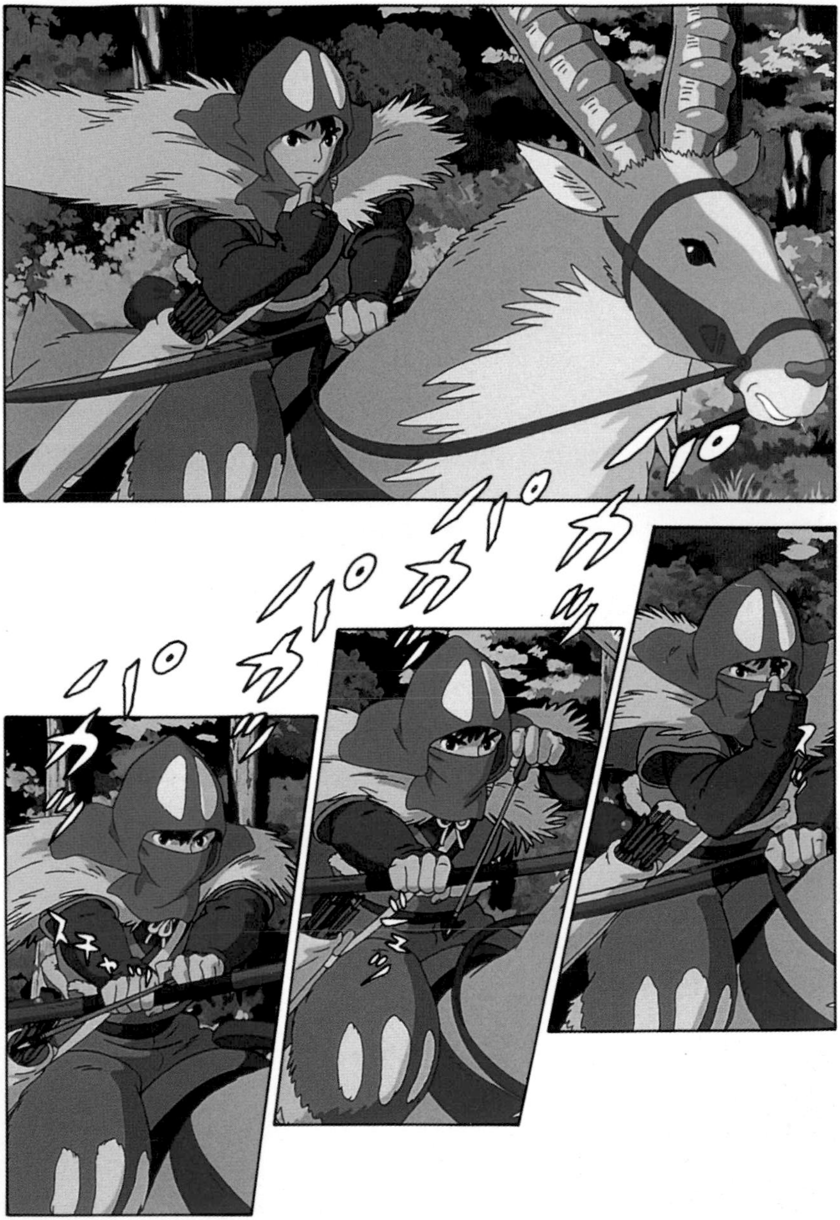
パカッ
パカッ
パカッ
パカッ

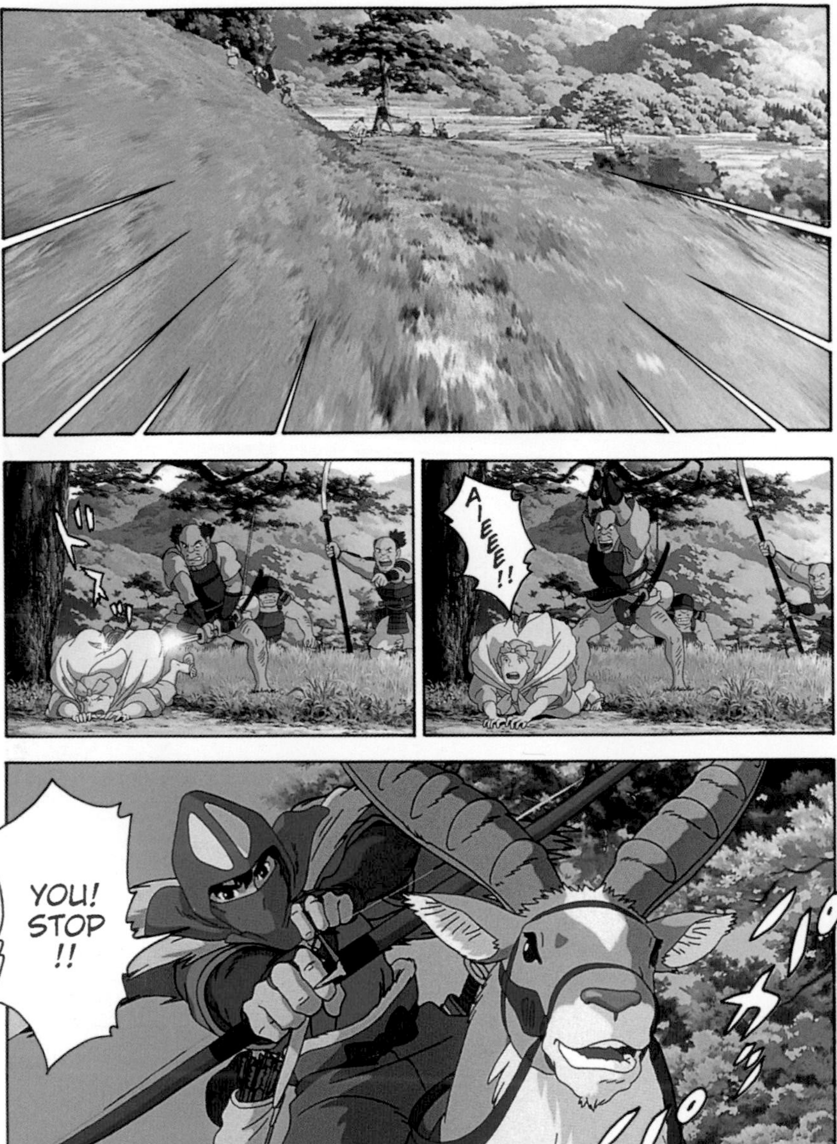
AIEEE!!
YOU! STOP !!

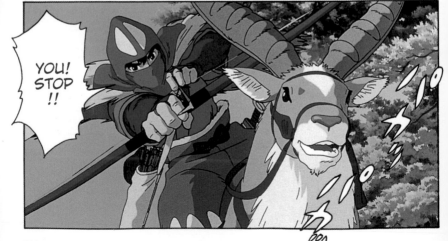

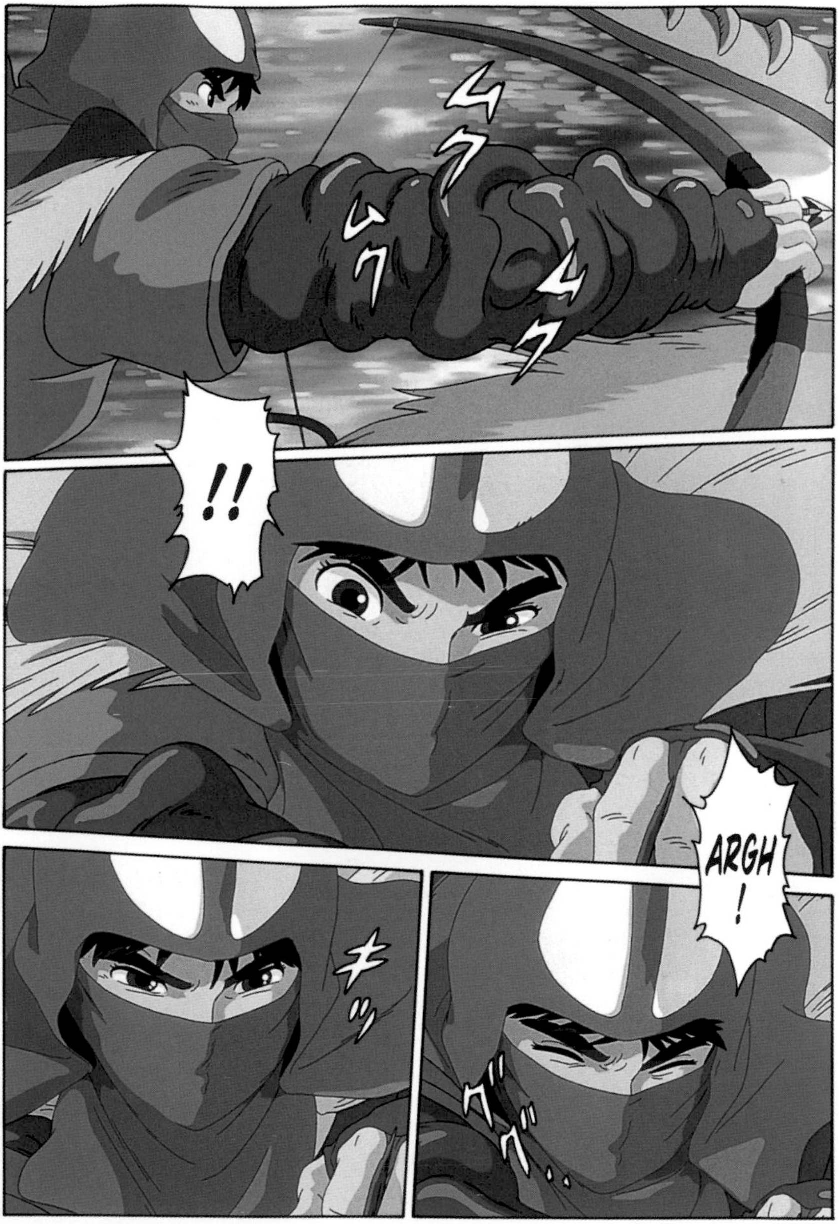
ムクムク
ムク
!!
キッ
ARGH!
グ…

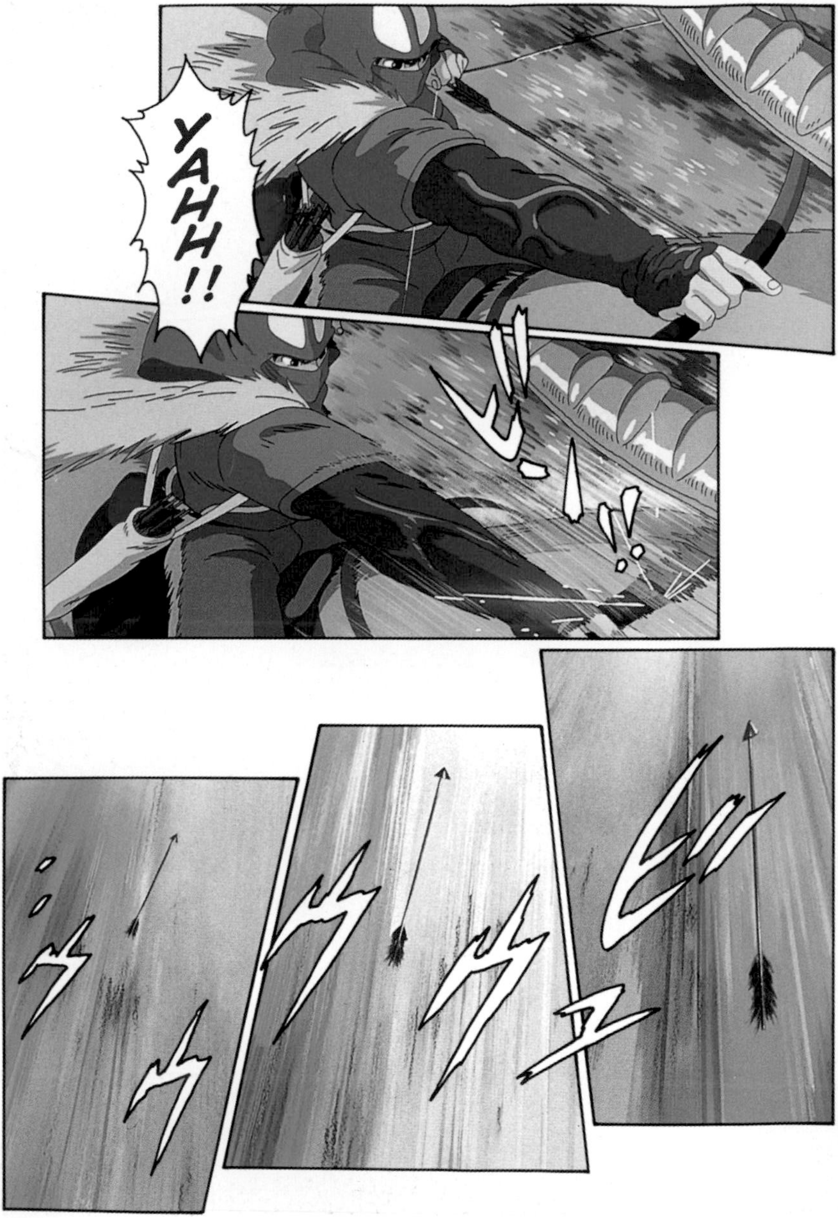
YAHHH!!

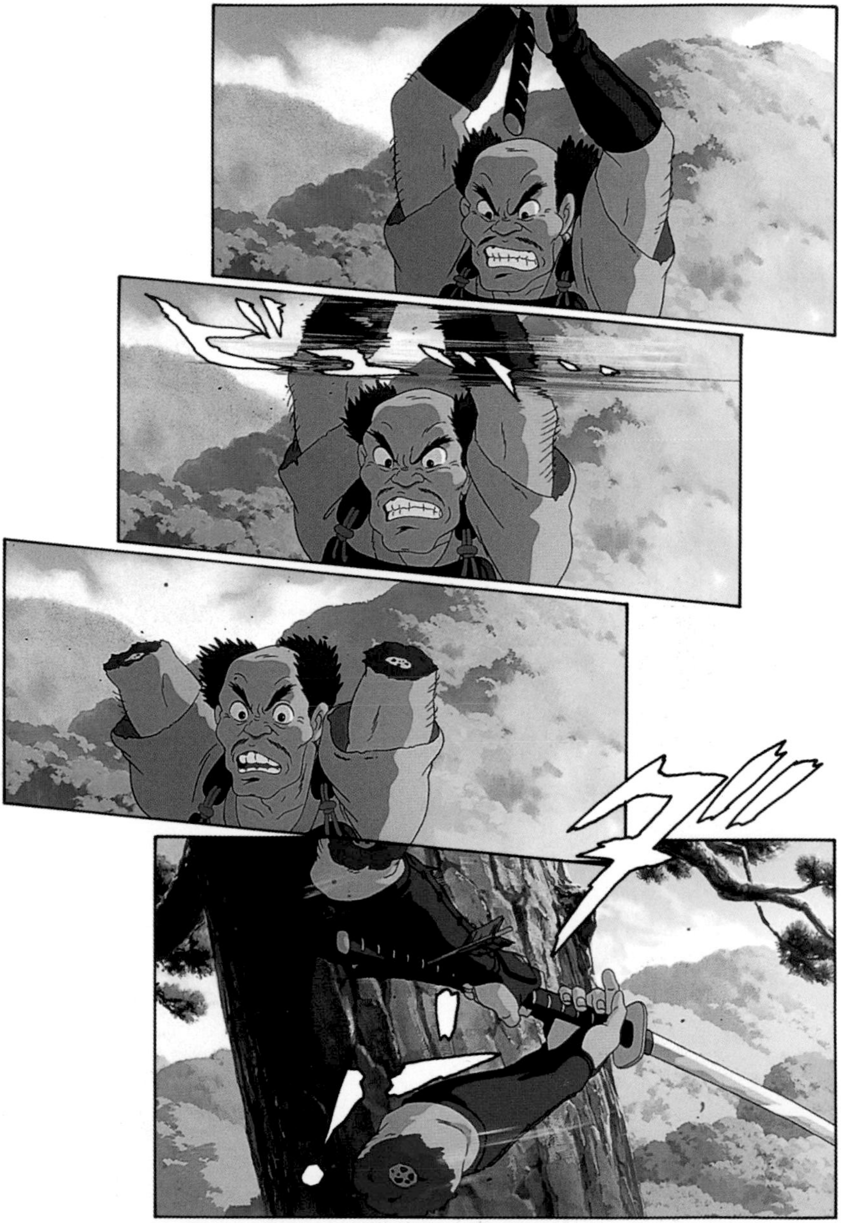
ダッ

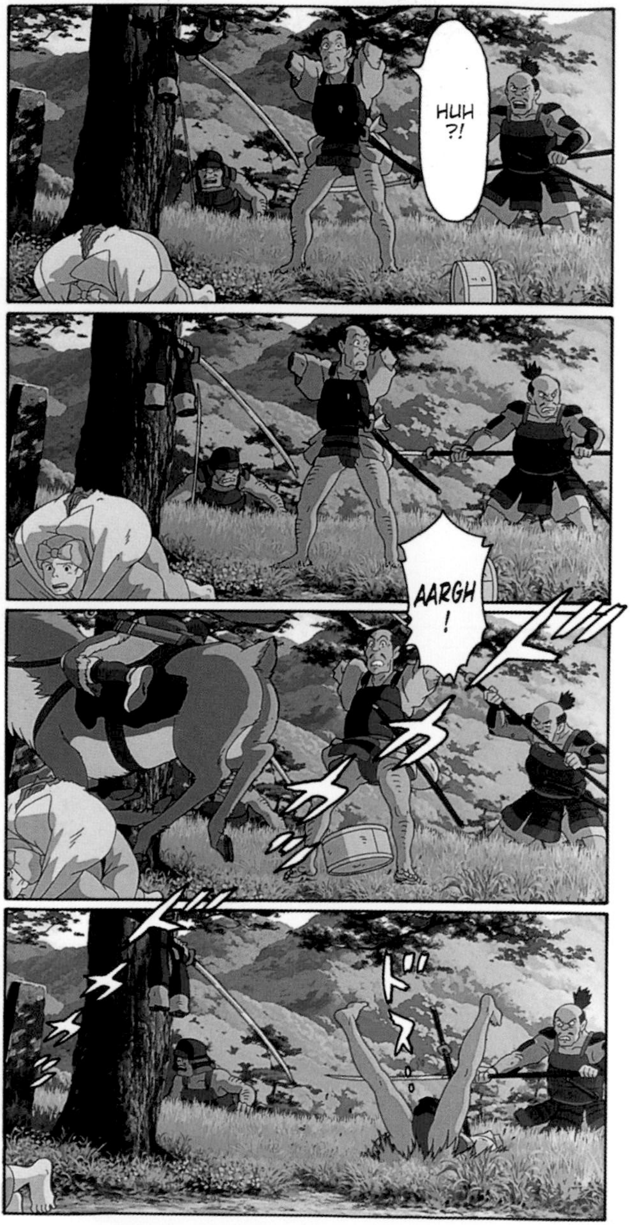
HUH ?!
AARGH !

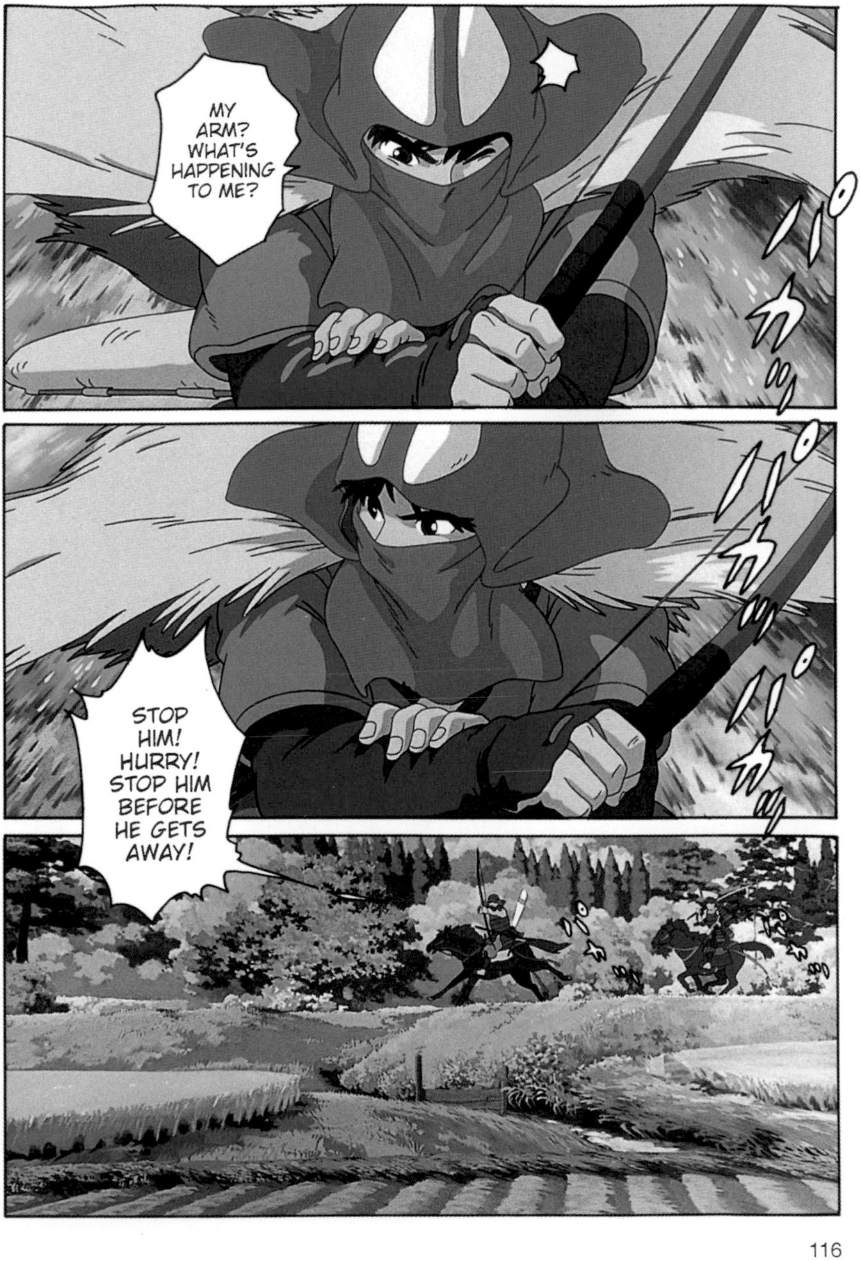
MY ARM? WHAT'S HAPPENING TO ME?
STOP HIM! HURRY! STOP HIM BEFORE HE GETS AWAY!

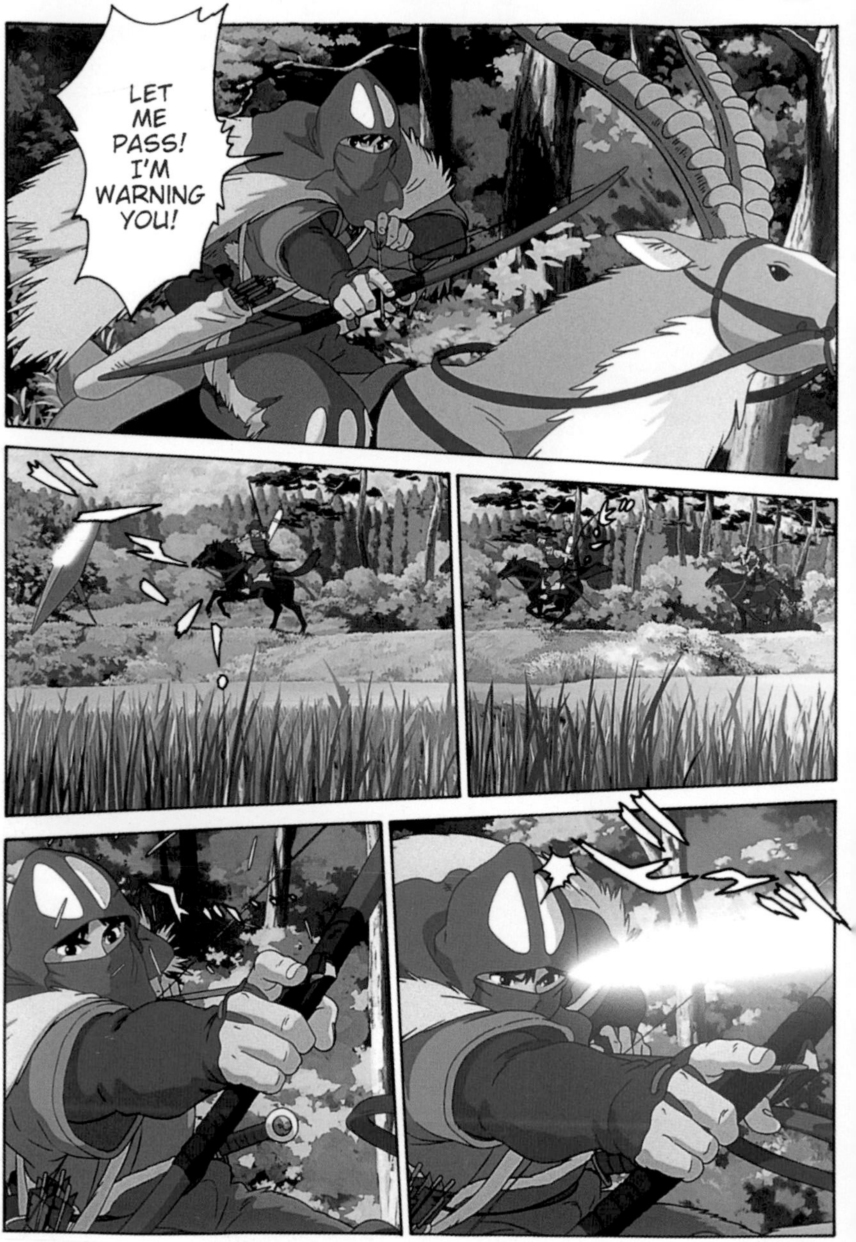
LET ME PASS! I'M WARNING YOU!

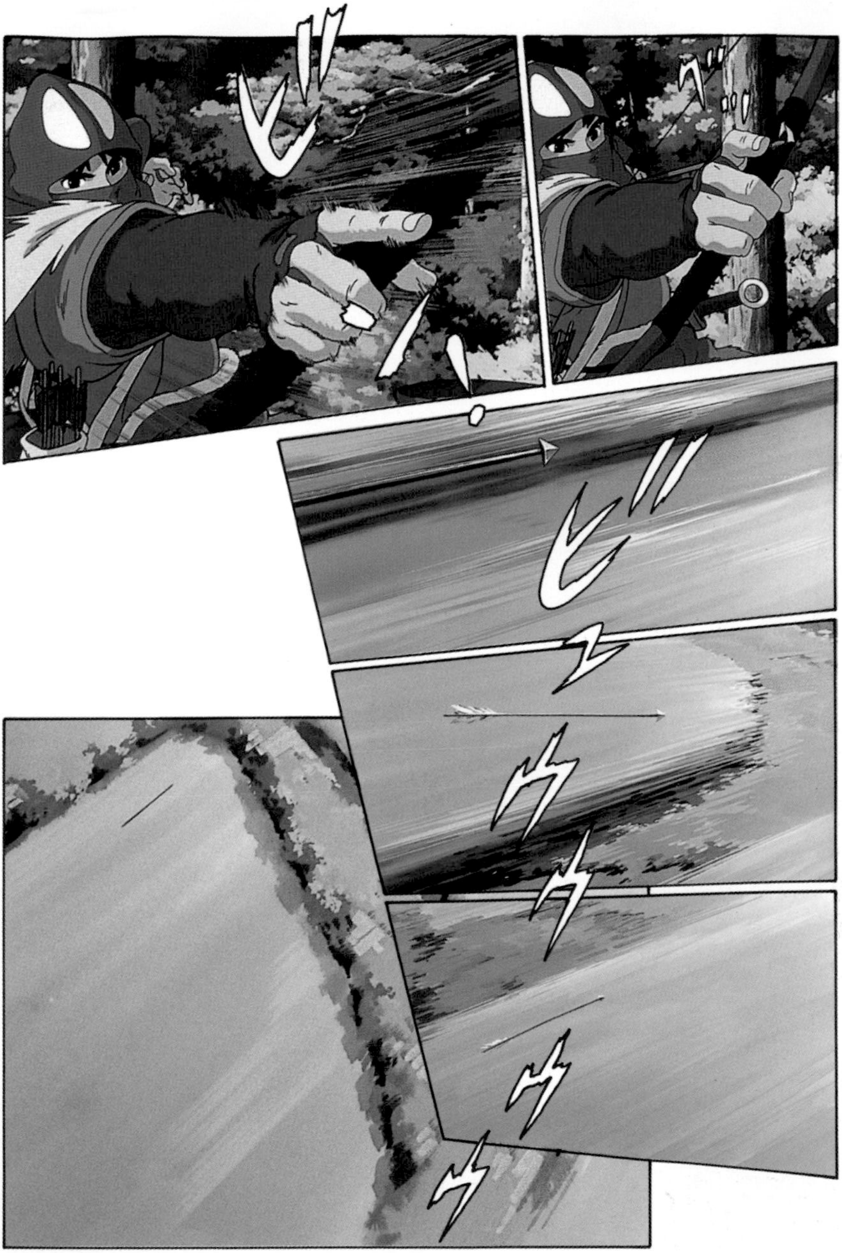
ビュウウウウ

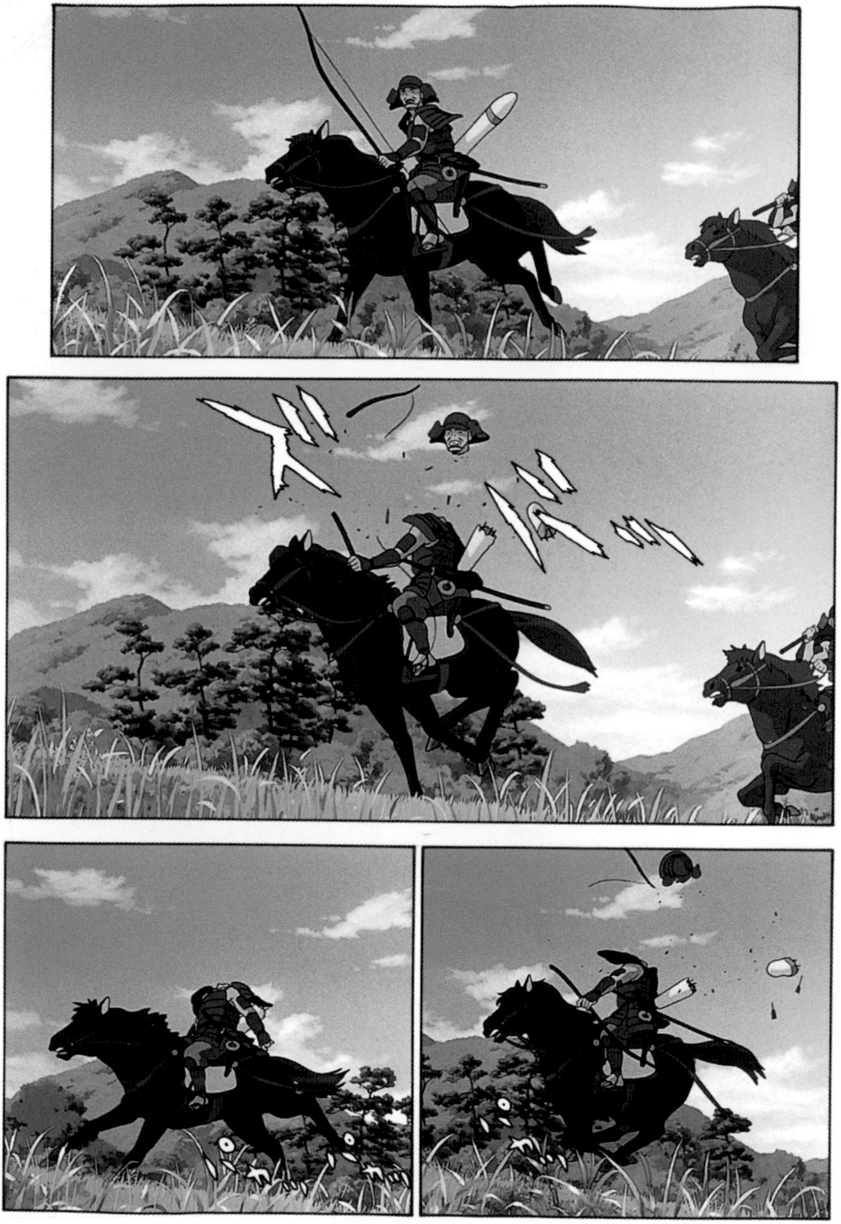

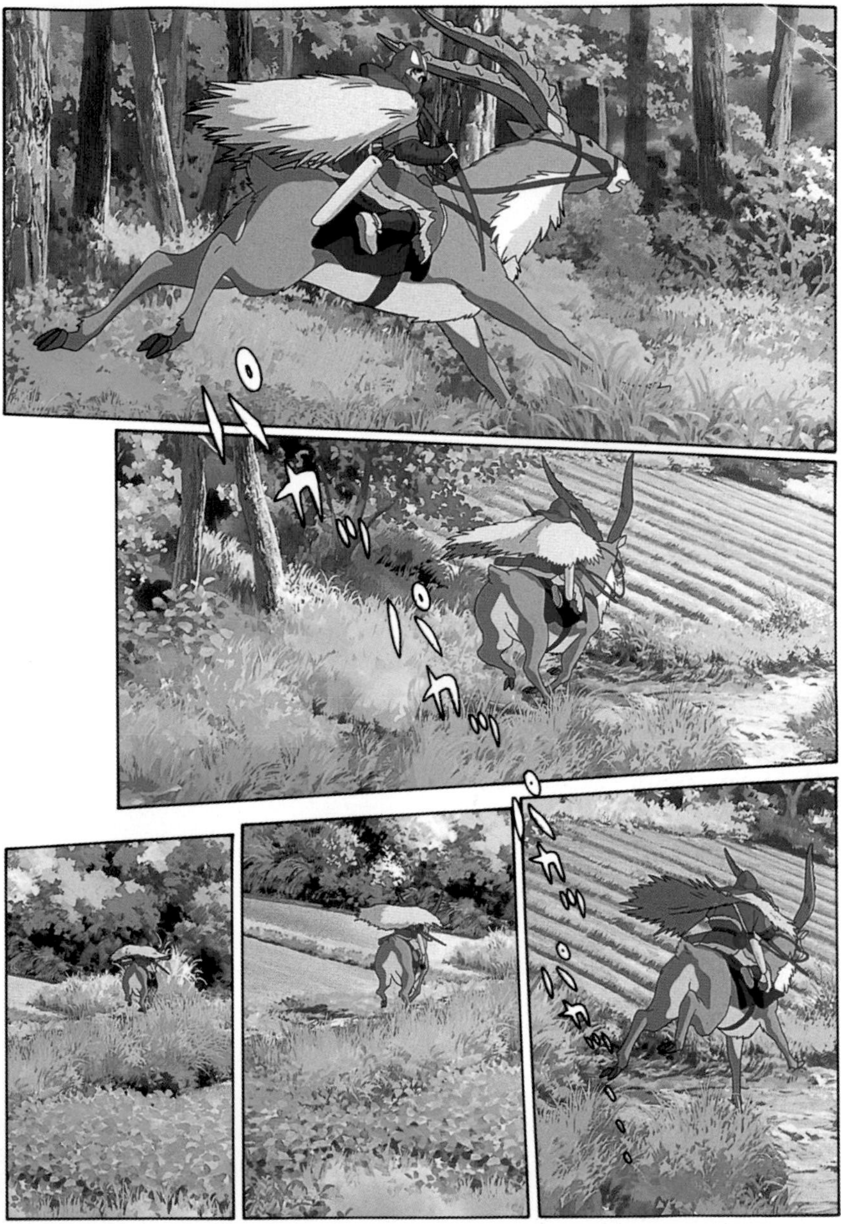

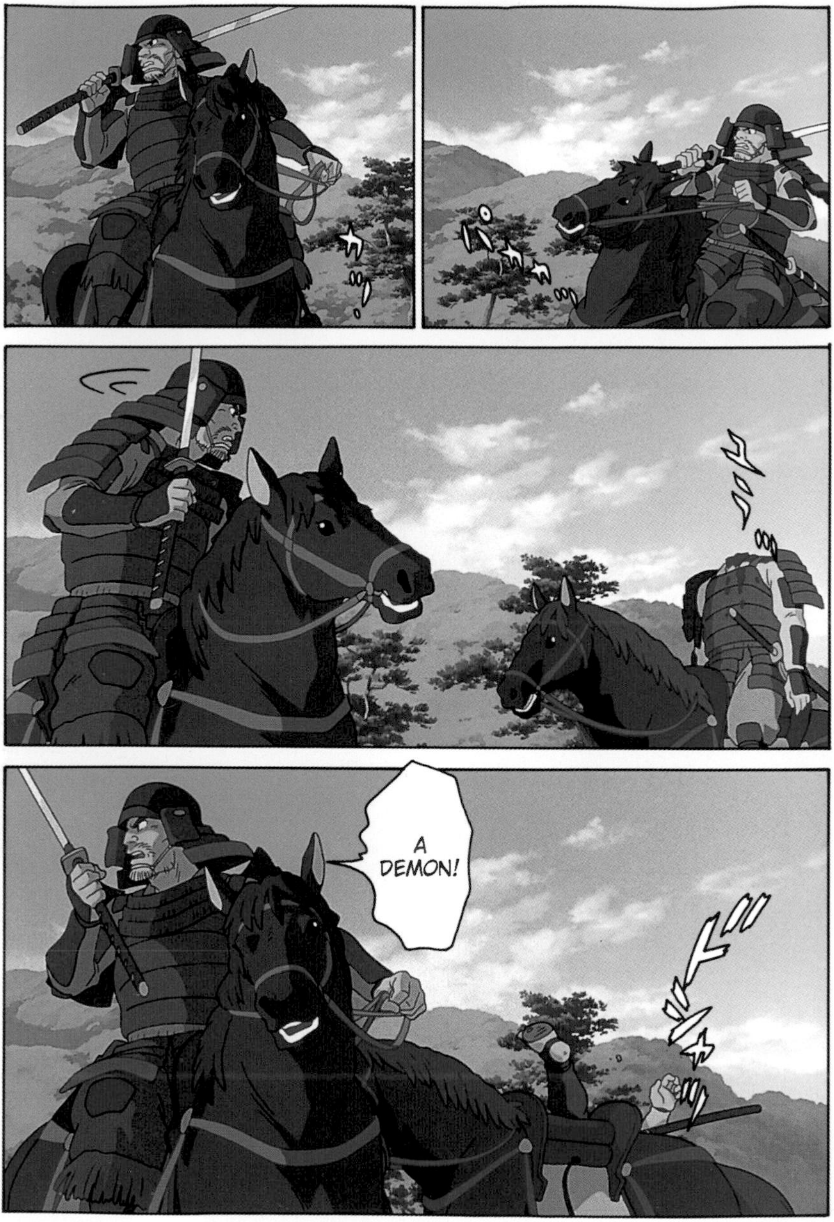
A DEMON!

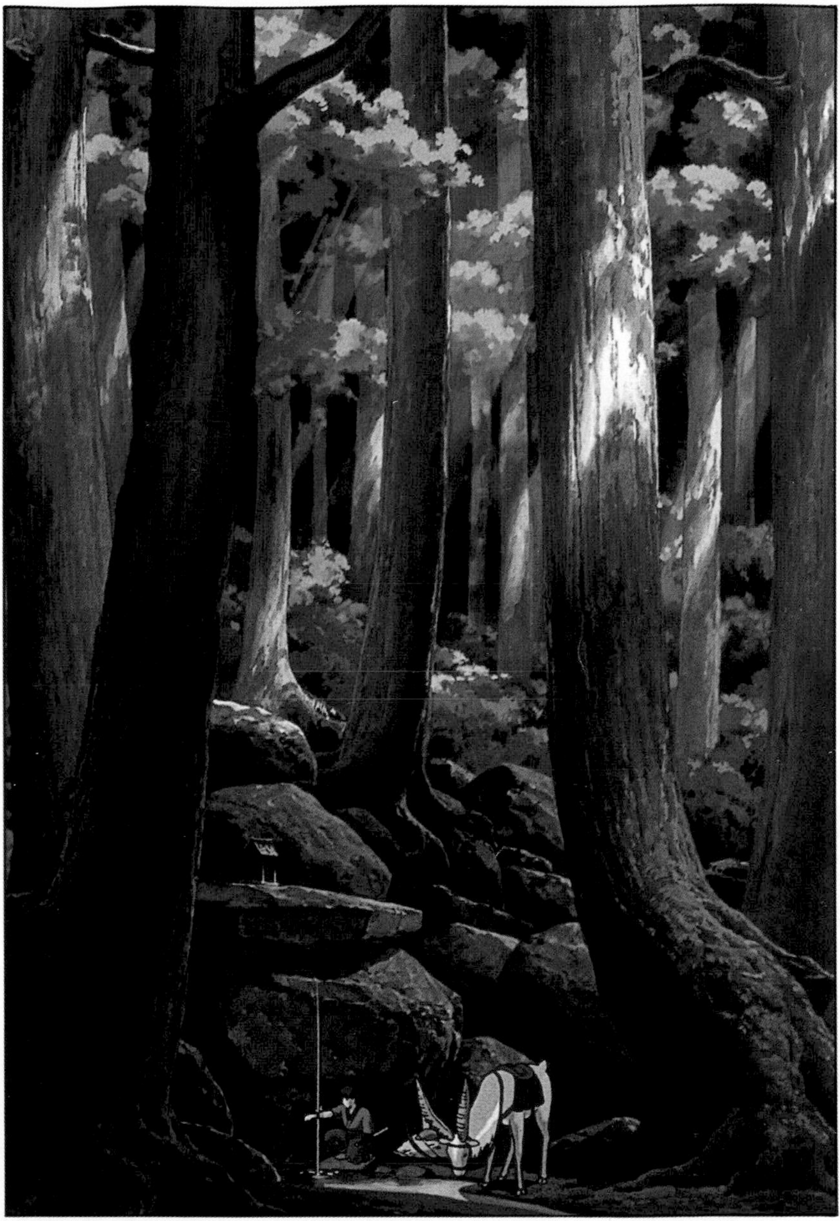

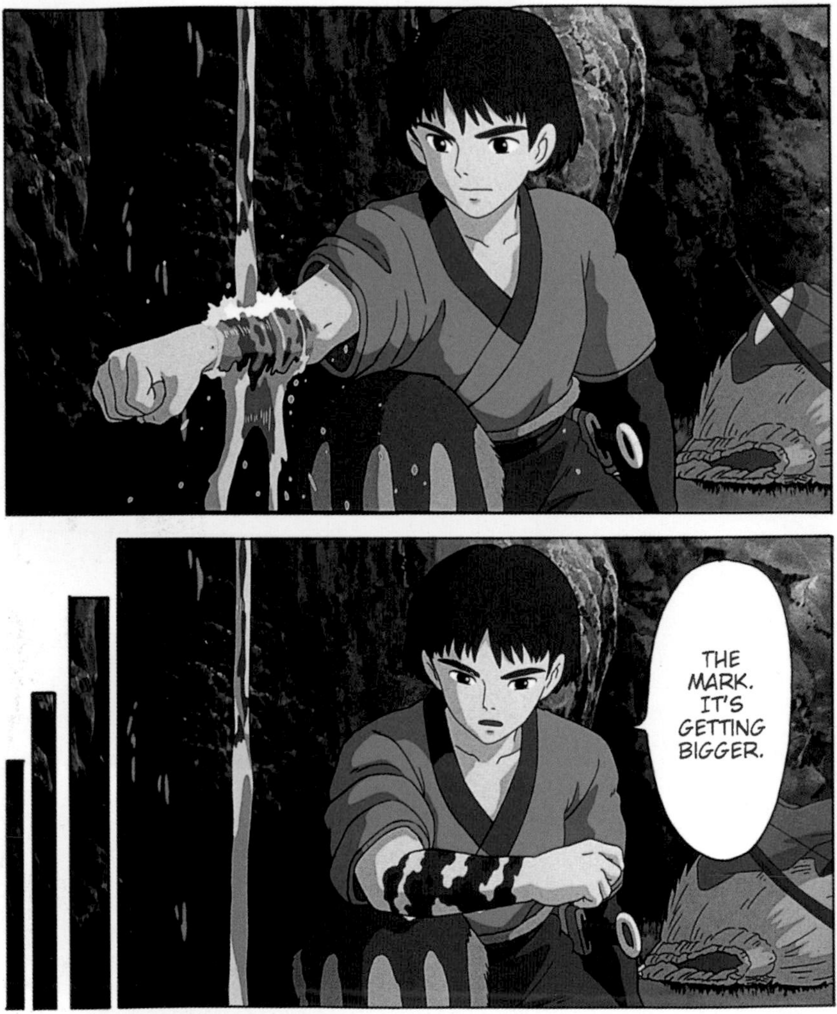
THE MARK. IT'S GETTING BIGGER.

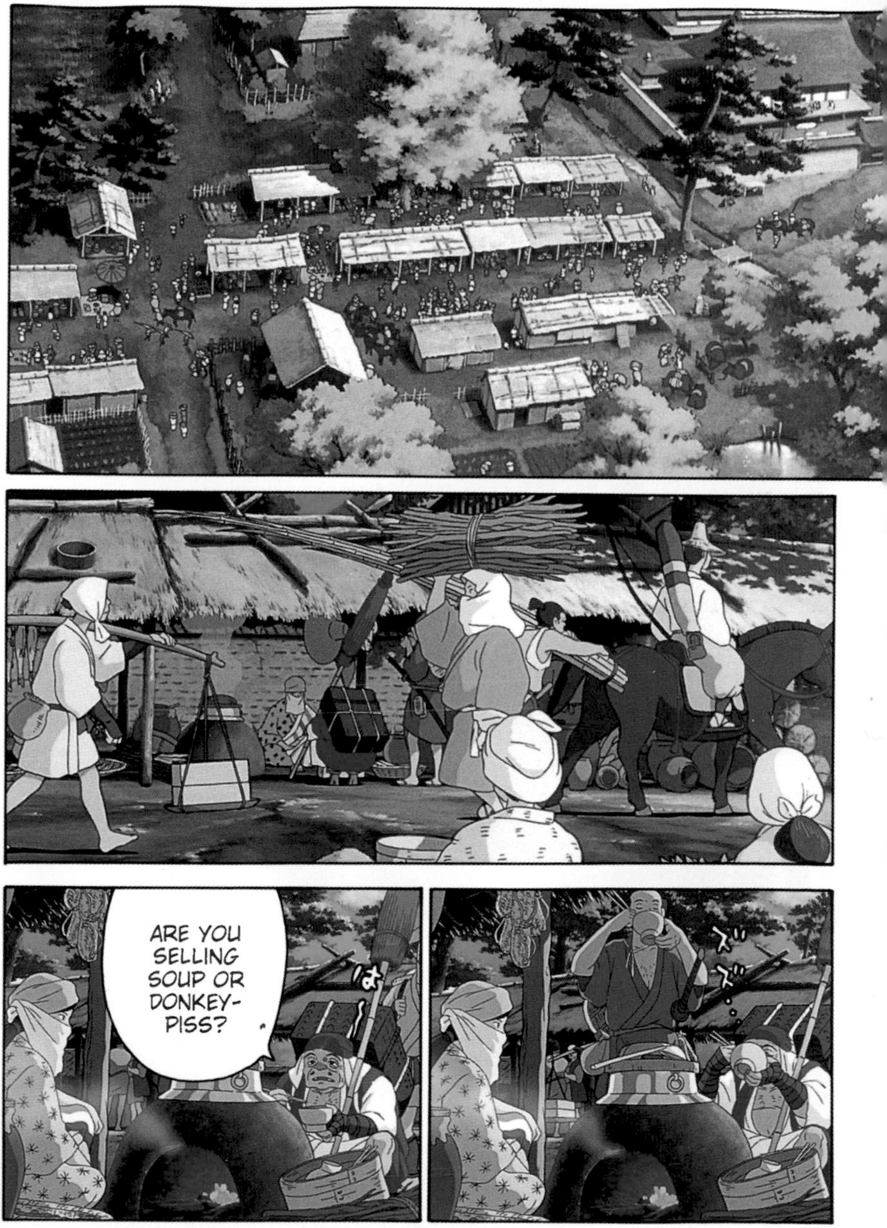
ズズ…
ARE YOU SELLING SOUP OR DONKEY-PISS?
は～

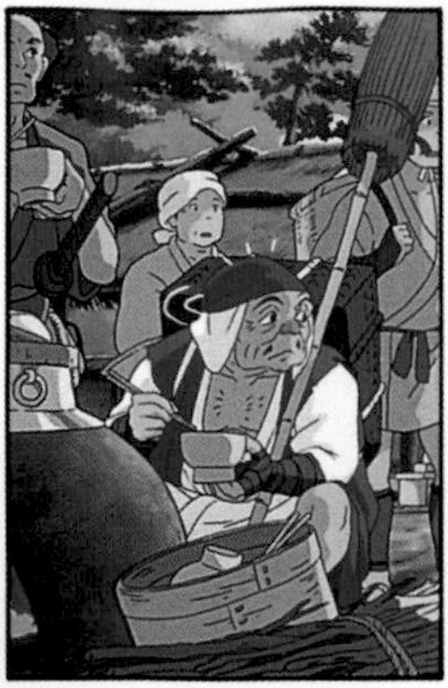
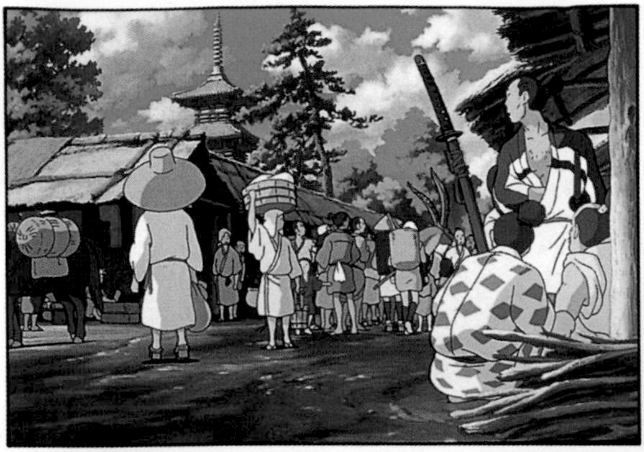
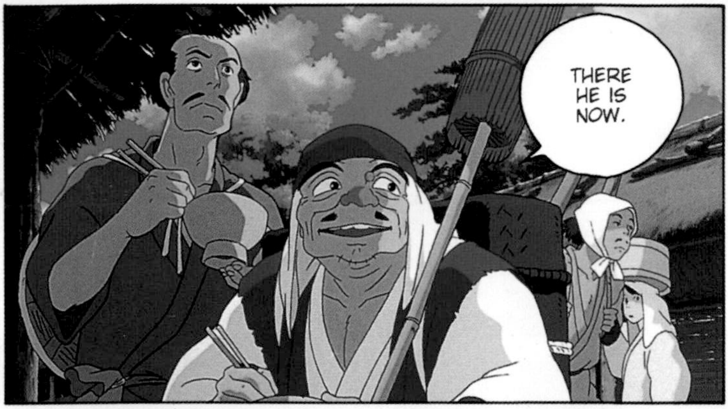
THERE HE IS NOW.
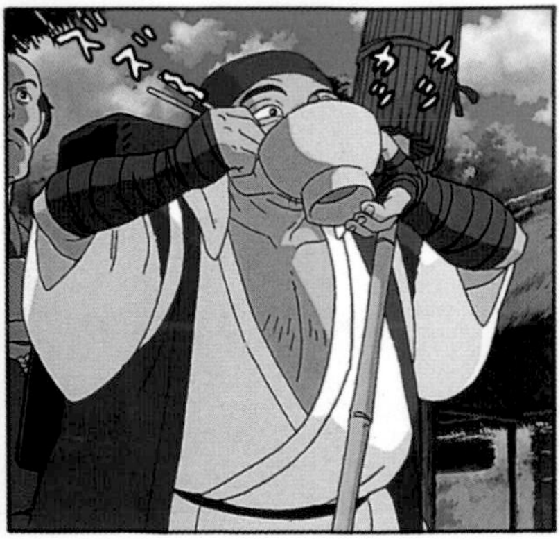
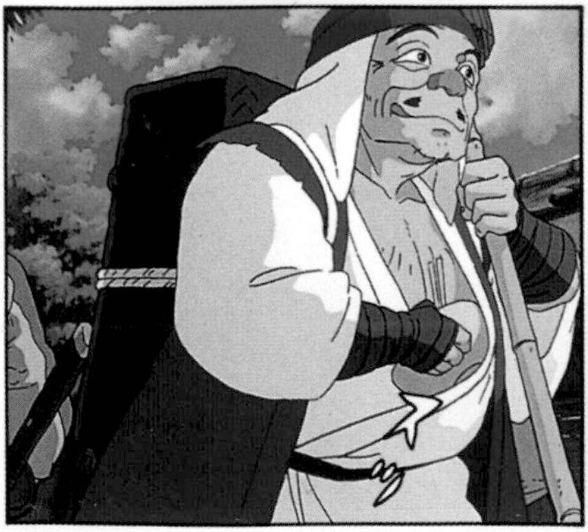

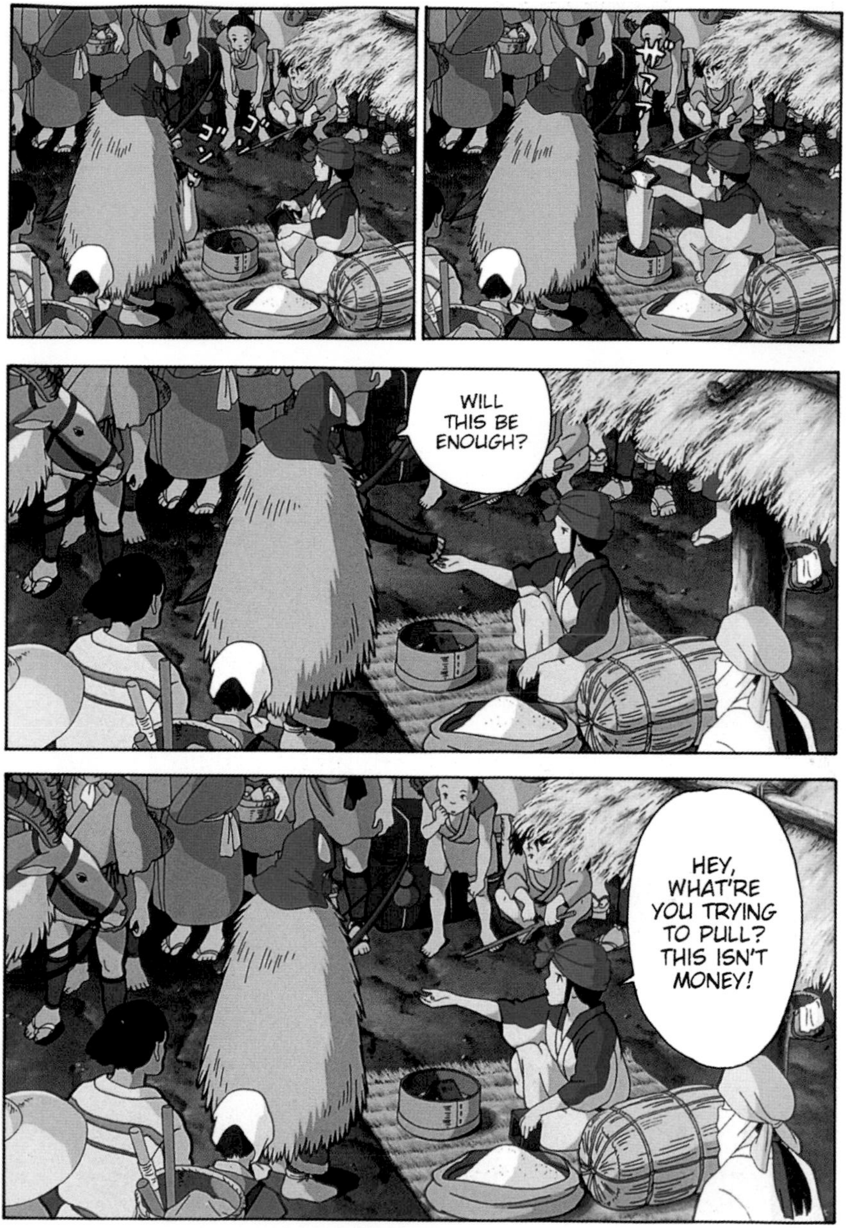
WILL THIS BE ENOUGH?
HEY, WHAT'RE YOU TRYING TO PULL? THIS ISN'T MONEY!

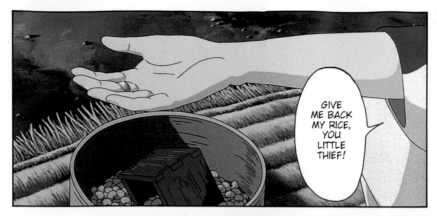

GIVE ME BACK MY RICE, YOU LITTLE THIEF!

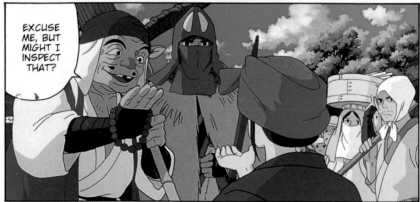

EXCUSE ME, BUT MIGHT I INSPECT THAT?

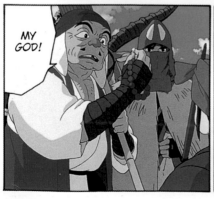

MY GOD!

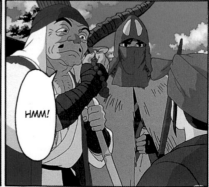

HMM!

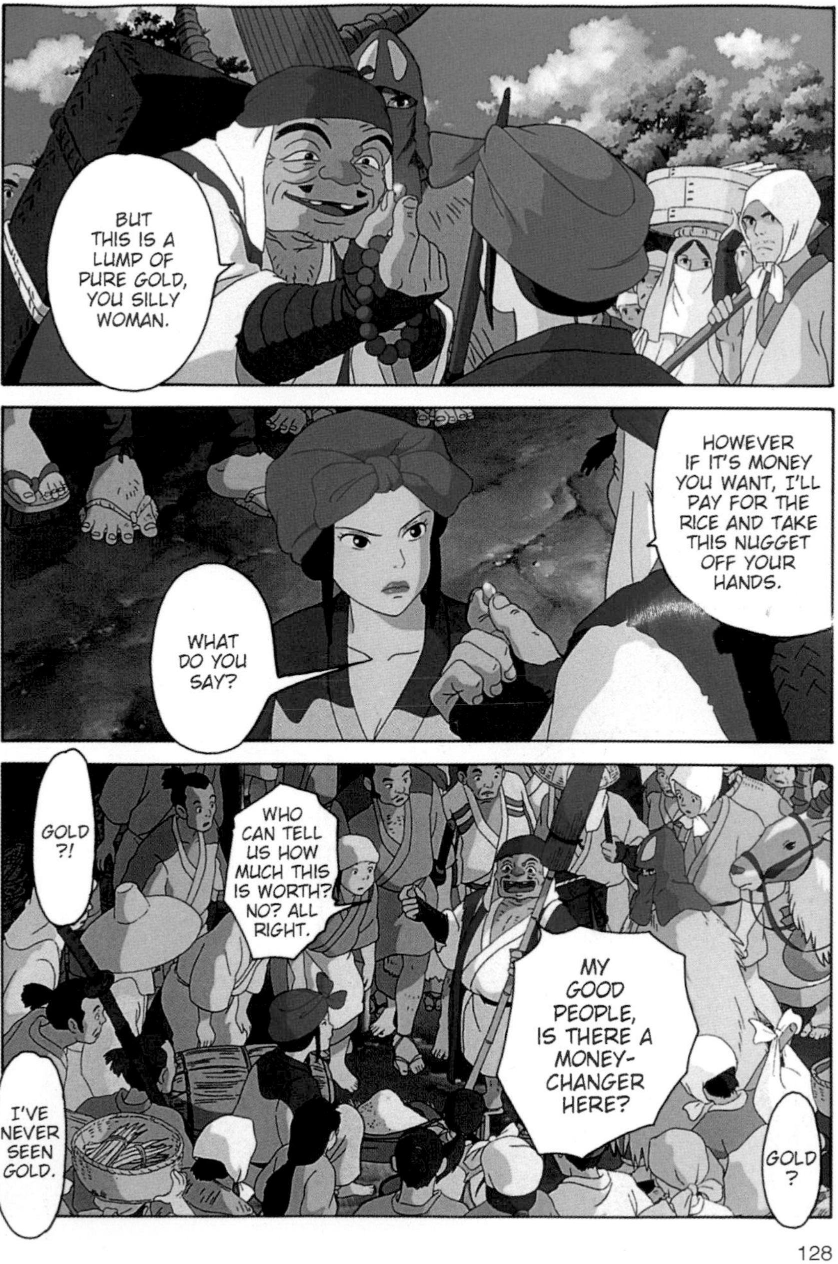
BUT THIS IS A LUMP OF PURE GOLD, YOU SILLY WOMAN.
HOWEVER IF IT'S MONEY YOU WANT, I'LL PAY FOR THE RICE AND TAKE THIS NUGGET OFF YOUR HANDS.
WHAT DO YOU SAY?
MY GOOD PEOPLE, IS THERE A MONEY-CHANGER HERE?
WHO CAN TELL US HOW MUCH THIS IS WORTH? NO? ALL RIGHT.
GOLD?!
GOLD?
I'VE NEVER SEEN GOLD.

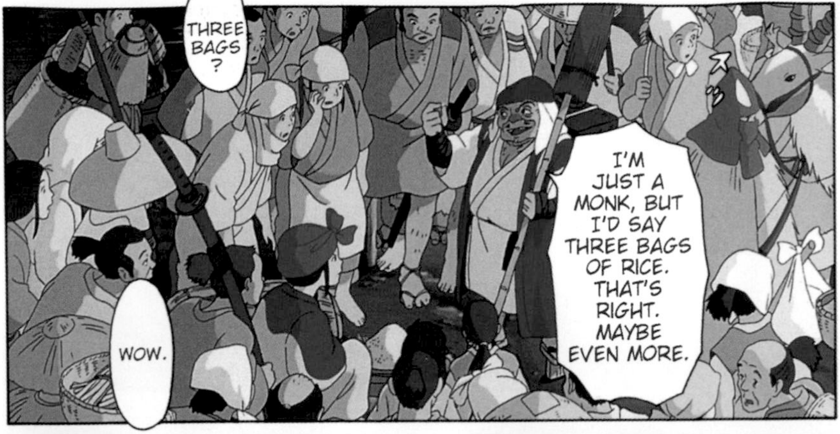
THREE BAGS?
I'M JUST A MONK, BUT I'D SAY THREE BAGS OF RICE. THAT'S RIGHT. MAYBE EVEN MORE.
WOW.

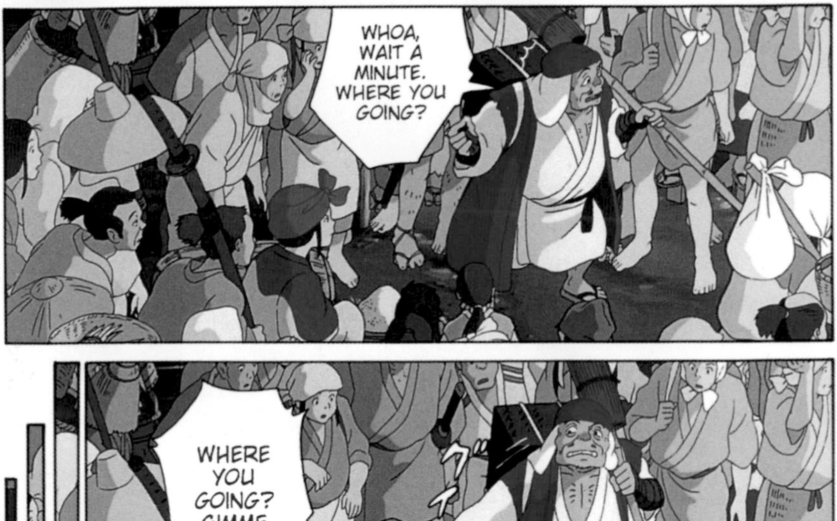
WHOA, WAIT A MINUTE. WHERE YOU GOING?

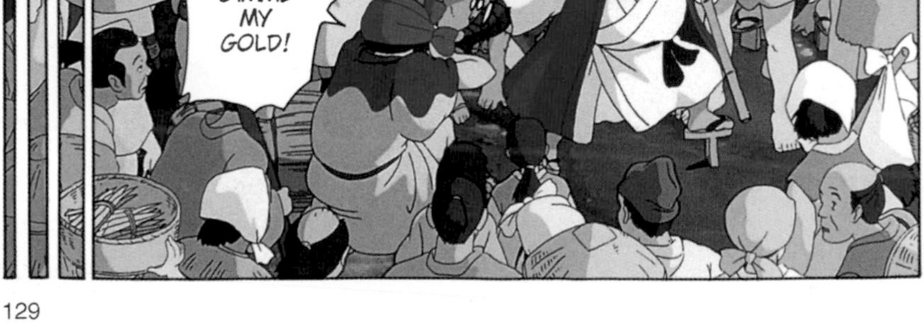
WHERE YOU GOING? GIMME MY GOLD!

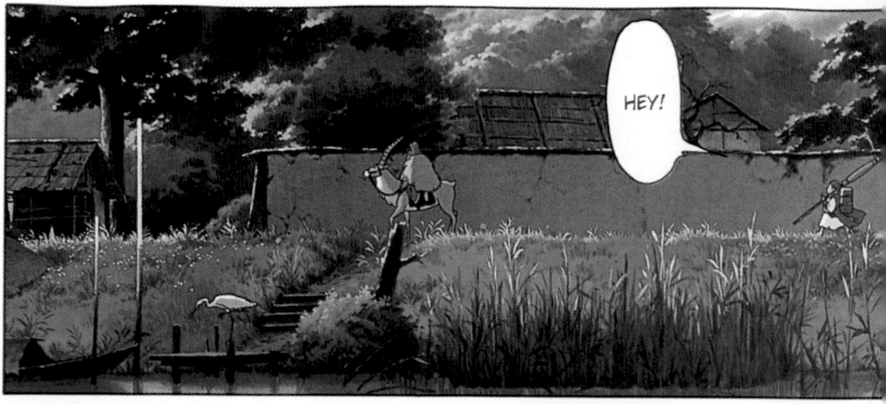
HEY!

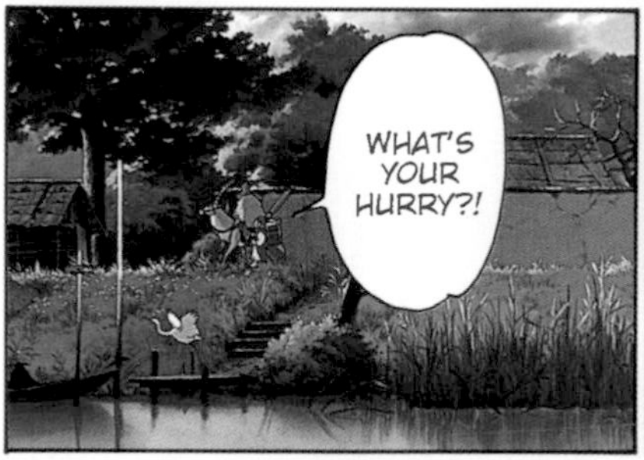
WHAT'S YOUR HURRY?!

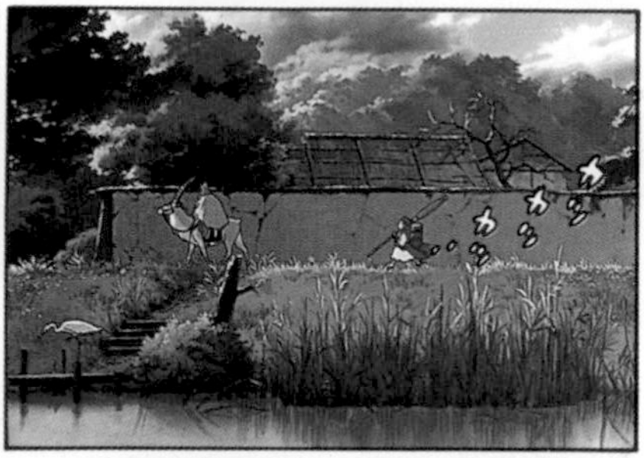

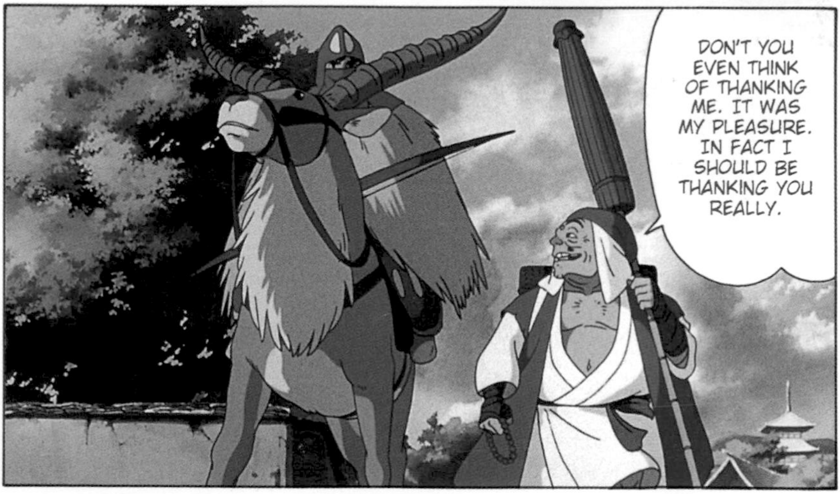
DON'T YOU EVEN THINK OF THANKING ME. IT WAS MY PLEASURE. IN FACT I SHOULD BE THANKING YOU REALLY.

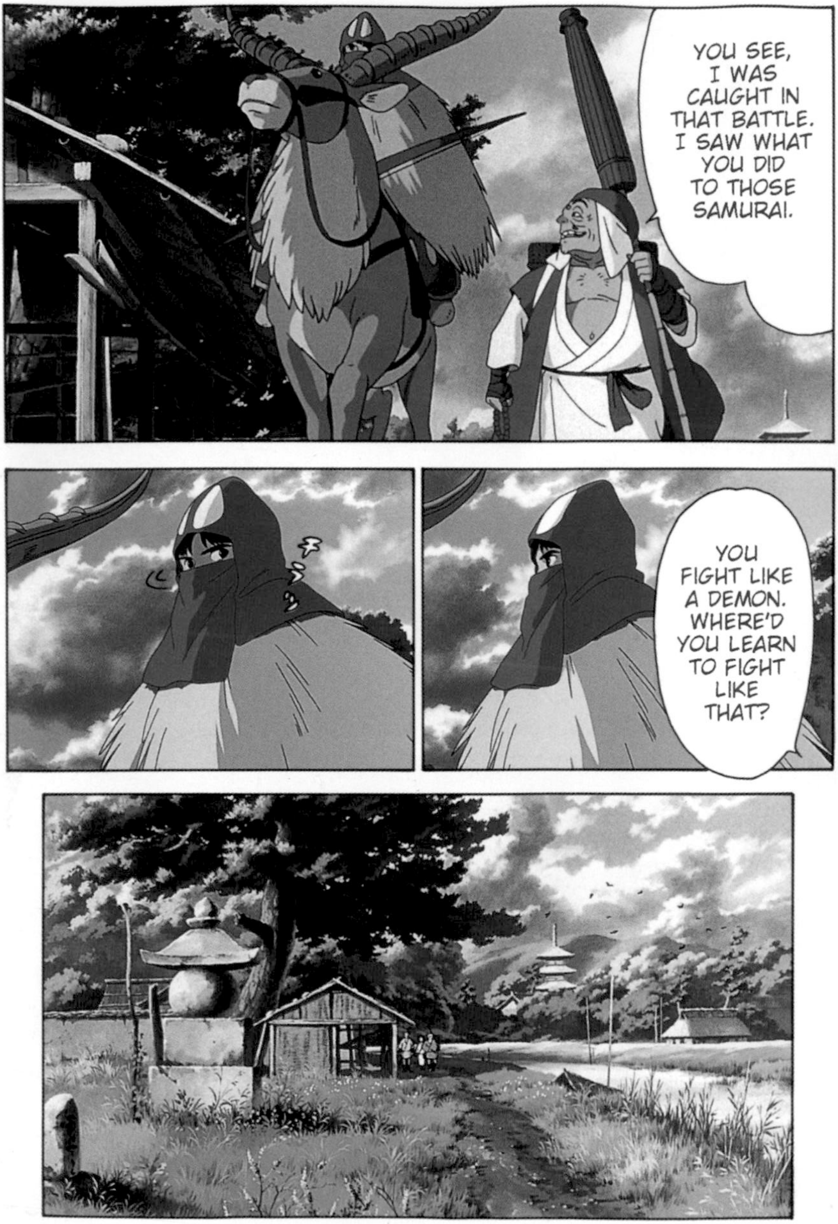
YOU SEE, I WAS CAUGHT IN THAT BATTLE. I SAW WHAT YOU DID TO THOSE SAMURAI.
YOU FIGHT LIKE A DEMON. WHERE'D YOU LEARN TO FIGHT LIKE THAT?

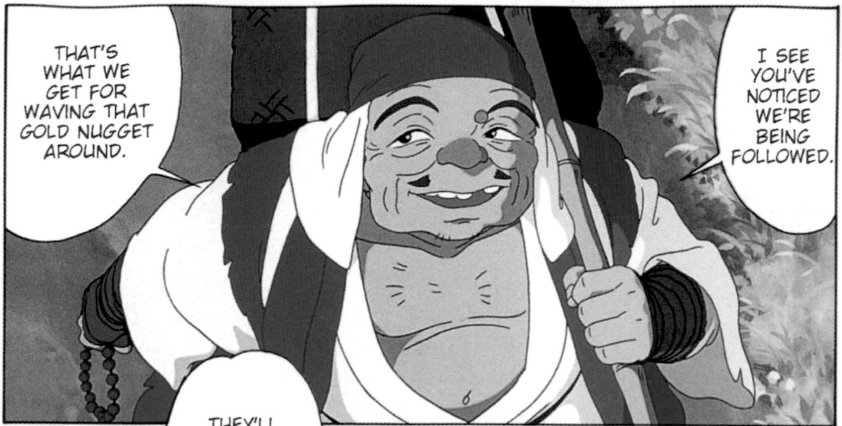
I SEE YOU'VE NOTICED WE'RE BEING FOLLOWED.
THAT'S WHAT WE GET FOR WAVING THAT GOLD NUGGET AROUND.

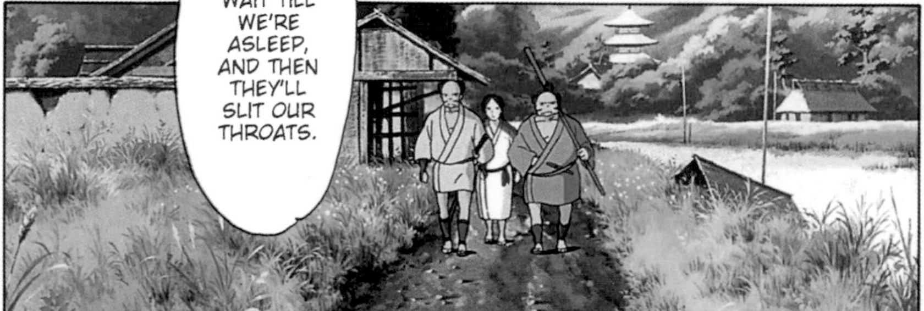
THEY'LL WAIT TILL WE'RE ASLEEP, AND THEN THEY'LL SLIT OUR THROATS.

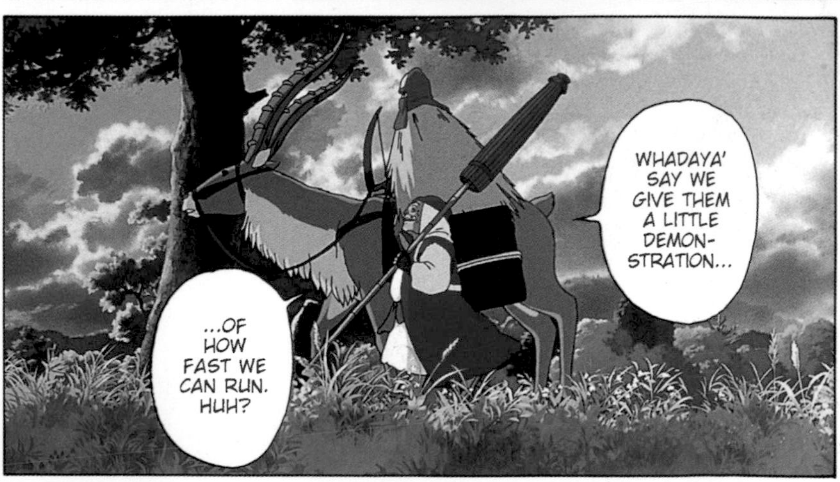
WHADAYA' SAY WE GIVE THEM A LITTLE DEMON-STRATION...
...OF HOW FAST WE CAN RUN. HUH?

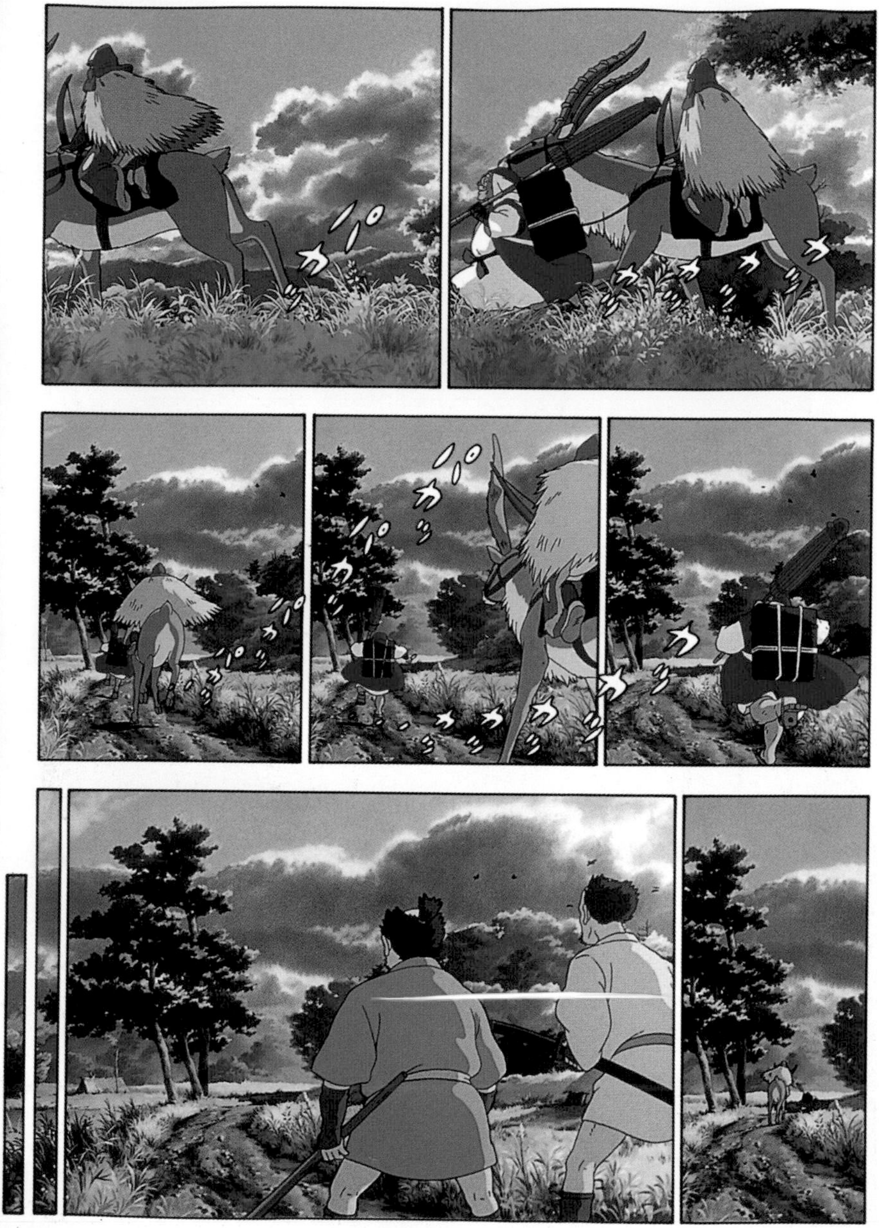
パカッ
パカッ
パカッ
パカッ

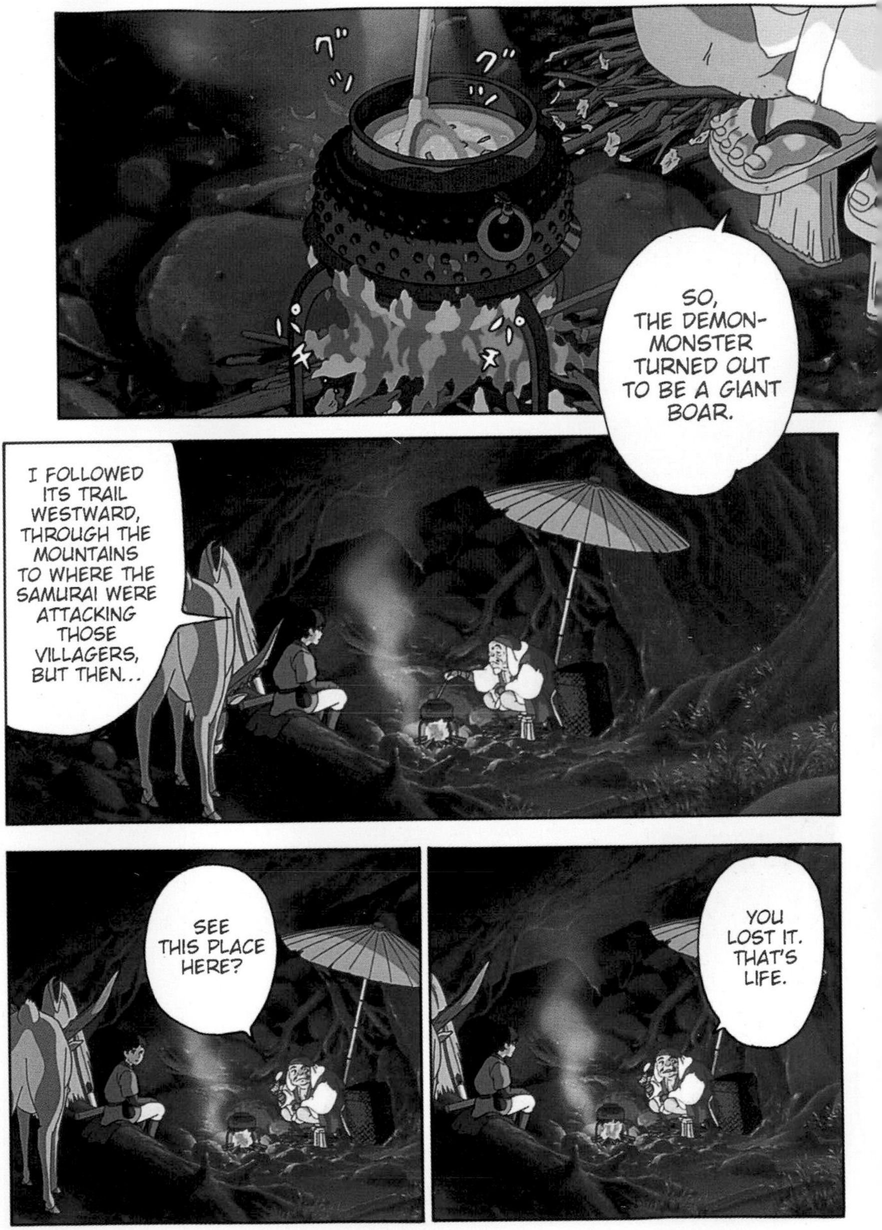
グツ
グツ
パチ
パチ
SO, THE DEMON-MONSTER TURNED OUT TO BE A GIANT BOAR.
I FOLLOWED ITS TRAIL WESTWARD, THROUGH THE MOUNTAINS TO WHERE THE SAMURAI WERE ATTACKING THOSE VILLAGERS, BUT THEN...
YOU LOST IT. THAT'S LIFE.
SEE THIS PLACE HERE?

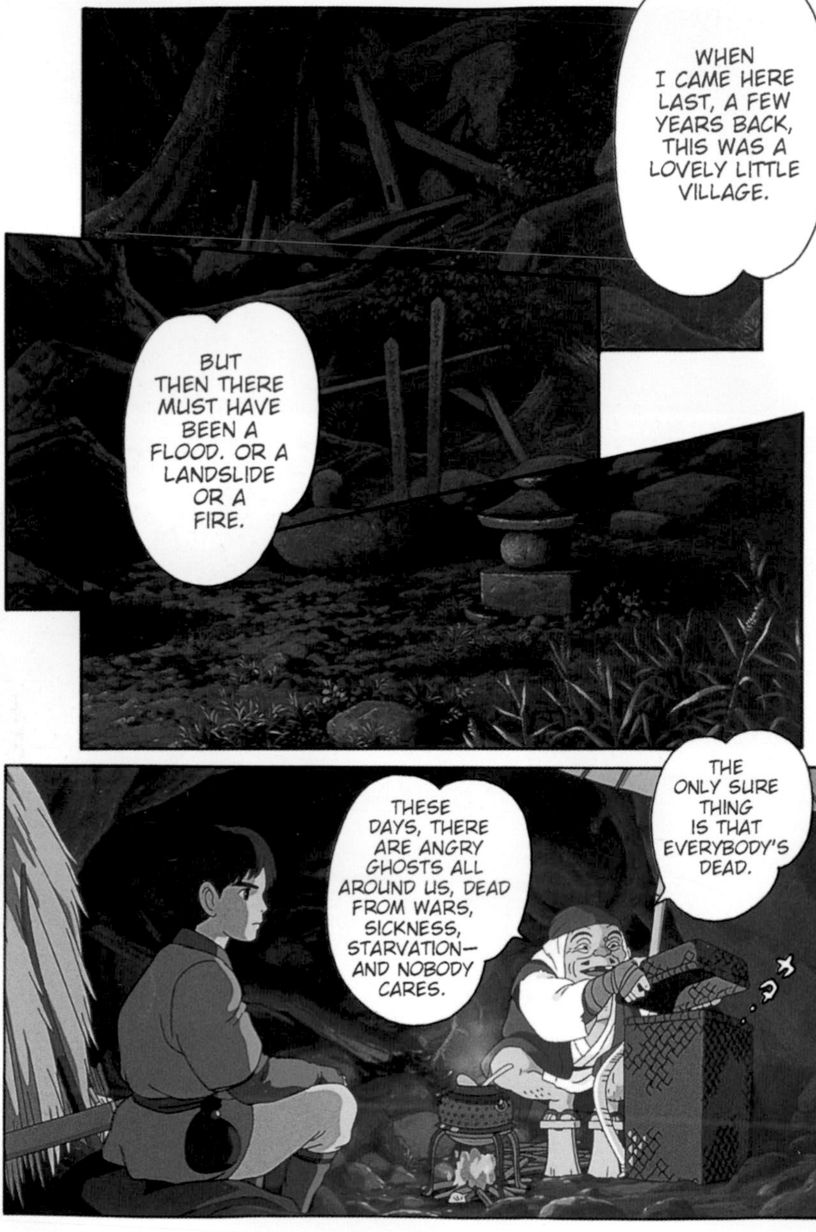
WHEN I CAME HERE LAST, A FEW YEARS BACK, THIS WAS A LOVELY LITTLE VILLAGE.
BUT THEN THERE MUST HAVE BEEN A FLOOD. OR A LANDSLIDE OR A FIRE.
THE ONLY SURE THING IS THAT EVERYBODY'S DEAD.
THESE DAYS, THERE ARE ANGRY GHOSTS ALL AROUND US, DEAD FROM WARS, SICKNESS, STARVATION— AND NOBODY CARES.

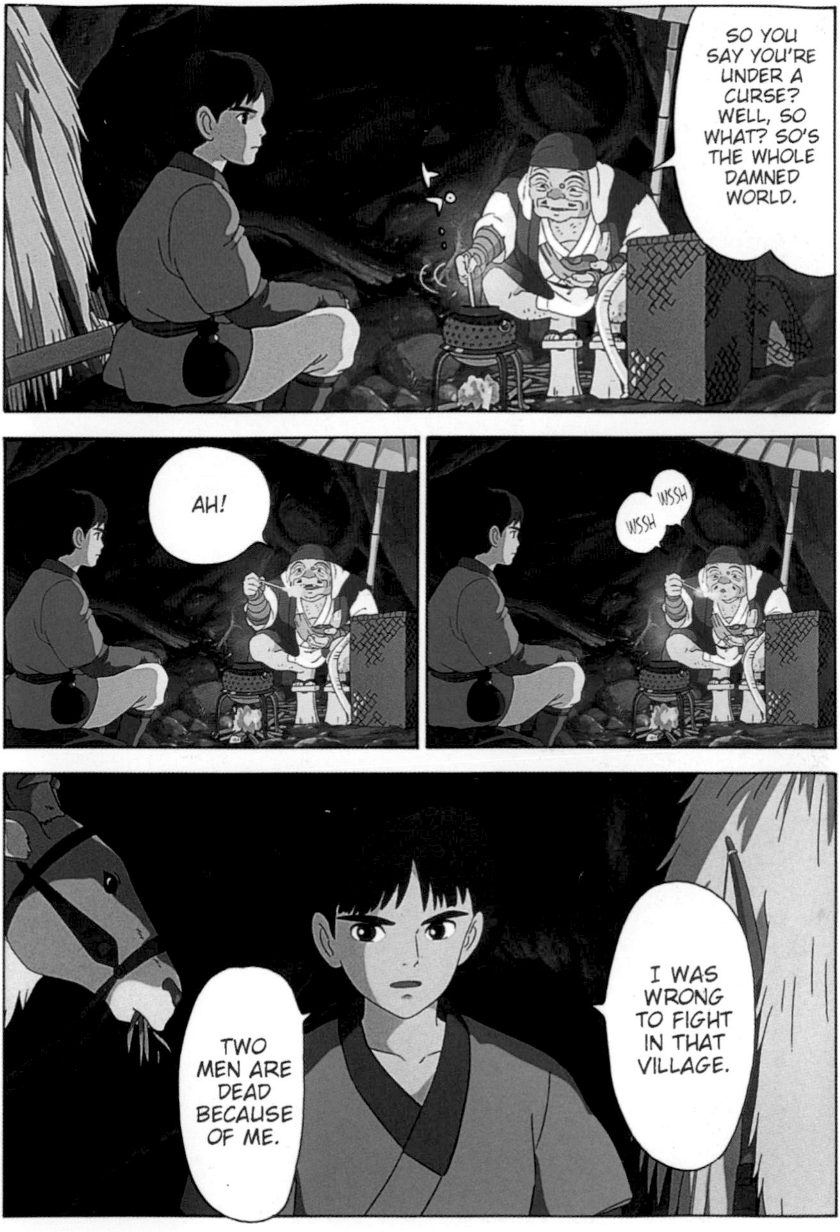
SO YOU SAY YOU'RE UNDER A CURSE? WELL, SO WHAT? SO'S THE WHOLE DAMNED WORLD.
AH!
WSSH
WSSH
I WAS WRONG TO FIGHT IN THAT VILLAGE.
TWO MEN ARE DEAD BECAUSE OF ME.

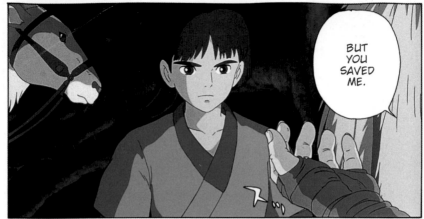

BUT YOU SAVED ME.

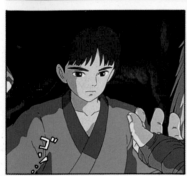

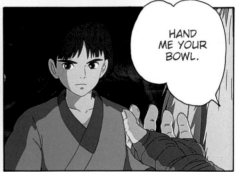

HAND ME YOUR BOWL.

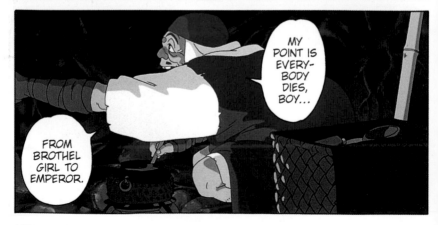

MY POINT IS EVERY-BODY DIES, BOY...

FROM BROTHEL GIRL TO EMPEROR.

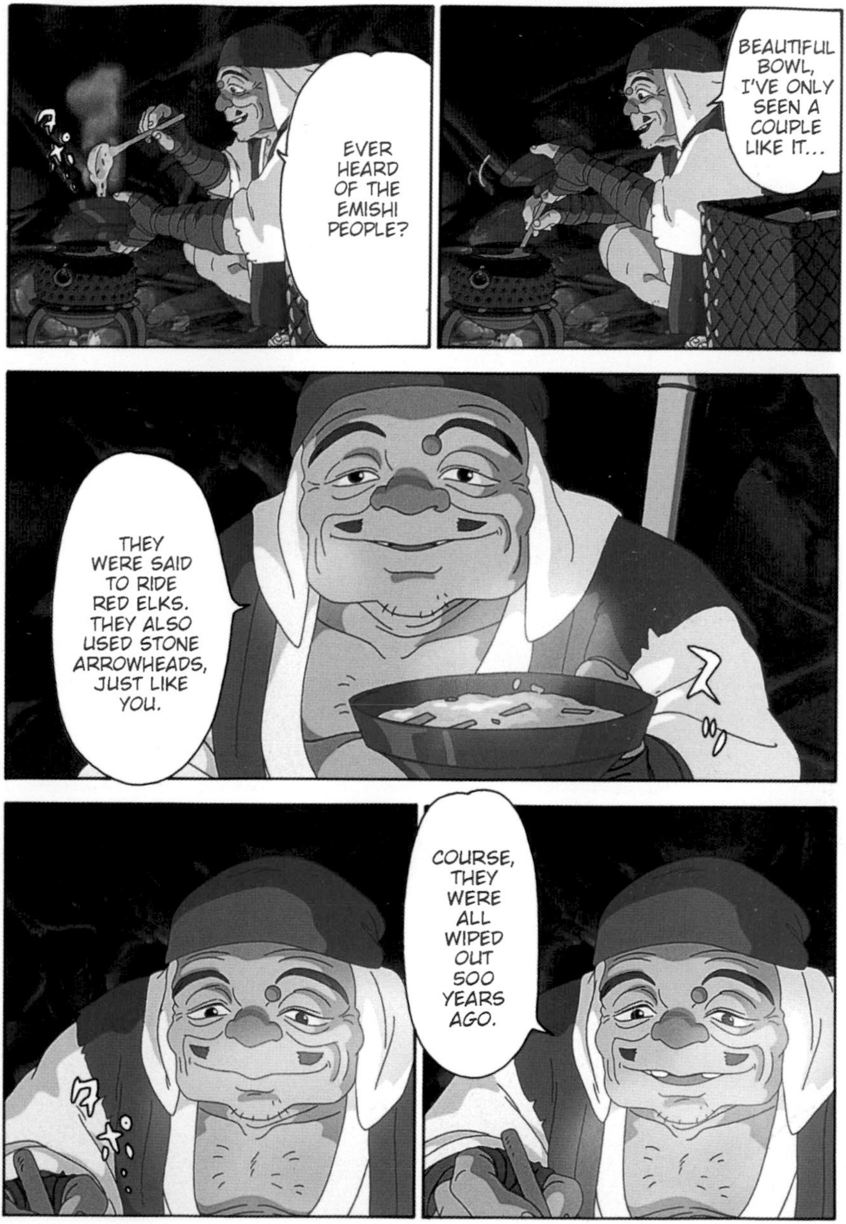
BEAUTIFUL BOWL, I'VE ONLY SEEN A COUPLE LIKE IT...
EVER HEARD OF THE EMISHI PEOPLE?
THEY WERE SAID TO RIDE RED ELKS. THEY ALSO USED STONE ARROWHEADS, JUST LIKE YOU.
COURSE, THEY WERE ALL WIPED OUT 500 YEARS AGO.

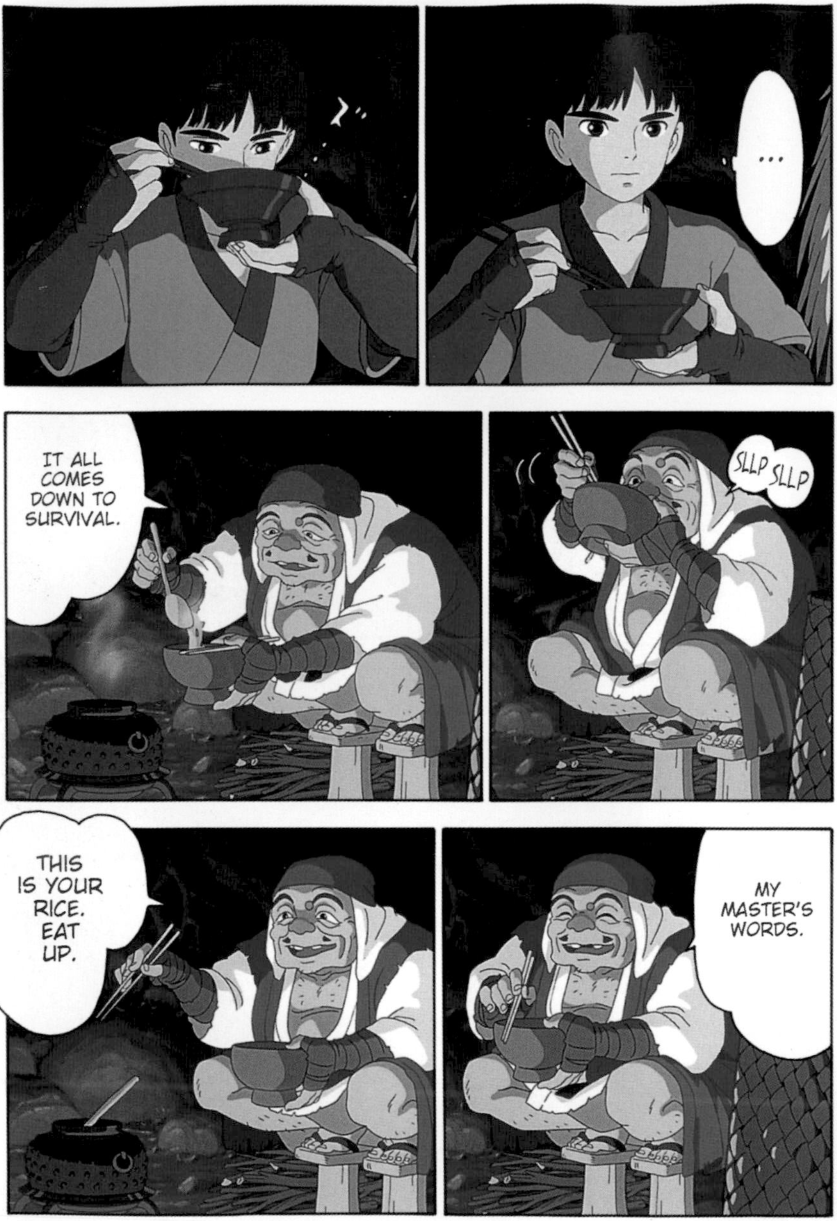

...
IT ALL COMES DOWN TO SURVIVAL.
SLLP SLLP
THIS IS YOUR RICE. EAT UP.
MY MASTER'S WORDS.

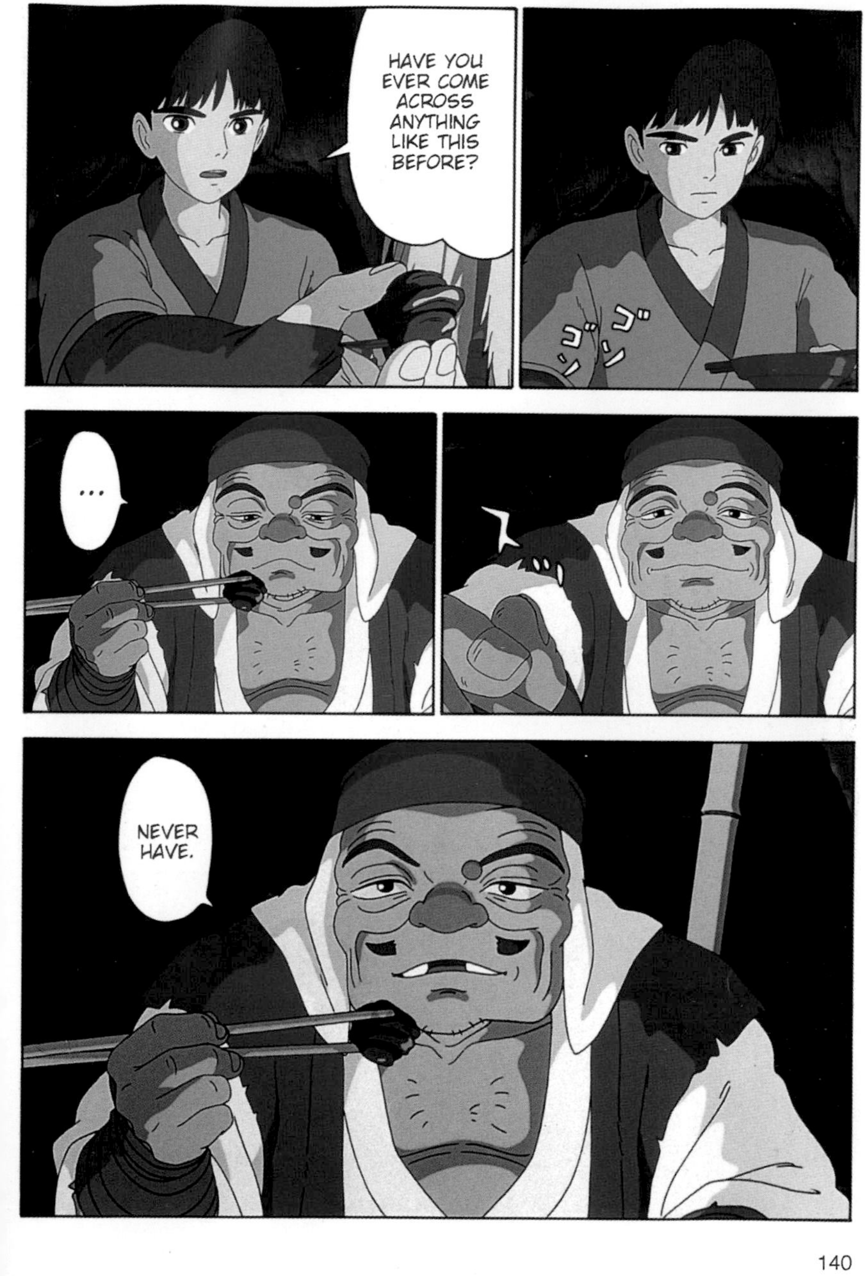
HAVE YOU EVER COME ACROSS ANYTHING LIKE THIS BEFORE?
...
NEVER HAVE.

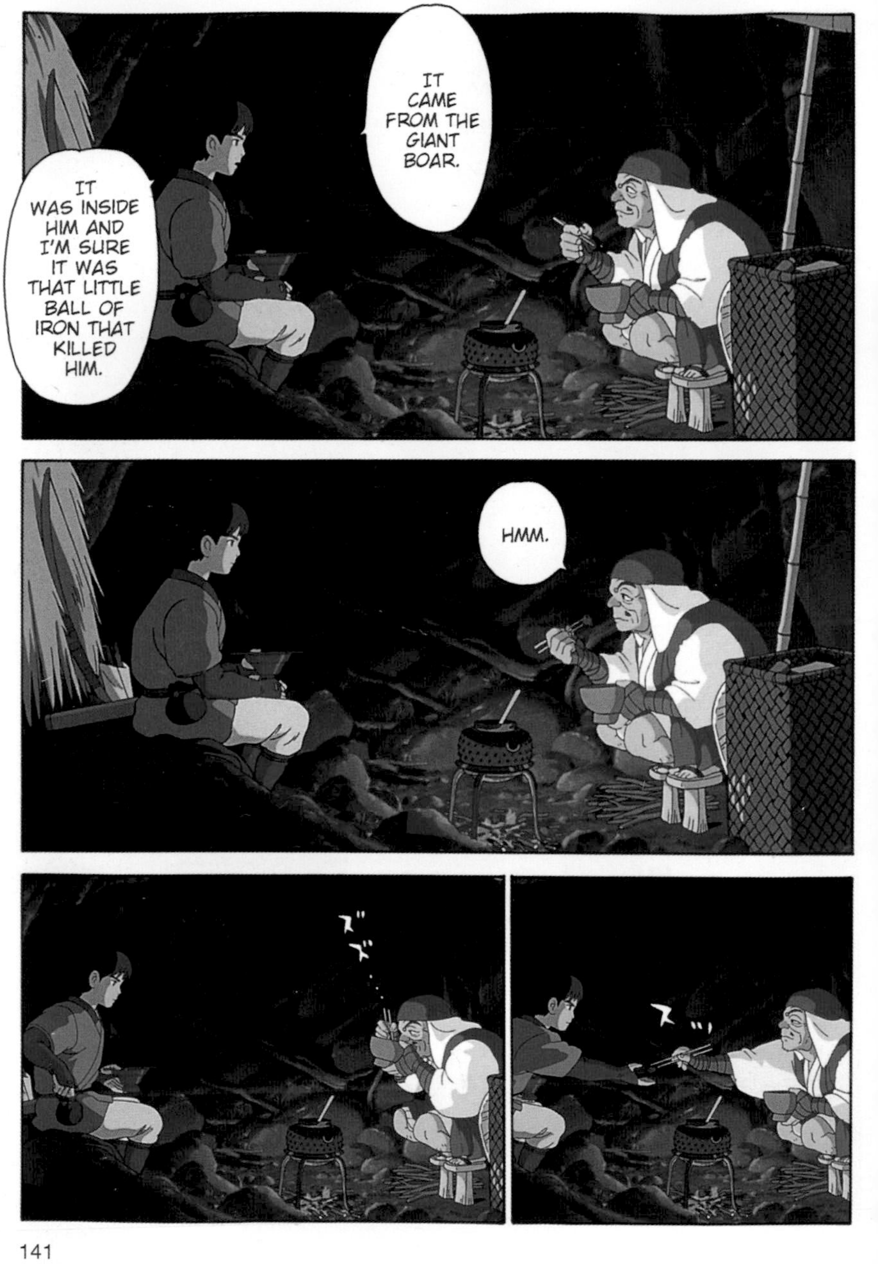
IT CAME FROM THE GIANT BOAR.
IT WAS INSIDE HIM AND I'M SURE IT WAS THAT LITTLE BALL OF IRON THAT KILLED HIM.
HMM.
ズッ
ズズ…

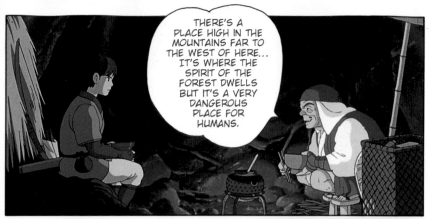

THERE'S A PLACE HIGH IN THE MOUNTAINS FAR TO THE WEST OF HERE... IT'S WHERE THE SPIRIT OF THE FOREST DWELLS BUT IT'S A VERY DANGEROUS PLACE FOR HUMANS.

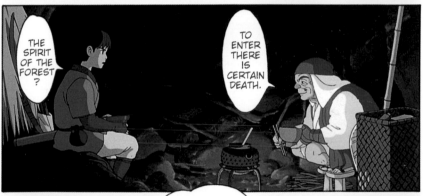

THE SPIRIT OF THE FOREST?

TO ENTER THERE IS CERTAIN DEATH.

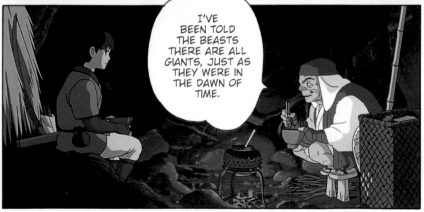

I'VE BEEN TOLD THE BEASTS THERE ARE ALL GIANTS, JUST AS THEY WERE IN THE DAWN OF TIME.

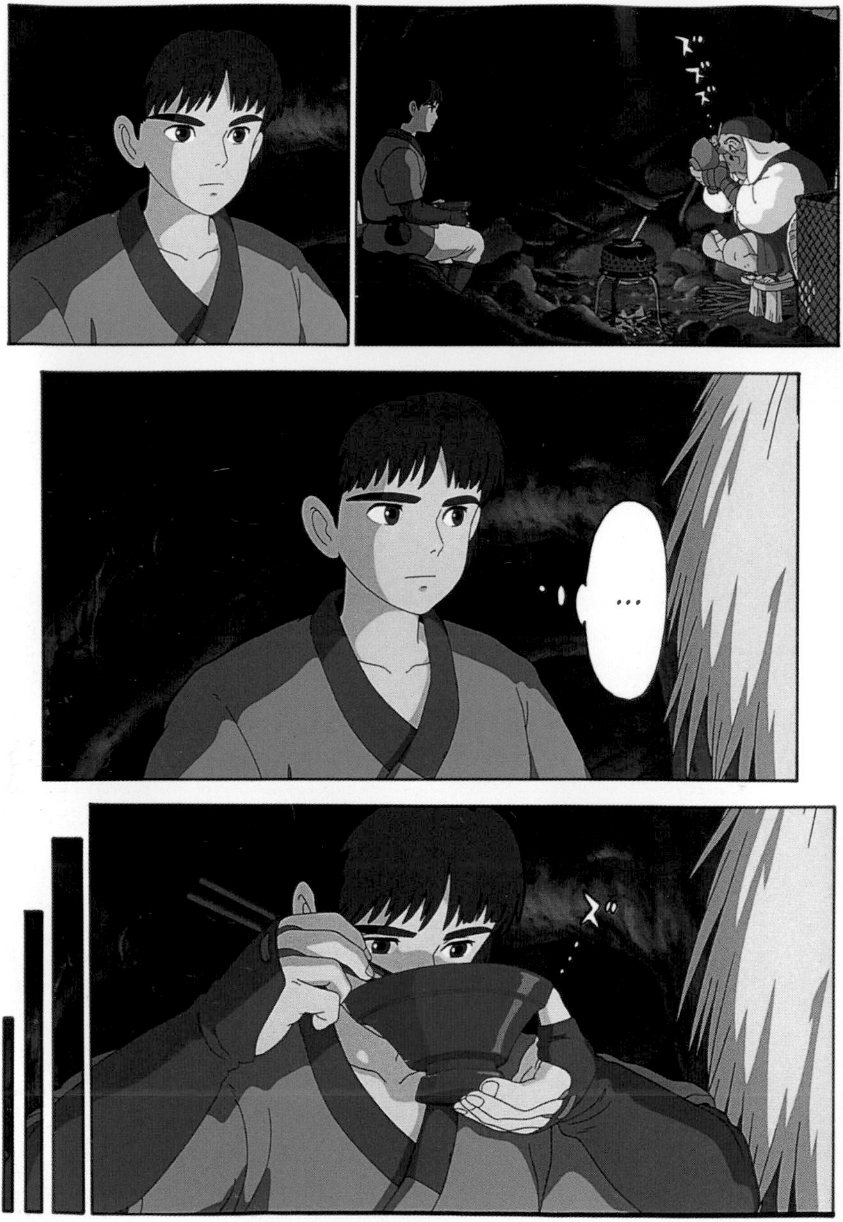
ズズズ…
…
ズ…

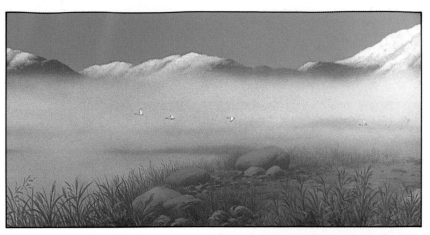

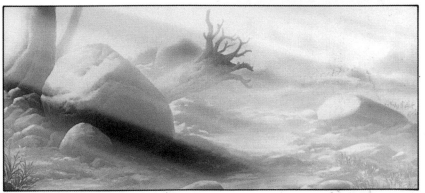

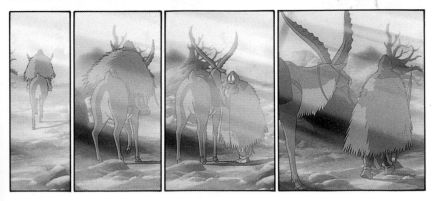

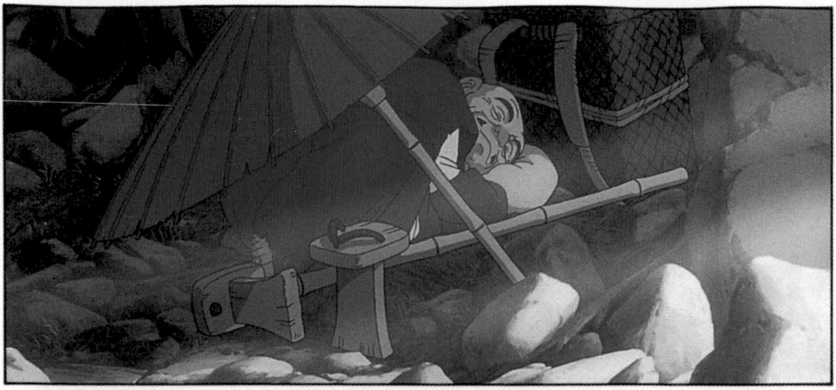
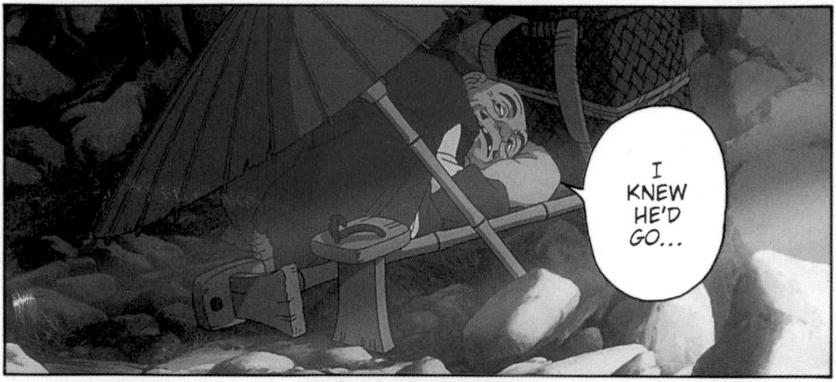
I KNEW HE'D GO...
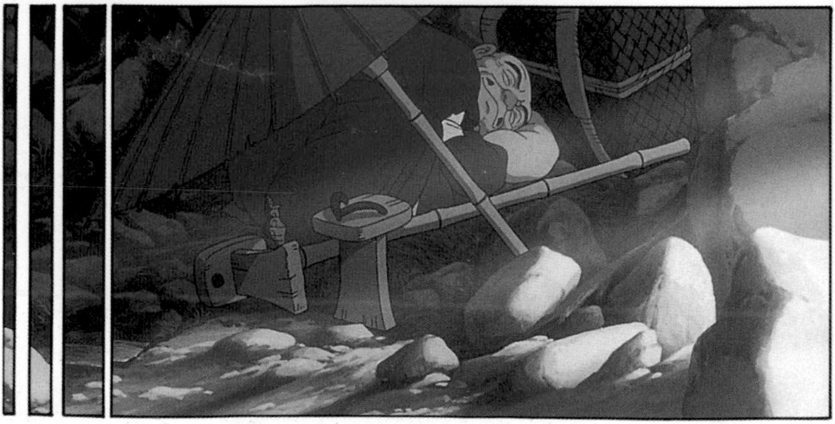

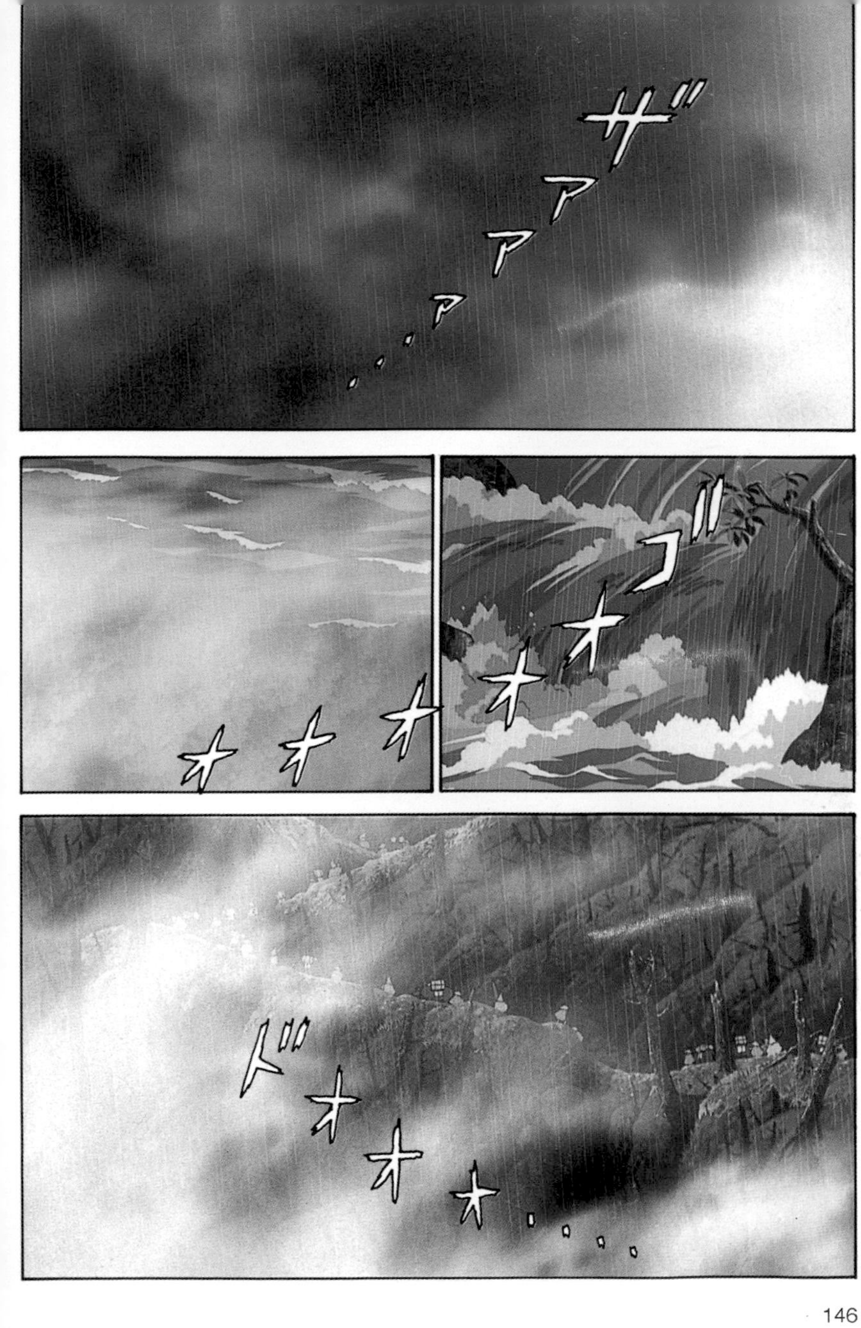
ザアアア…
ゴオオ
オオオ
ドオオオ…

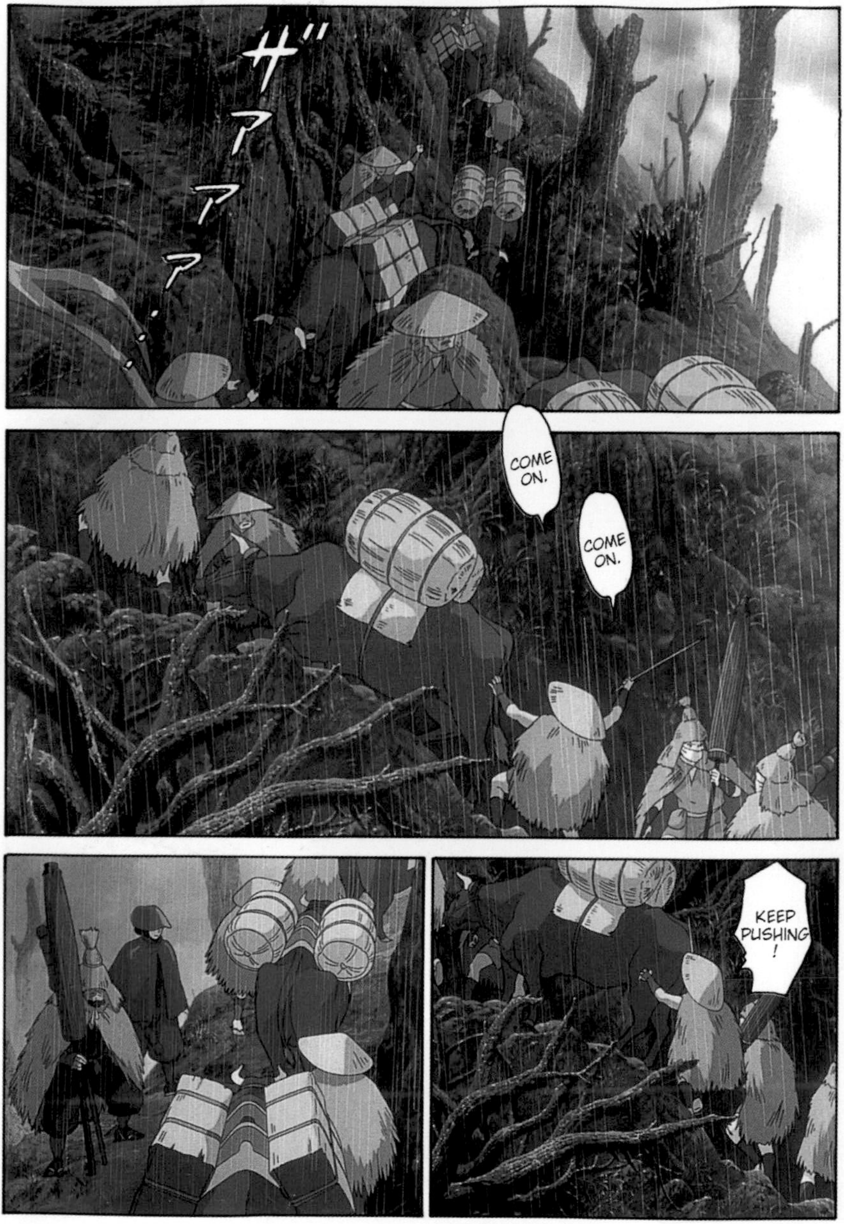
ザアアア…
COME ON.
COME ON.
KEEP PUSHING!

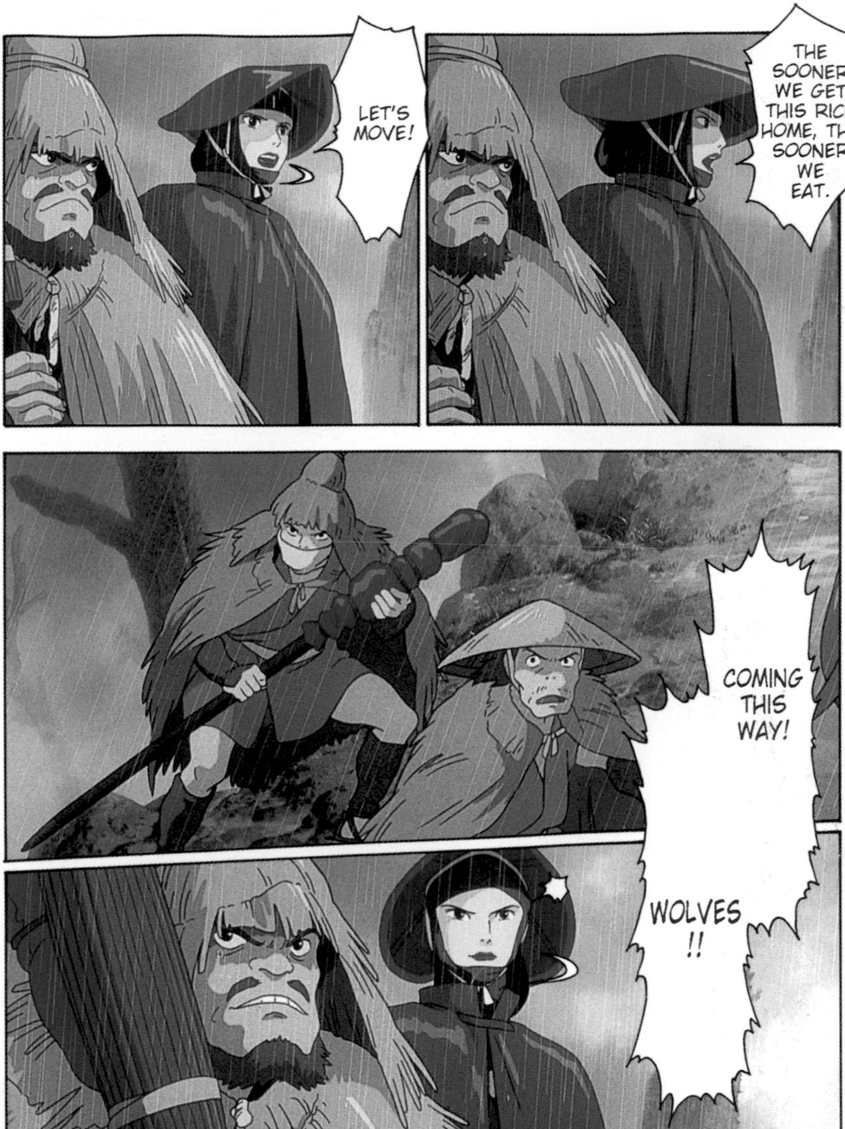
LET'S MOVE!
THE SOONER WE GET THIS RICE HOME, THE SOONER WE EAT.
COMING THIS WAY!
WOLVES !!

ダッ
ダダッ

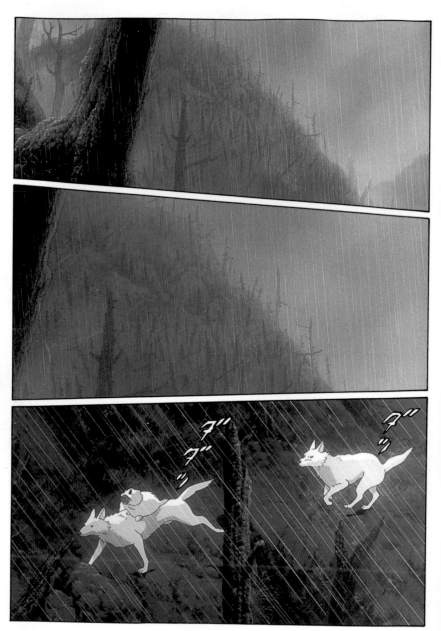

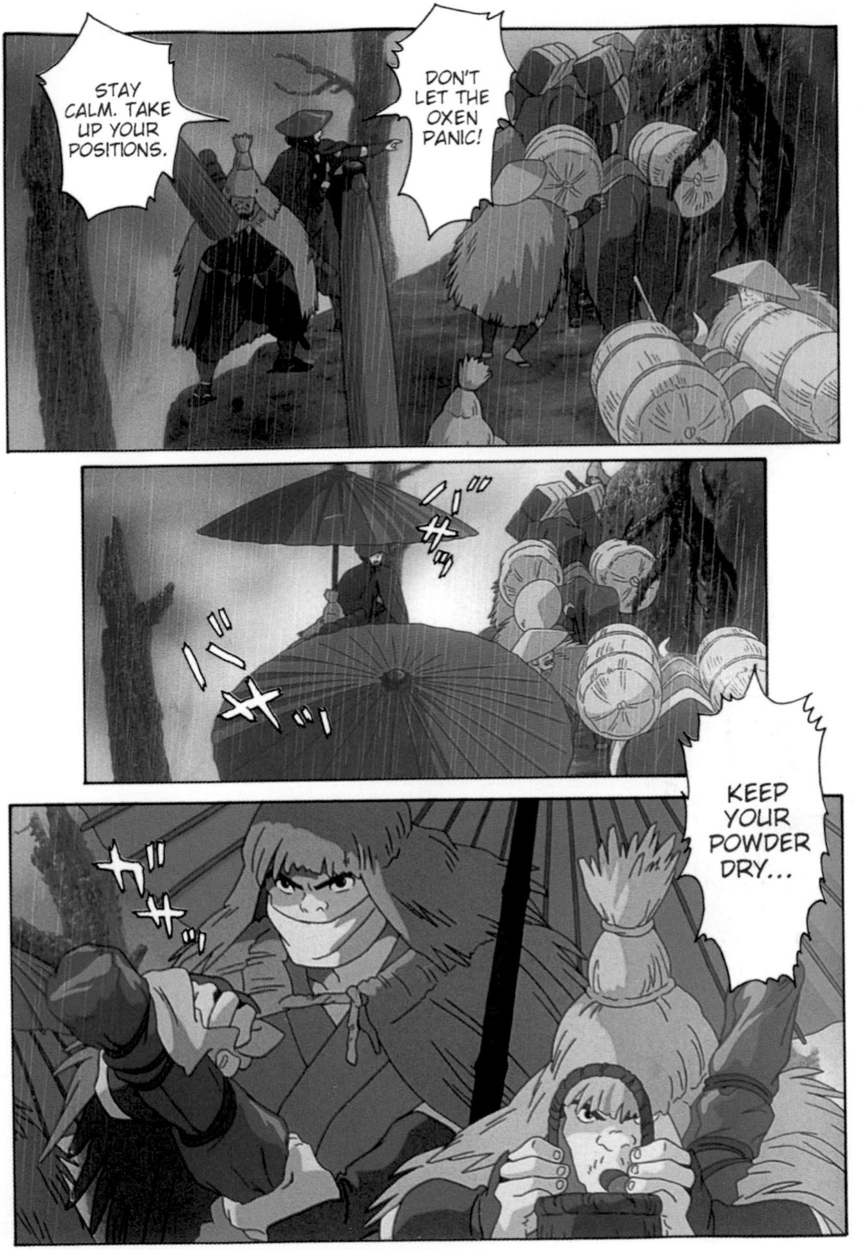
DON'T LET THE OXEN PANIC!
STAY CALM. TAKE UP YOUR POSITIONS.
KEEP YOUR POWDER DRY...

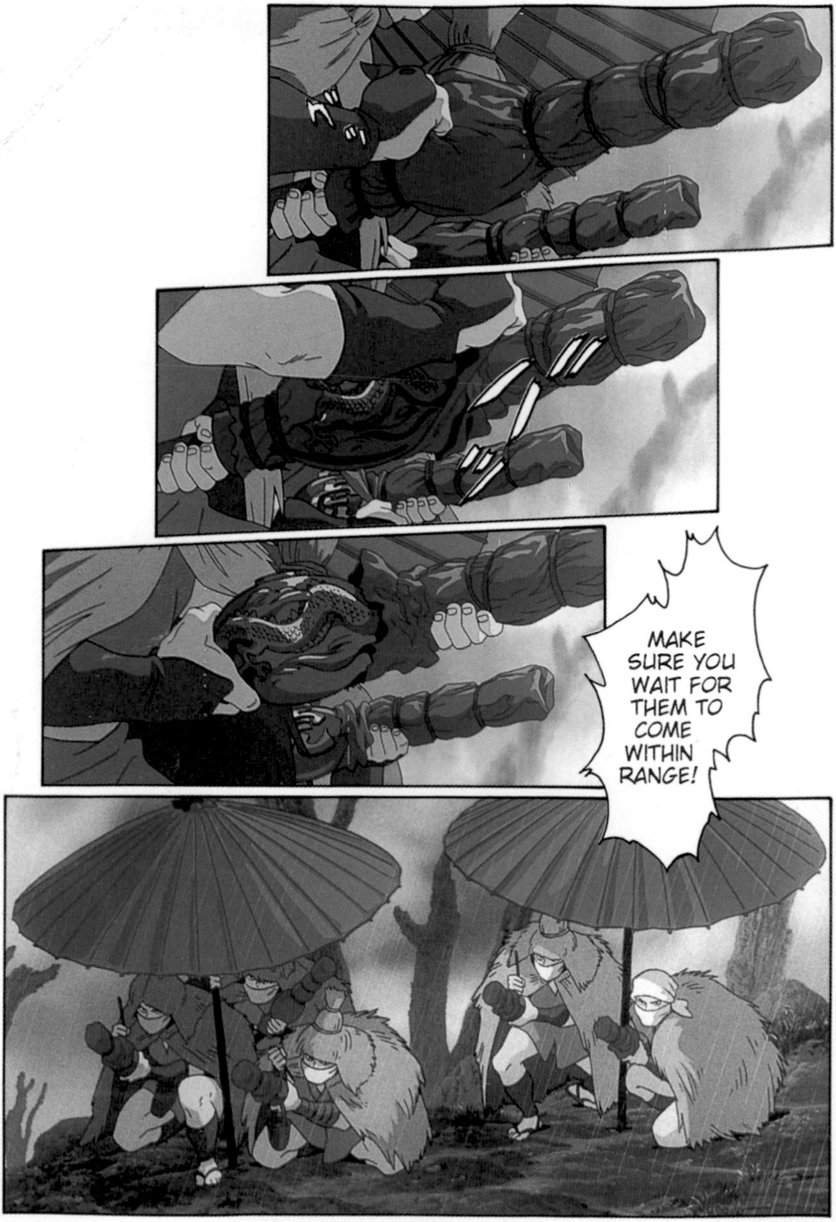
MAKE SURE YOU WAIT FOR THEM TO COME WITHIN RANGE!

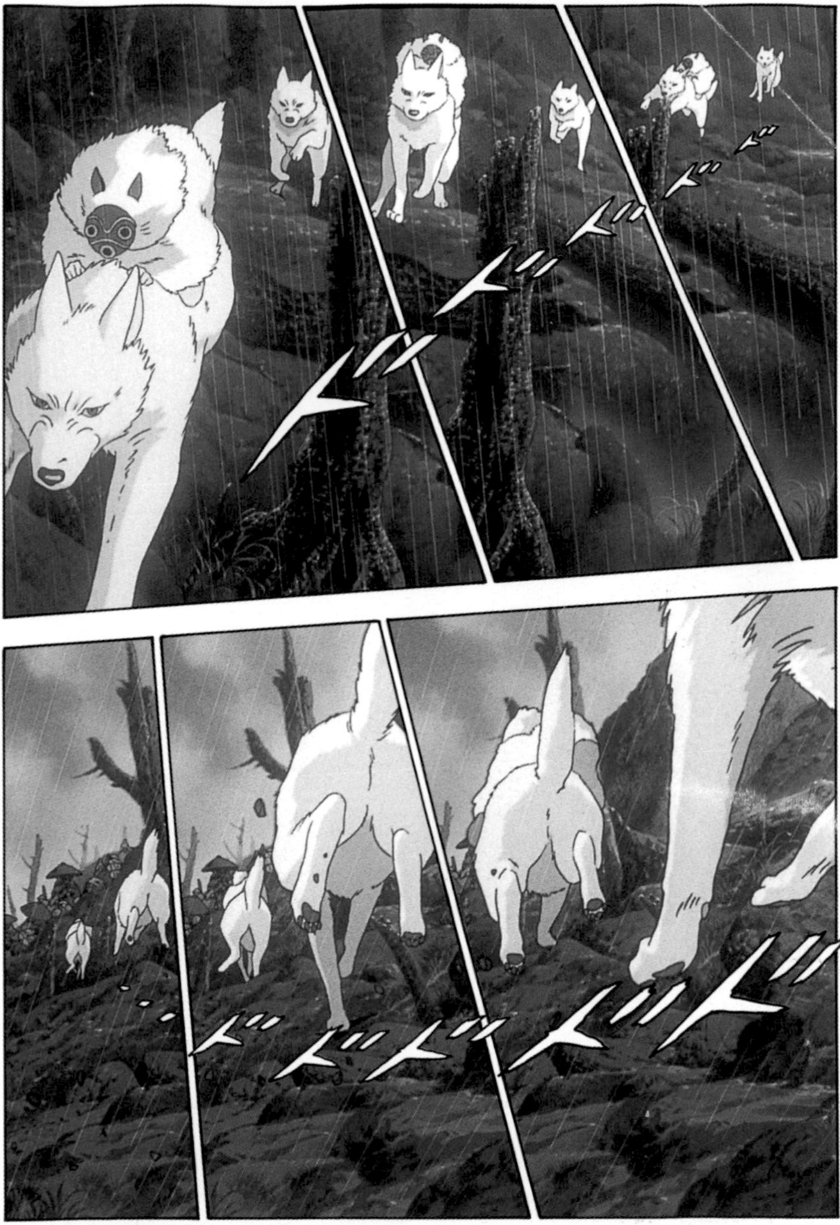
ドドドドド
ドドドドド

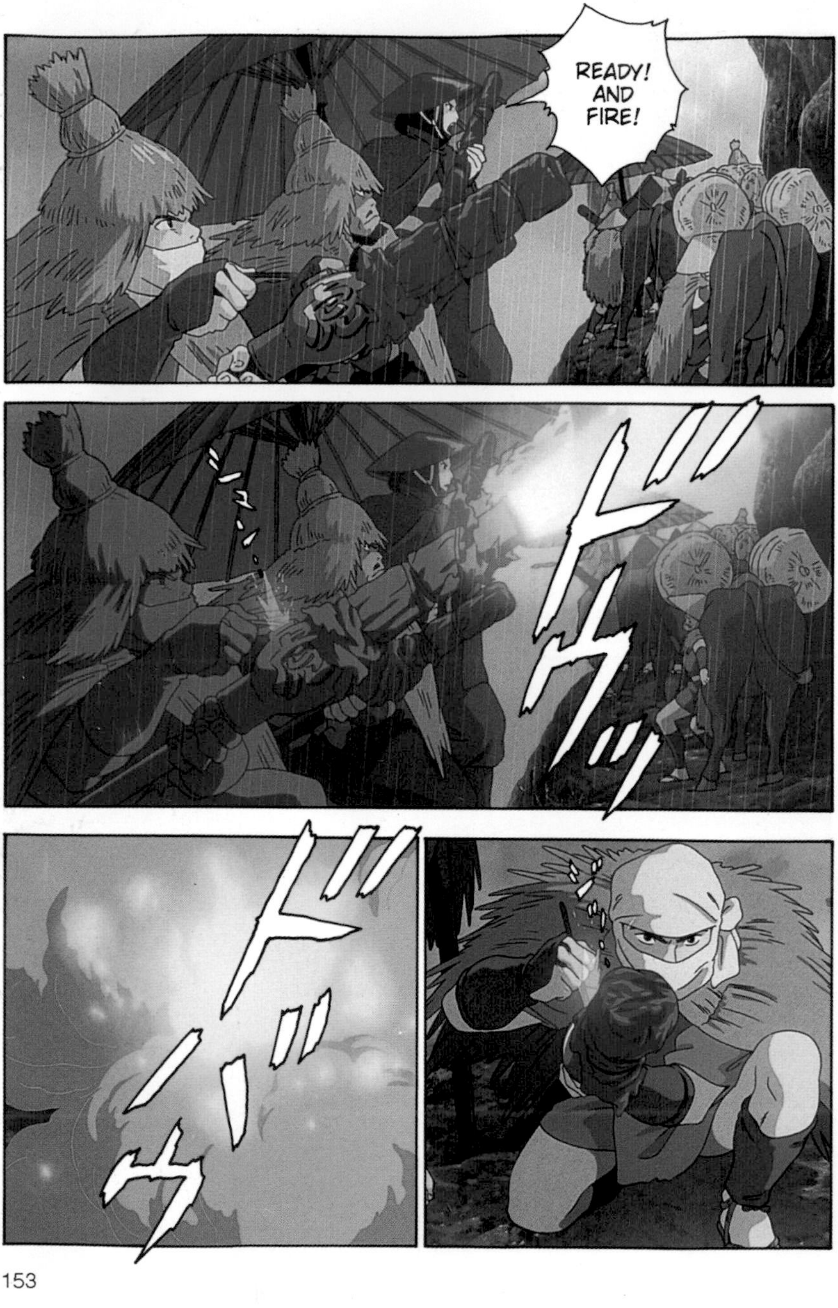
READY! AND FIRE!

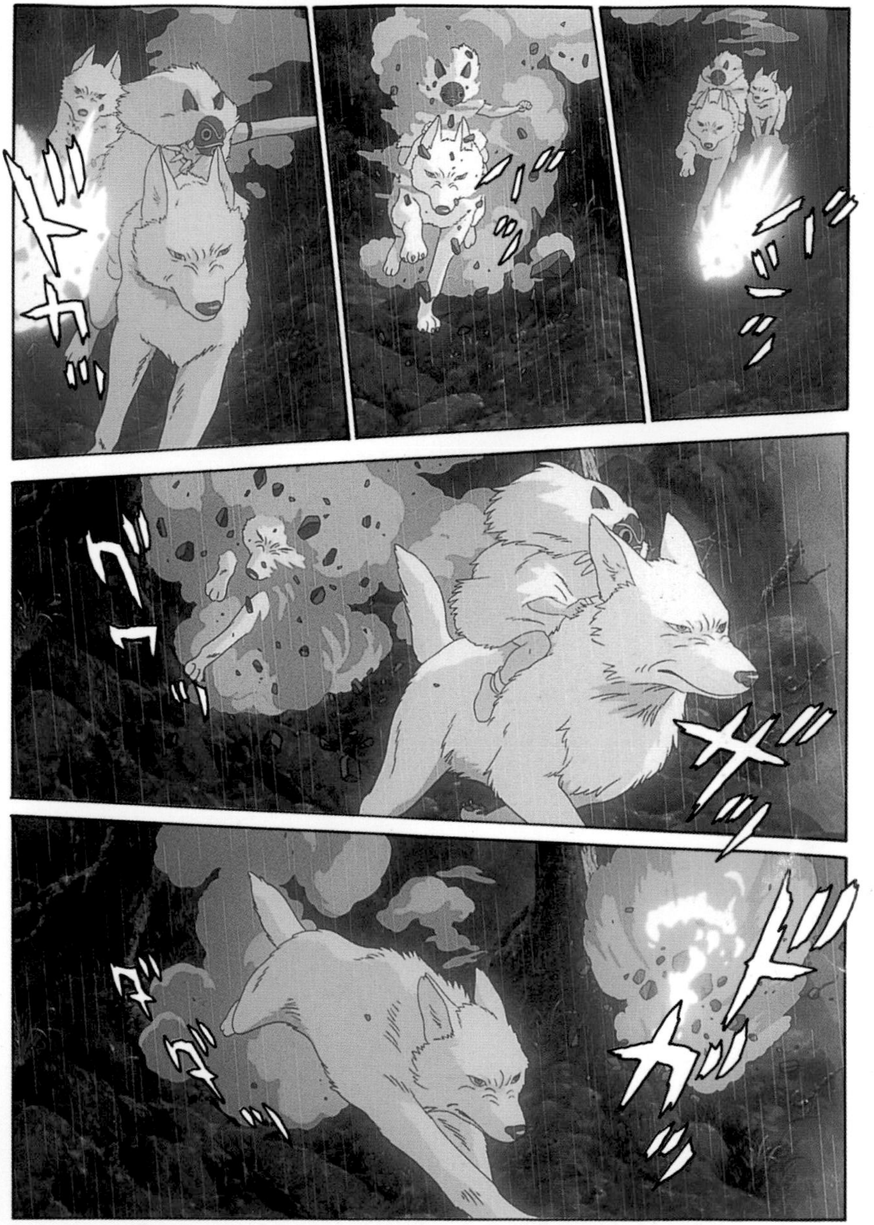
ザッ
ドガッ

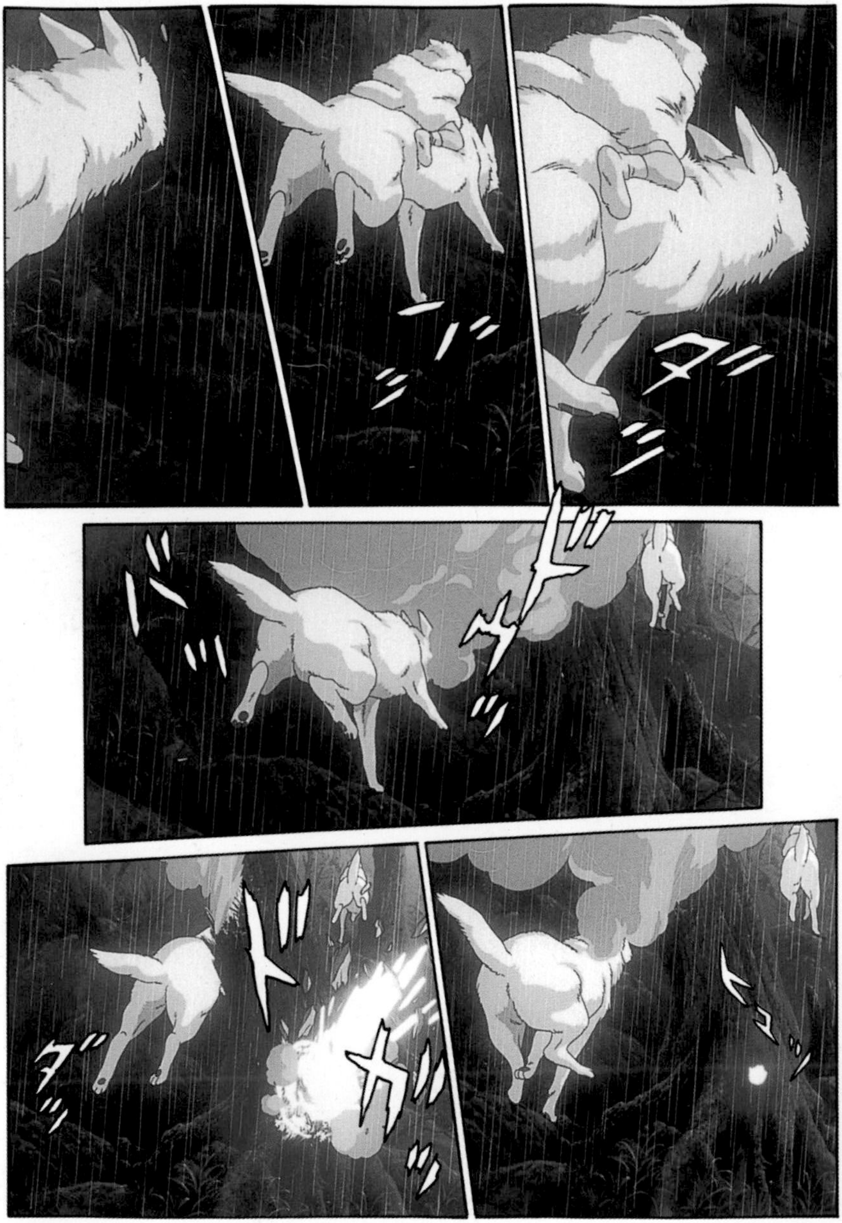
ダッ
バッ
ドッ
バッ
ヒュッ
ガッ
ドッ
ダッ

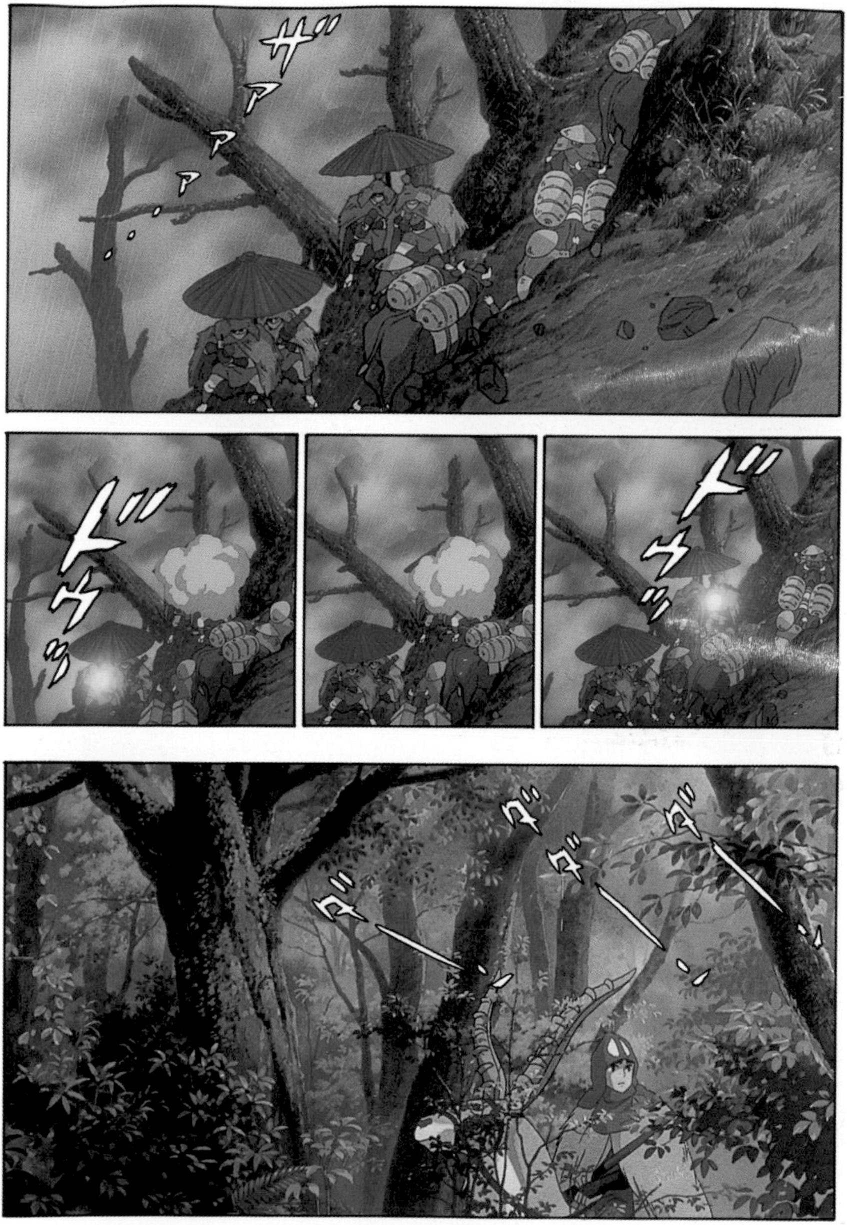
ザァァァ
ドゥッ
ドゥッ
ヴー
ヴー
ヴー
ヴー

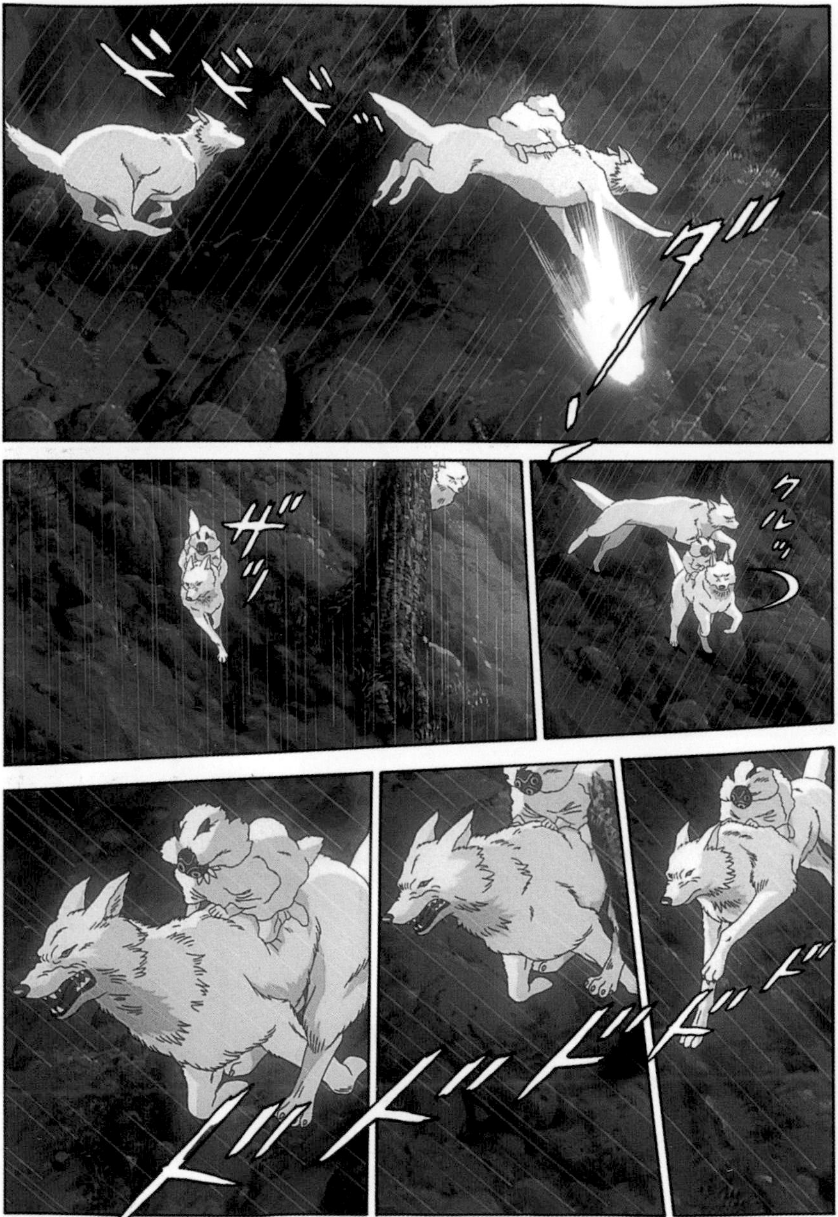
ズズズッ
ダッ
クルッ
ザッ
ドドドドド

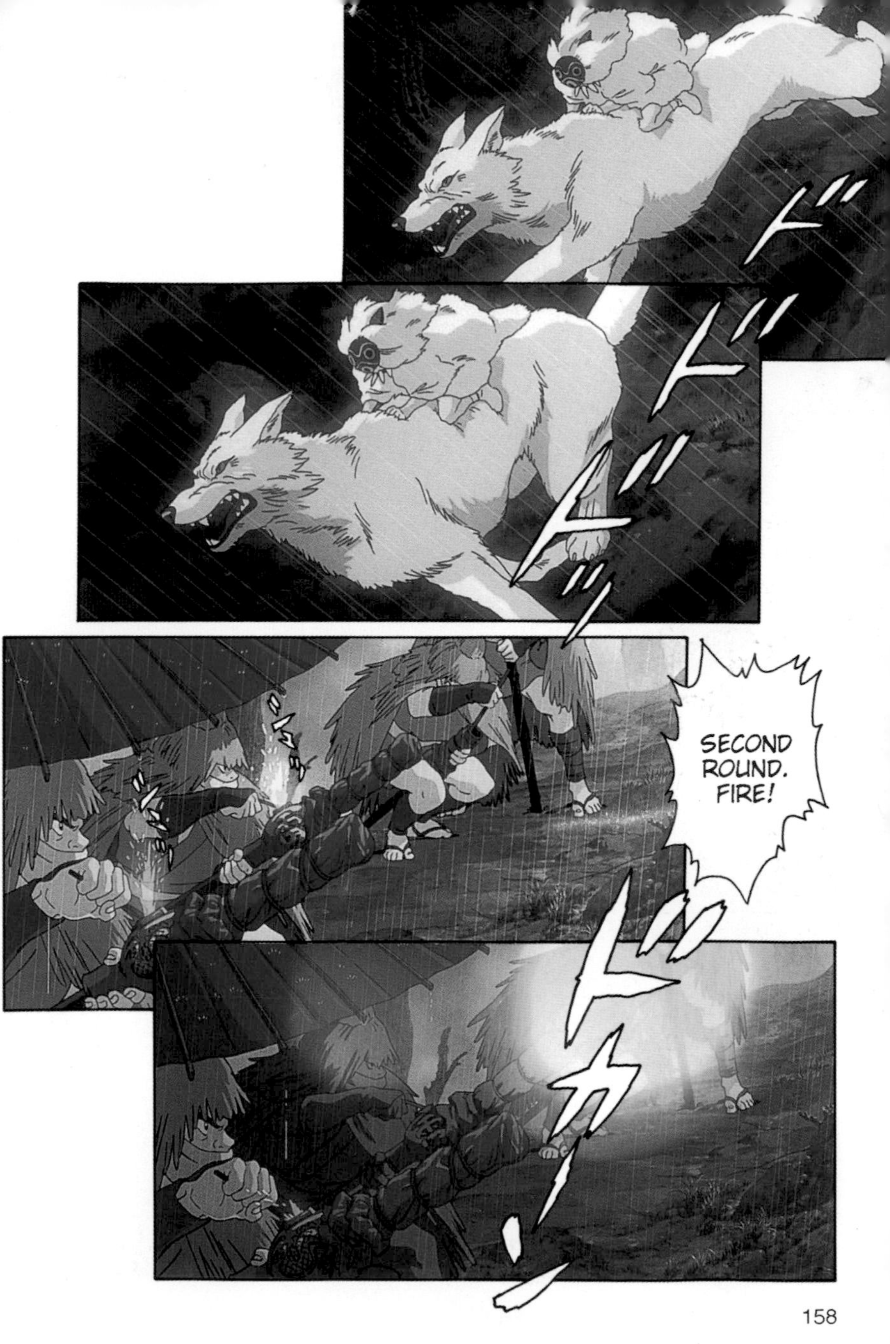
SECOND ROUND. FIRE!

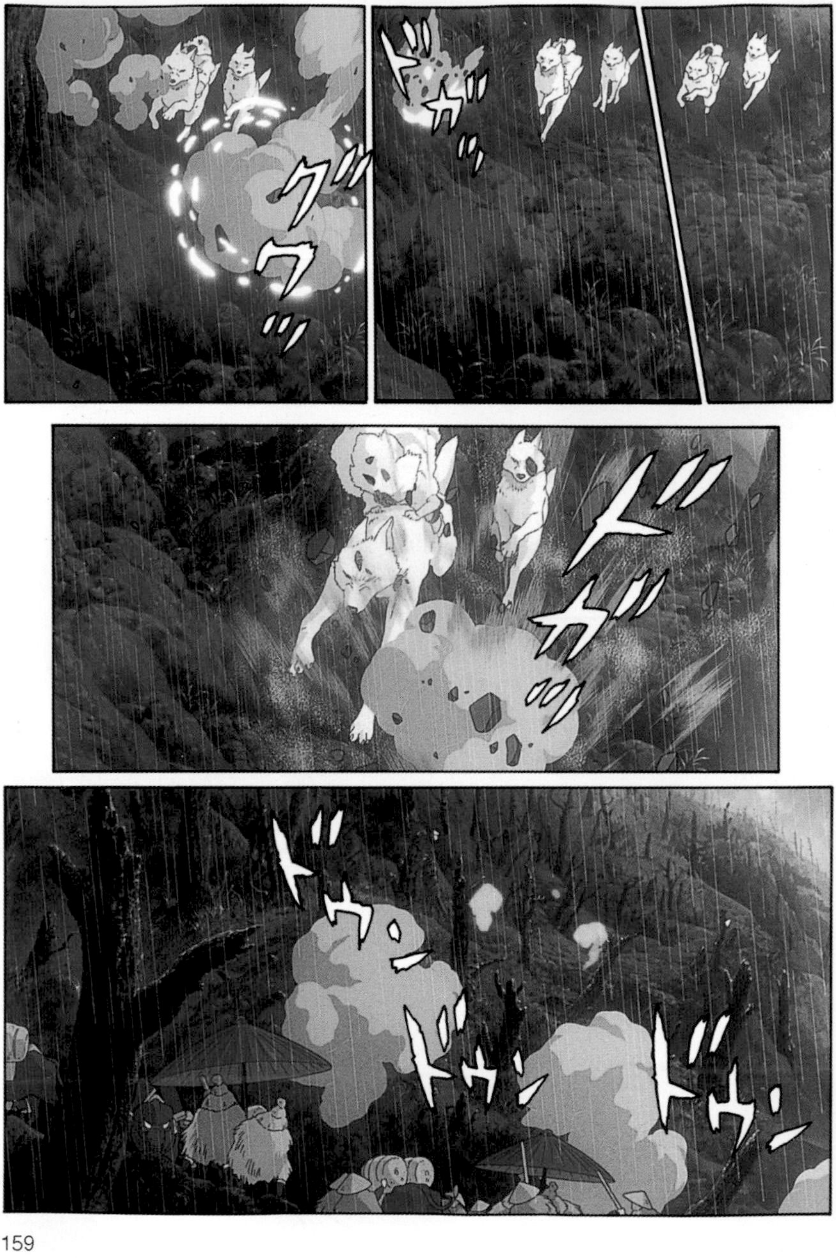
ドガッ
グワッ
ドガッ
ドウン
ドウン
ドウン

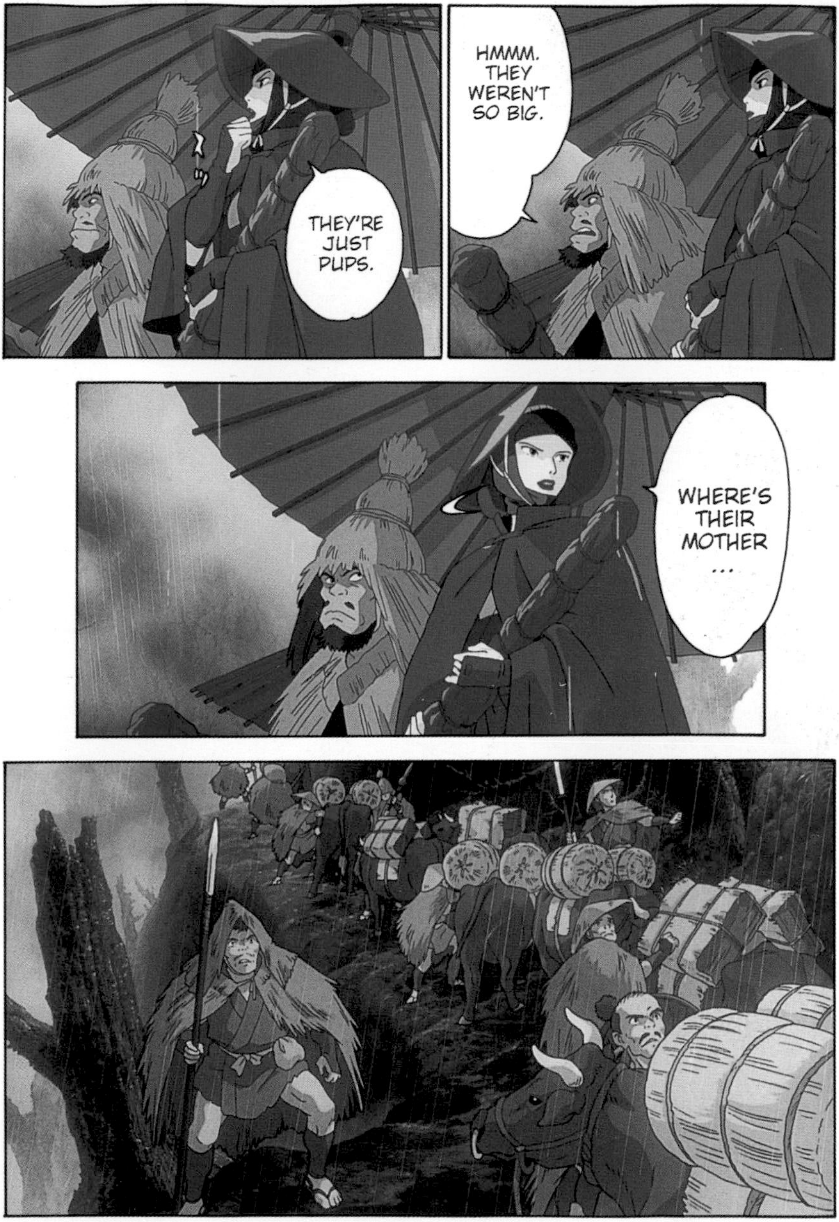
THEY'RE JUST PUPS.
HMMM. THEY WEREN'T SO BIG.
WHERE'S THEIR MOTHER ...

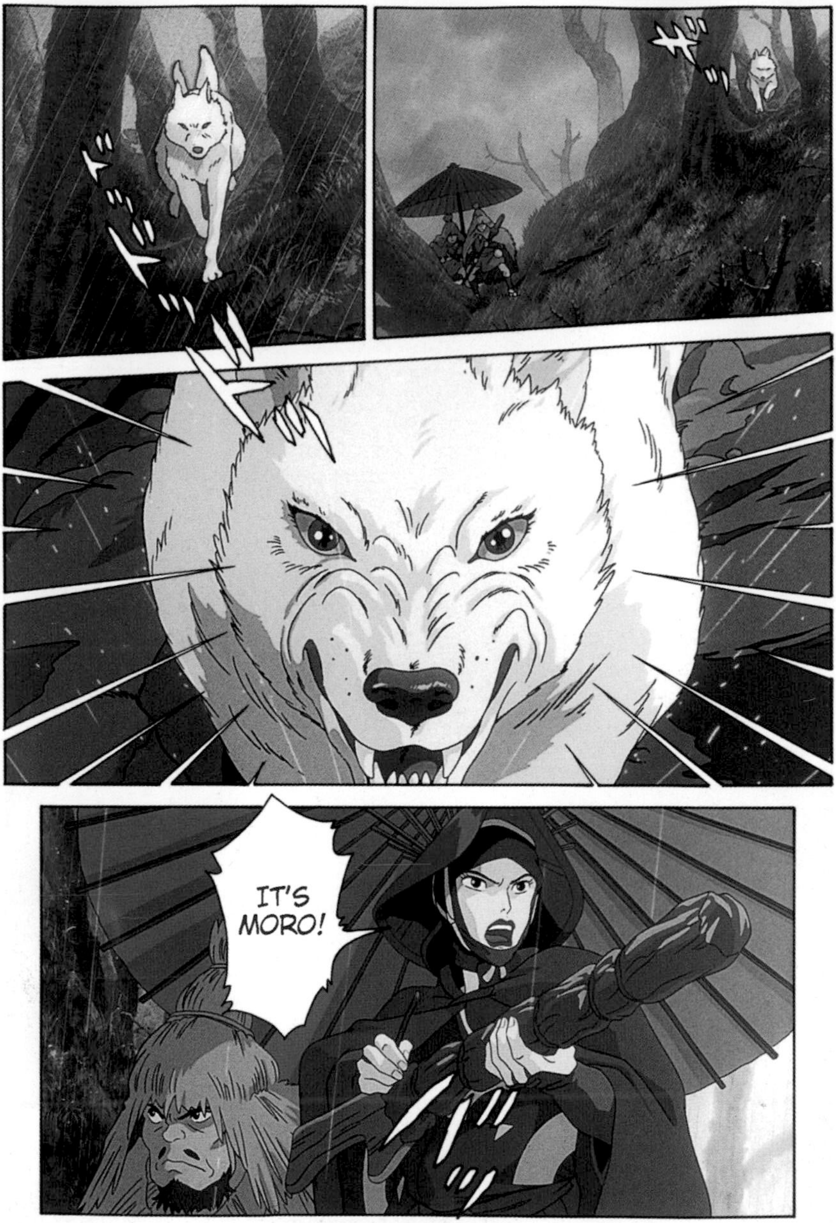
IT'S
MORO!

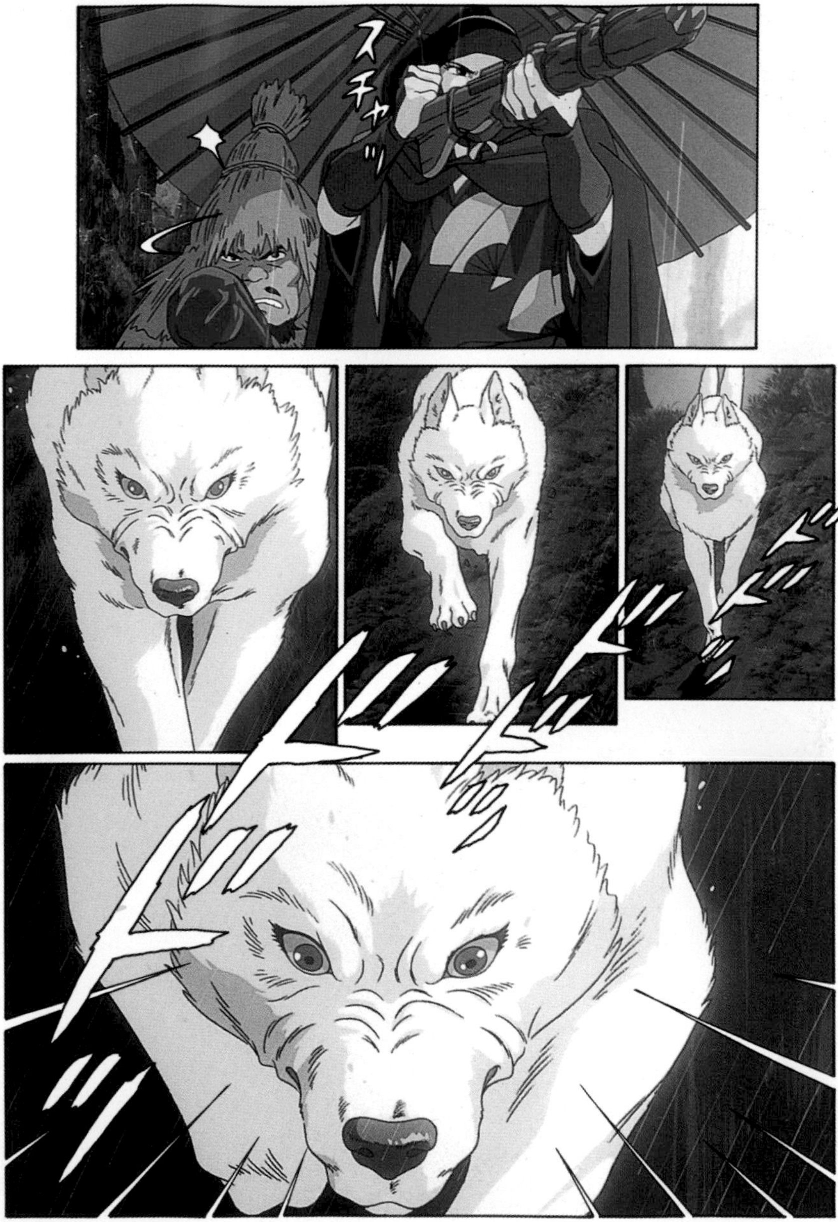
スチャッ
ドッ
ドッ
ドッ
ドッ
ドドッ

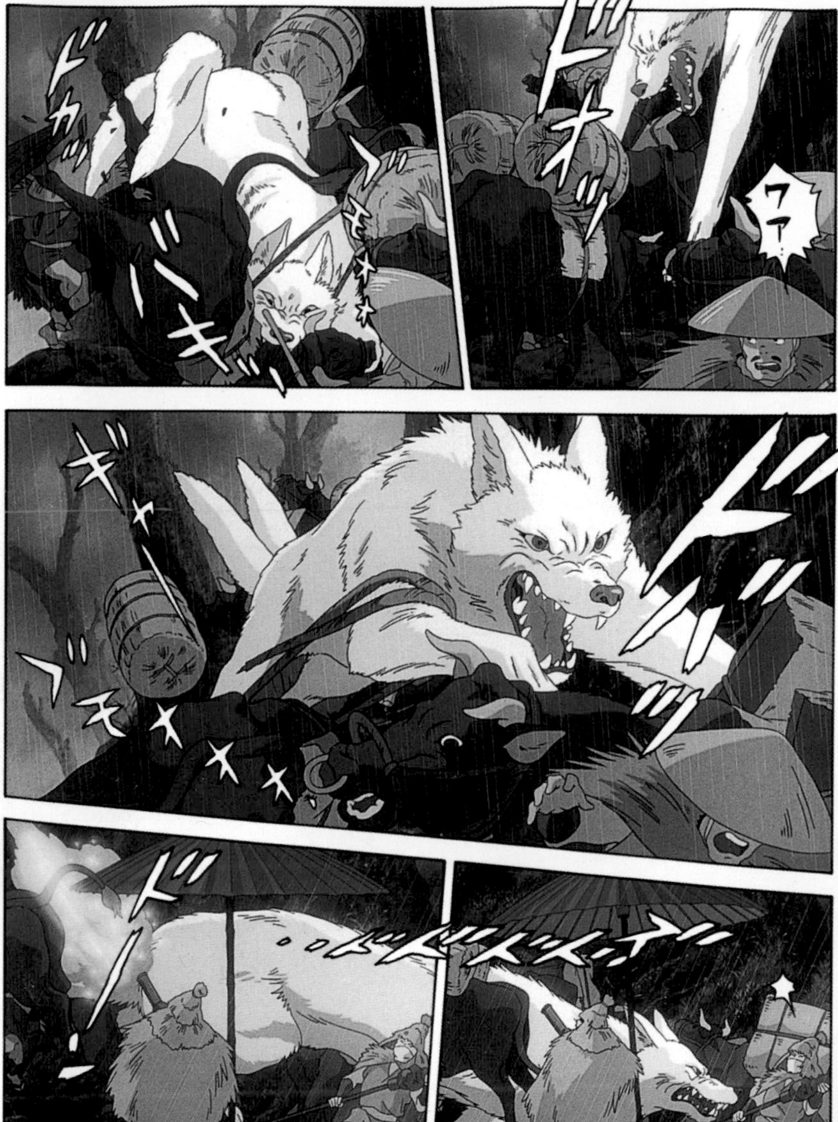
ドドォッ
ワァ!
ドカッ
ドドッ
ギャーッ
ドン

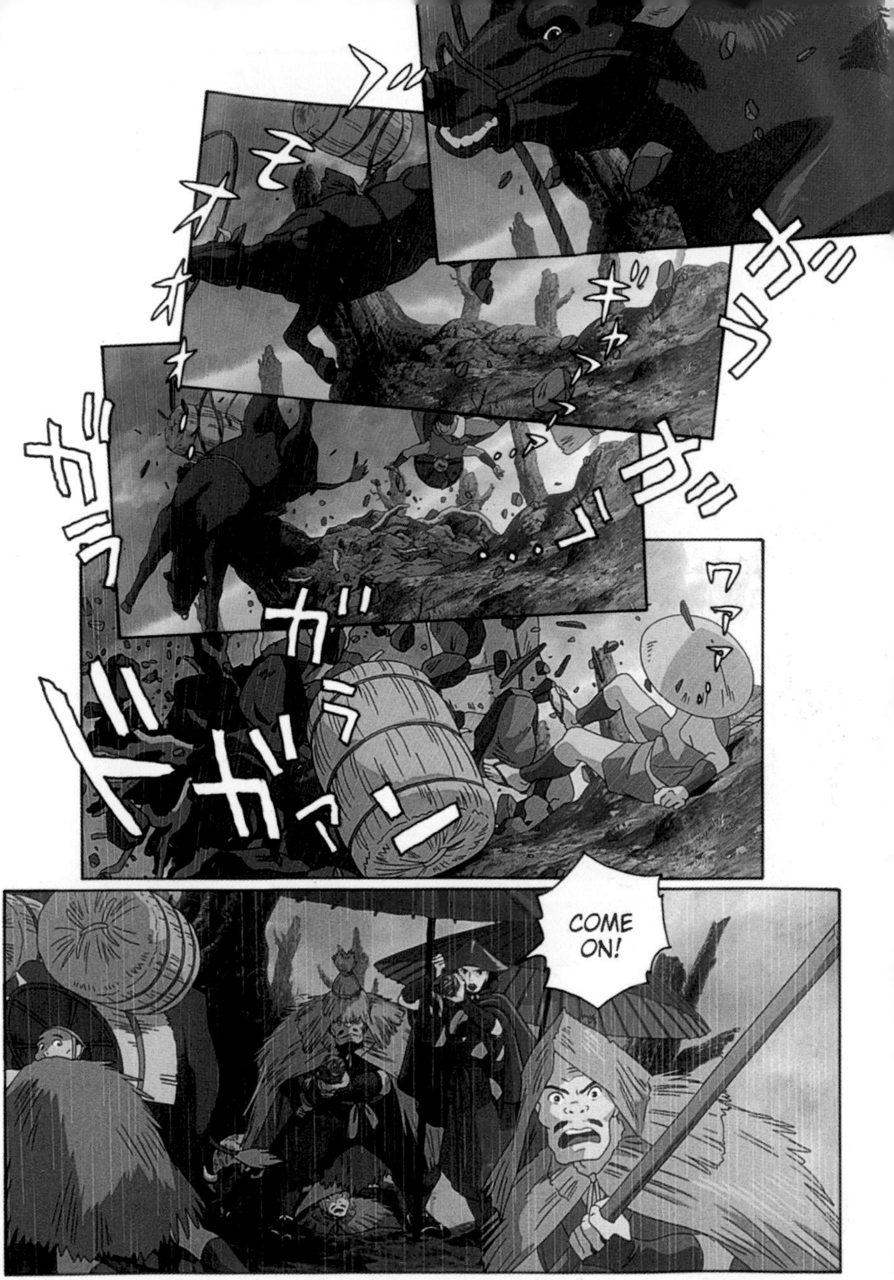
COME ON!

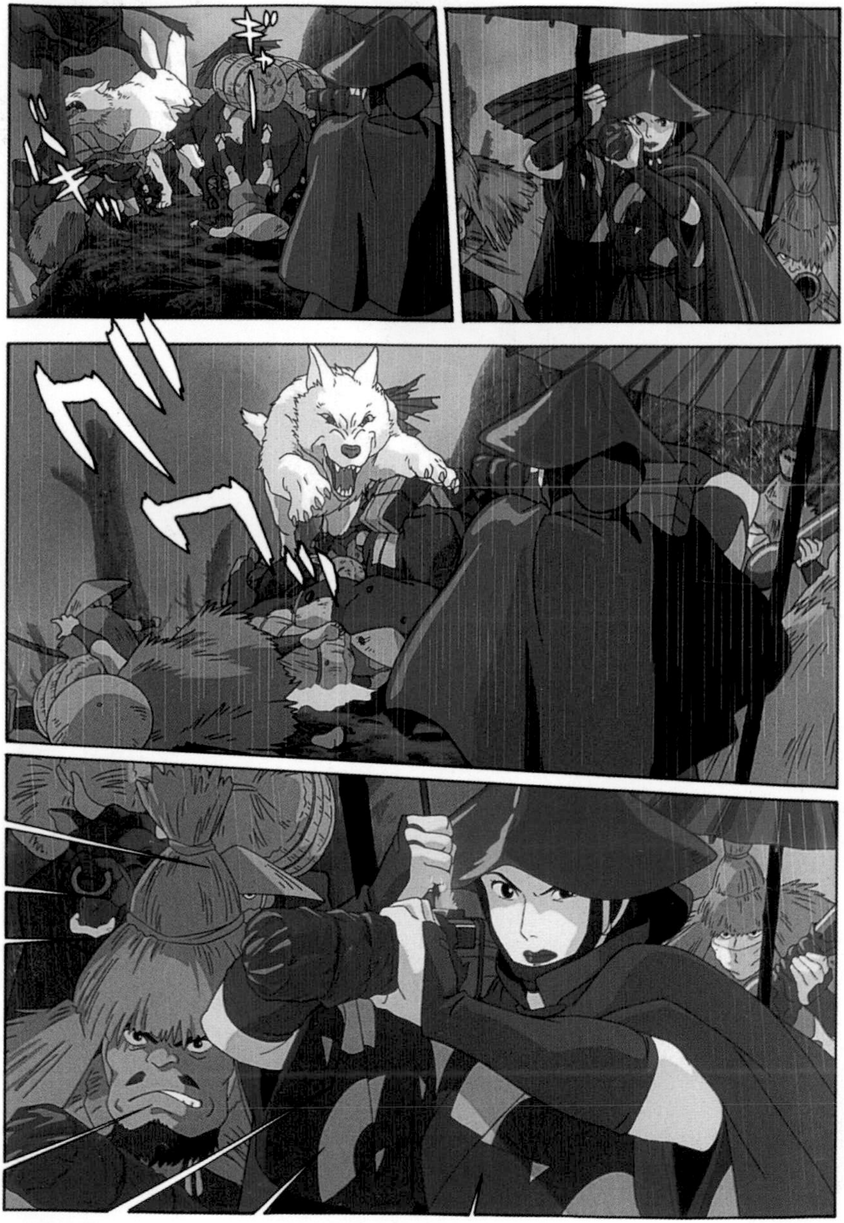

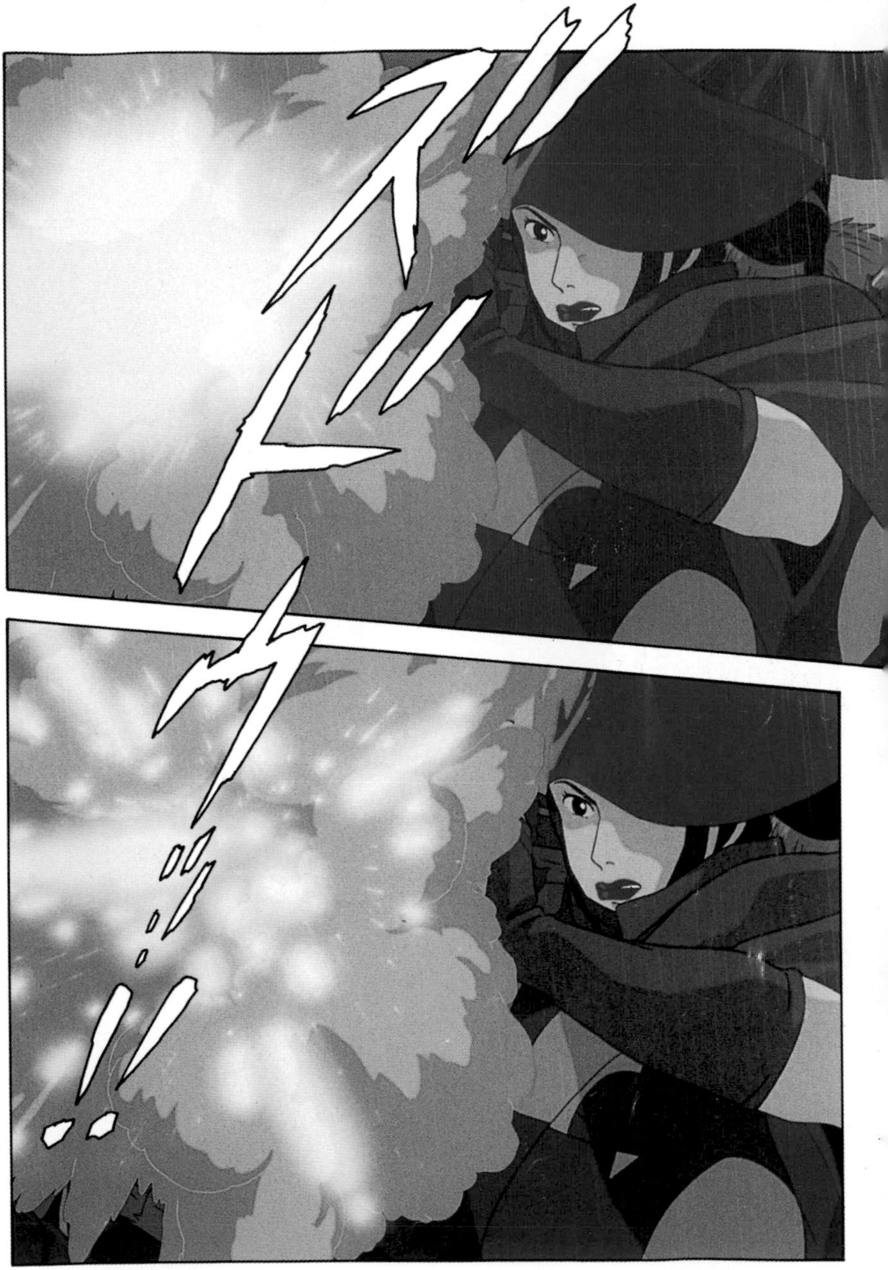
ズドクッ…!!

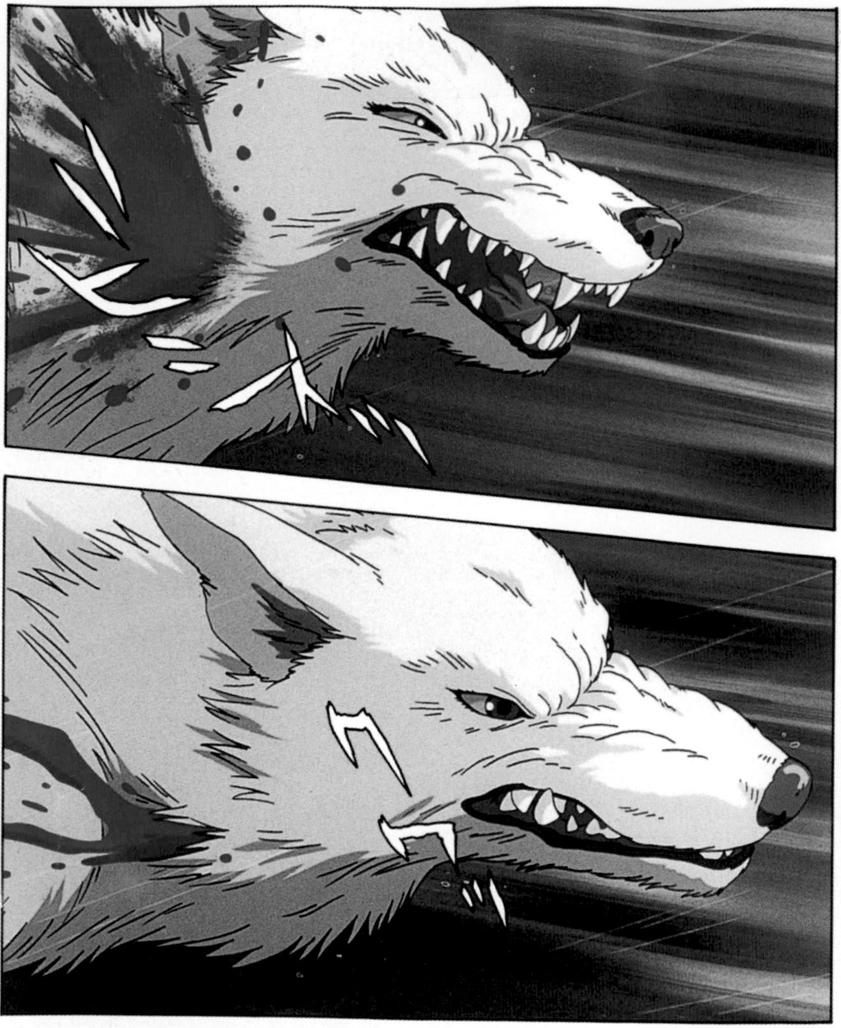

TO BE CONTINUED...

## Your Guide to *Princess Mononoke* Sound Effects!

To increase your enjoyment of the distinctive Japanese visual style of *Princess Mononoke* we've included a listing of and guide to the sound effects used in this comic adaptation of the movie. In the comic, these sound effects are written in the Japanese phonetic characters called katakana.

In the sound effects glossary for *Princess Mononoke*, sound effects are listed by page and panel number. For example, 9.1 means page 9, panel 1. And if there is more than one sound effect in a panel, the sound effects are listed in order (so, 106.1.1 means page 106, panel 1, first sound effect). Remember that all numbers are given in the original Japanese reading order: right-to-left.

After the page and panel numbers, you'll see the literally translated sound spelled out by the katakana, followed by how the sound effect might have been spelled out, or what it stands for, in English—it is interesting to see the different ways Japanese people describe the sounds of things!

You'll sometimes see a long dash at the end of a sound effects listing. This is just a way of showing that the sound is the kind that lasts for a while; similarly, a hyphen and number indicate the panels affected.

Now you are ready to use the *Princess Mononoke* Sound Effects Guide!

| | |
|---|---|
| 29.1 | FX: DOSU [thunk] |
| 29.1-2 | FX: ZUZUZUZUZU [zwisssshhh] |
| 29.2 | FX: DOSU [thunk] |
| 30.2-3 | FX: ZUZUZUZU [fwisssshhh] |
| 30.3-4 | FX: ZAWAWAWA [fwoowoosh] |
| 31.1-2 | FX: GUEEEH [uehhh] |
| 32.1-3 | FX: ZUZUZUZU [fwisssh] |
| 32.3-5 | FX: ZAZAZAZA [zwisssshhh] |
| 33.1 | FX: BUWA [ploosh] |
| 33.1-3 | FX: ZAZAZAAA [zwisssshhh] |
| 33.4 | FX: ZAZA [fsssshhh] |
| 33.5-6 | FX: ZUZAZAZAAA [zwisssshhh] |
| 34.1-3 | FX: ZUZAZAZAZAAA [zwisssshhh] |
| 35.2.1 | FX: BIKU [urk] |
| 35.2.2 | FX: BURURU [hween] |
| 35.3-5 | FX: ZUZAZAZAAA [zwizwisshhh] |
| 36.1 | FX: BYU [fwipp] |
| 36.2 | FX: TAN! [tump!] |
| 36.3 | FX: BA [fwoosh] |
| 36.4 | FX: DA [tmp] |
| 36.4-5 | FX: ZUZAZAA [zwisssshh] |
| 36.5 | FX: DON [thunk] |
| 37.1 | FX: BEKI BEKI [krakk krakk] |
| 37.2.1 | FX: BOKI BAKI [krakk krakk] |
| 37.2.2 | FX: PAKKA PAKKA [klop klop] |
| 37.3 | FX: BAKI [krakk] |

| | |
|---|---|
| 13.3.2 | FX: GISHI GISHI [kreech kreech] |
| 13.4 | FX: TA [tmp] |
| 13.5.1 | FX: PAKKA PAKKA [klop klop] |
| 13.5.2 | FX: SU [fsh] |
| 13.6.1 | FX: PAKKA [klop] |
| 13.6.2 | FX: BA [fwoosh] |
| 16.2 | FX: DA [tmp] |
| 16.3 | FX: PAKA [klop] |
| 16.4 | FX: PAKA [klop klop] |
| 16.5 | FX: PAKA [klop] |
| 16.6 | FX: PAKA PAKA [klop klop] |
| 21.3 | FX: PIKU [urk] |
| 22.1 | FX: TON [tp] |
| 22.2 | FX: TA [tmp] |
| 24.3 | FX: SU [fsh] |
| 25.1 | FX: GIRI GIRI [fwiwich] |
| 25.2 | FX: SUUU [fssh] |
| 26.1 | FX: YURA [fwom] |
| 26.2 | FX: ZAWA ZAWA [fwish fwish] |
| 26.3 | FX: ZAWA ZAWA ZAWA [fwish fwish fwish] |
| 26.4 | FX: ZUUU [fshhh] |
| 27.1 | FX: DOGA [thwunk] |
| 27.2-3 | FX: ZUZAZAZAZA [zwisssshhh] |
| 28.1-4 | FX: ZUZAZAZAZAZA [zwisssshhh] |

| | |
|---|---|
| 7.1.1 | FX: HUU HUU [huuf huuf] |
| 7.1.2 | FX: BEKI BEKI [krak krak] |
| 7.1.3 | FX: BOKI [thrak] |
| 7.1.4 | FX: BAKI [krakk] |
| 8.1.1 | FX: BEKI BEKI [krak krak] |
| 8.1.2 | FX: BOKI [thrak] |
| 8.2.1 | FX: BEKI BEKI [krak krak] |
| 8.2.2 | FX: ZA ZA ZAAA [fssshhh] |
| 8.3 | FX: ZUUN [fummp] |
| 9.1 | FX: HUUU [huuf] |
| 9.2 | FX: ZUZA [fich] |
| 9.3.1 | FX: HUUU [huff] |
| 9.3.2 | FX: ZUZU [zwissh] |
| 9.4 | FX: ZUZAZAZA [zwisssshhh] |
| 10.1 | FX: FUU [huuf] |
| 10.2.1 | FX: ZUZAZAZA [zwisssshhh] |
| 10.2.2 | FX: HUU [huuf] |
| 10.3 | FX: ZU ZU ZU ZU [zwissh zwissh] |
| 12.1 | FX: PAKKA PAKKA [klop klop] |
| 12.2.1 | FX: ZA [fich] |
| 12.2.2 | FX: PAKKA PAKKA [klop klop] |
| 12.3 | FX: PAKKA PAKKA [klop klop] |
| 12.4.1 | FX: CHA [thup] |
| 12.4.2 | FX: PAKKA PAKKA [klop klop] |
| 12.5.1 | FX: PAKKA PAKKA [klop klop] |
| 12.5.2 | FX: TA [tmp] |
| 12.6 | FX: TA TA TA [tmp tmp tmp] |
| 13.1 | FX: TA TA TA [tmp tmp tmp] |
| 13.3.1 | FX: PAKA PAKA [klop klop] |

| | | |
|---|---|---|
| 66.2 | FX: GIRIRI [kririnch] | |
| 66.4 | FX: BYU [fwoosh] | |
| | | |
| 67.1 | FX: TAN! [thunk!] | |
| 67.3-4 | FX: ZUZUZU [fwish fwish fwish] | |
| 67.4 | FX: PAKA PAKA [klop klop] | |
| | | |
| 68.1-5 | FX: PAKA PAKA PAKA PAKA PAKA [klop klop klop klop klop] | |
| 68.7-9 | FX: ZUZUZUZUZU [zwoosssh] | |
| | | |
| 69.1 | FX: ZUZUZU [zwoosh] | |
| | FX: HUU [hooof] | |
| 69.1.2 | FX: ZUZUZU [zwoosh] | |
| 69.5 | FX: TOSU [tunk] | |
| | | |
| 70.1 | FX: JUUU [sizzz] | |
| 70.2 | FX: GU [tugg] | |
| 70.4 | FX: GURA [fwom] | |
| 70.5 | FX: ZUU [zwoosh] | |
| | | |
| 71.1.1 | FX: DOH [thunk] | |
| 71.1.2 | FX: ZUZUUN [thuddd] | |
| 71.2 | FX: OOOH [ahh] | |
| 71.3 | FX: OOH [ahh] | |
| 71.4 | FX: TA [tmp] | |
| | | |
| 72.2 | FX: DA [tmp] | |
| 72.3 | FX: BA [fwoosh] | |
| 72.4 | FX: TATATA [tmp tmp tmp] | |
| | | |
| 73.4 | FX: ZA [fich] | |
| 73.5 | FX: BASAA [fshh] | |
| | | |
| 74.1 | FX: TATATA [tmp tmp tmp] | |
| | | |
| 75.1 | FX: SUU [fsh] | |
| 75.2 | FX: TOKU TOKU [glug glug] | |
| 75.3 | FX: JUU [sizzz] | |
| | | |
| 78.1-2 | FX: JUWAAH [fizzz] | |
| 78.2 | FX: SHUU [fsssh] | |
| | | |
| 79.1 | FX: ZUZUZU [fssshhh] | |
| | | |
| 80.3.1 | FX: CHARA [fip] | |
| 80.3.2 | FX: KAN KARAN [klak klak] | |
| | | |
| 81.2 | FX: KARAN [klak] | |
| | | |
| 82.1 | FX: KARAN [klak] | |
| 82.4 | FX: SU [fsh] | |
| 82.5 | FX: SA [fsh] | |

| | | |
|---|---|---|
| 49.1.1 | FX: DOKAKA [klolopp] | |
| 49.1.2 | FX: ZUZAZAAA [zwissshhh] | |
| 49.2 | FX: ZUZAAN [fwuuum] | |
| | | |
| 52.2-4 | FX: ZUZAZAZAZA [zwissshhh] | |
| | | |
| 53.2 | FX: TA [tmp] | |
| 53.3 | FX: ZUZAZAZAAA [zwissshhh] | |
| | | |
| 54.1-3 | FX: DODODODODODODO [whud whud whud whud whud whud] | |
| | | |
| 55.1-3 | FX: DODODODODODODO [whud whud whud whud whud whud] | |
| | | |
| 56.1 | FX: TATA [tmp tmp] | |
| 56.2.1 | FX: DODODO [whud whud whud] | |
| 56.2.2 | FX: TATATA [tmp tmp tmp] | |
| 56.3 | FX: DODO [whud whud] | |
| | | |
| 57.1 | FX: DOSA [whud] | |
| 57.3 | FX: ZAA [fichh] | |
| 57.4 | FX: SUCHA [fwish] | |
| | | |
| 58.1-4 | FX: DODODODO [whud whud whud whud] | |
| | | |
| 59.1 | FX: BYU [fwee] | |
| 59.2 | FX: TAN! [thunk!] | |
| 59.3 | FX: GUEHH [ehhh!] | |
| | | |
| 60.1-2 | FX: GUEEEHHH [ehhhh] | |
| 60.2 | FX: TATATA [tmp tmp tmp] | |
| 60.3 | FX: ZUZUZU [foom] | |
| 60.4 | FX: DOBA [ploosh] | |
| | | |
| 61.1-3 | FX: BYUOHH [fwooom] | |
| 61.4-6 | FX: BYURURURU [fweeesh] | |
| 61.6 | FX: PAKA PAKA [klop klop] | |
| | | |
| 62.1.1 | FX: ZUBYURU [ploosh] | |
| 62.1.2 | FX: PAKA PAKA [klop klop] | |
| 62.2 | FX: ZUZU [swoosh] | |
| 62.3 | FX: GU [tugg] | |
| 62.4 | FX: GUGUGU [tugg tugg] | |
| | | |
| 63.1-2 | FX: GUGU [tugg tugg] | |
| 63.3 | FX: BUCHI BUCHI [plipp plipp] | |
| | | |
| 64.2-5 | FX: PAKA PAKA PAKA PAKA PAKA [klop klop klop klop klop] | |
| | | |
| 65.1 | FX: GIRI [krinch] | |
| 65.2-4 | FX: DODODODODO [whud whud whud whud] | |

| | | |
|---|---|---|
| 38.1 | FX: BEKI BAKI [krakk krakk] | |
| 38.2.1 | FX: BAKI BAKI [krakk krakk] | |
| 38.2.2 | FX: BA [fsh] | |
| 38.3 | FX: BARA [fwoom] | |
| 38.3-4 | FX: WAAA [aieeee] | |
| 38.5 | FX: ZA [fich] | |
| | | |
| 39.1.1 | FX: BARI BARI [thrak thrak] | |
| 39.1.2 | FX: GARA GARA [klak klak] | |
| 39.2 | FX: HAAAAH [haaah] | |
| 39.3 | FX: ZUZAZAA [zwissshh] | |
| | | |
| 40.1 | FX: ZU [fssh] | |
| 40.2-3 | FX: ZUZAZAZAAA [zwisssshhh] | |
| | | |
| 41.1.1 | FX: BASA [fich] | |
| 41.1.2 | FX: DOSU [thunk] | |
| 41.2 | FX: DA [tmp] | |
| | | |
| 42.1 | FX: SU [fsh] | |
| 42.2 | FX: TAA [tmp] | |
| 42.3 | FX: PII [tweep] | |
| | | |
| 43.1 | FX: CHA [chak] | |
| 43.2 | FX: KURU [fwip] | |
| 43.3 | FX: GU [tugg] | |
| 43.4-5 | FX: PAKAKA [kloklop] | |
| 43.5.1 | FX: BA [fwoosh] | |
| 43.5.2 | FX: PAKA [klop] | |
| | | |
| 44.1 | FX: TA [tmp] | |
| 44.2 | FX: BA [fwoosh] | |
| 44.3 | FX: DOKA [klopp] | |
| 44.4 | FX: DOKAKA [klopp] | |
| | | |
| 45.1 | FX: GAKA [kloklopp] | |
| 45.2 | FX: TAN [tmp] | |
| 45.3 | FX: ZUZAZA [zwissshh] | |
| 45.4 | FX: ZA [fich] | |
| 45.5 | FX: ZAZA [fssh] | |
| 45.6 | FX: ZA [fich] | |
| | | |
| 46.1.1 | FX: BAKI BAKI [krak krak] | |
| 46.1.2 | FX: ZUZAZAZAA [zwissshh] | |
| 46.2 | FX: ZAZA [fich fich] | |
| | | |
| 47.1-2 | FX: ZAZAZAZA [fich fich fich fich] | |
| 47.2 | FX: BAKI [krakk] | |
| 47.3.1 | FX: ZUZAZAZAAA [zwissshhh] | |
| 47.3.2 | FX: BAKI BAKI [krak krak] | |
| | | |
| 48.1 | FX: ZUZAZA [zwisshh] | |
| 48.1-2 | FX: UOOH [wohhhh] | |
| 48.4 | FX: ZA ZA [fich fich] | |
| | FX: ZUZAZAZAAA [zwissshhh] | |

124.3 FX: ZUZU [slurrp]
124.4 FX: HAA [urrgh]

125.4.1 FX: KA KA [klak klak]
125.4.2 FX: ZUZUU [slurrp]
125.5 FX: SU [fsh]

126.1 FX: ZAAA [fsssh]
126.2 FX: GOSO GOSO [fip fip]

129.3 FX: GUI [tugg]

130.2 FX: KA KA KA [klak klak klak]

131.3 FX: CHIRA [sound of a glance]

133.1 FX: KA KA KA KA
    [klak klak klak klak]
133.2 FX: PAKA [klop]
133.3-4 FX: KA KA KA KA KA
    [klak klak klak klak klak]
133.4-5 FX: PAKA PAKA PAKA PAKA
    [klop klop klop klop]

134.1.1 FX: GUTSU GUTSU [glug glug]
134.1.2 FX: PACHI PACHI [krakkl krakkl]

135.4 FX: KATA [chak]

136.1 FX: TOPUU [plipp]

137.1 FX: SU [fsh]
137.3 FX: GOSO [fip]

138.2 FX: TAPO [plipp]
138.3 FX: SUU [fshh]
138.5 FX: TAPOO [plipp]

139.2 FX: ZUU [sipp]

140.1 FX: GOSO GOSO [fip fip]
140.3 FX: SU [fsh]

141.3 FX: SU [fsh]
141.4 FX: ZUZU [slurrp]

143.1 FX: ZUZUZU [slurrrp]
143.4 FX: ZUU [sipp]

146.1 FX: ZAAA [fssshh]
146.2-3 FX: GOOOHH [rrrrrrr]
146.4 FX: DOOOHH [rrrrrrrr]

147.1 FX: ZAAA [fssshh]

109.1-3 FX: PAKA PAKA PAKA
    [klop klop klop]
109.4-7 FX: PAKA PAKA PAKA PAKA
    [klop klop klop klop]
109.5 FX: TOSU TOSU [thup thup]

110.1-4 FX: PAKA PAKA PAKA PAKA
    [klop klop klop klop]
110.2 FX: SU [fsh]
110.3 FX: SHU [fwip]
110.4 FX: SUCHA [chak]

111.3 FX: DOSU [thunk]
111.4 FX: PAKA PAKA [klop klop]

112.1 FX: MUKU MUKU MUKU
    [wom wom wom]
112.3 FX: GUGU [ungh]
112.4 FX: KI [hmm]

113.2 FX: BIN [zwing]
113.3-5 FX: BYUUU [fweeee]

114.2 FX: BYU [fwee]
114.4 FX: DAN! [thunk!]

115.3 FX: DOKAKA [klopp klopp klopp]
115.4.1 FX: DOSU [whudd]
115.4.2 FX: DOKAKA [klopp klopp klopp]

116.1-2 FX: PAKA PAKA PAKA
    [klop klop klop]
116.3 FX: PAKA [klop]

117.2 FX: BIN [zwing]
117.3 FX: SHUN! [fwoosh!]
117.4 FX: BYU [fweee]
117.5 FX: SUU [fshh]

118.1 FX: GU [tugg]
118.2 FX: BIN! [zwing!]
118.3-6 FX: BYUUUU [fweeeee]

119.2 FX: ZUBA [slissh]
119.3 FX: PAKA [klop]
119.4 FX: PAKA PAKA [klop klop]

120.1-3 FX: PAKA PAKA PAKA PAKA
    [klop klop klop klop]

121.1 FX: PAKAKA [klopp klopp]
121.2 FX: KA [klip]
121.3 FX: YURA [fwom]
121.4 FX: DOSHA [krrsh]

86.1 FX: SU [fsh]
86.2 FX: GOTON [tunk]

88.4 FX: SU [fsh]

89.2.1 FX: GU [tugg]
89.2.2 FX: ZAKU [slish]

90.1 FX: BASA [fwisk]

91.3 FX: SU [fsh]

92.2 FX: PIKU [irl]
92.3 FX: KOTO [kluk]

93.2 FX: TA TA TA [tmp tmp tmp]
93.3 FX: TA TA TA [tmp tmp tmp]

95.2 FX: SU [fsh]

96.3 FX: SU [fsh]

97.3 FX: SA [fich]

98.1 FX: KA [klip]
98.3 FX: KA KA [klip klip]
98.4 FX: TA [tmp]

99.1-3 FX: PAKA PAKA PAKA PAKA PAKA
    PAKA [klop klop klop klop klop
    klop klop]

104.2 FX: WAAHH WAAHH [ahhh ahhh]

105.3 FX: KYAA [aieee]
105.4.1 FX: WAAHH [aaah]
105.4.2 FX: KYAA [aieee]

106.1.1 FX: KYAA [aieee]
106.1.2 FX: TATATA [tmp tmp tmp]
106.2 FX: BA [fwoosh]
106.3 FX: ZUBA [slissh]
106.4 FX: GUSA [thunk]

107.2 FX: HA [hm!]
107.3 FX: WAA WAA [ahhh ahhh]
107.4 FX: WAAA [ahhh]

108.2.1 FX: SHU [fwish]
108.2.2 FX: BYU [fwoosh]
108.2.3 FX: TON! [tunk!]
108.3.1 FX: TON! [tunk!]
108.3.2 FX: PAKA PAKA [klop klop]
108.3.3 FX: SHU [fwoosh]

149.3.1 FX: DA [tmp]
149.3.2 FX: DA DA [tmp tmp]

150.2.1 FX: BASA [fwip]
150.2.2 FX: BASA [fwip]
150.3 FX: GASA [fwich]

151.1 FX: GU [tugg]
151.2 FX: BA [fwoosh]

152.1-3 FX: DODODODODO [whud whud whud whud whud]
152.4-6 FX: DODODODODO [whud whud whud whud whud]

153.2.1 FX: SHUN [fsh]
153.2.2 FX: DOUH [blamm]
153.3 FX: JIII [sizzz]
153.4 FX: DOBAU [boomsh]

154.1 FX: BASHI [plissh]
154.2 FX: BA [fwoosh]
154.3 FX: DOKA [tunk]
154.4.1 FX: ZA [fich]
154.4.2 FX: GUWA [thrak]
154.5.1 FX: DOGA [boomsh]
154.5.2 FX: DADA [tmp tmp]

155.1 FX: DA [tmp]
155.2 FX: BA [fwoosh]
155.4.1 FX: DOU [boom]
155.4.2 FX: BA [fwoosh]
155.5 FX: HYU [fwee]
155.6.1 FX: DOGA [boomsh]
155.6.2 FX: DA [tmp]

156.1 FX: ZAAA [fssshh]
156.2 FX: DOU [blamm]
156.4 FX: DOU [blamm]
156.5.1 FX: DAAN [baam]
156.5.2 FX: DADAAN [babaam]
156.5.3 FX: DAAN [baam]

157.1.1 FX: DAAN [baam]
157.1.2 FX: DODODO [whud whud whud]
157.2 FX: KURU [fwip]
157.3 FX: ZA [fich]
157.4-6 FX: DODODODODO [whud whud whud whud whud]

158.1-2 FX: DODODO [whud whud whud]
158.3 FX: SHU SHU [fsh fsh]
158.4 FX: DOKAAN [blaam]

159.2 FX: DOGA [boomsh]
159.3 FX: GUWA [thrak]
159.4 FX: DOGA [boomsh]
159.5 FX: DOUN DOUN DOUN [blamm blamm blamm]

161.2-3 FX: DO DO DO [whud whud whud]
161.1 FX: ZA [fich]
161.4 FX: BA [fwoosh]

162.1 FX: SUCHA [chak]
162.2-5 FX: DODO DODO DODO [whud whud whud whud whud whud]

163.1 FX: DOH [whudd]
163.2.1 FX: BUMOHH [moooo]
163.2.2 FX: DOKA [thudd]
163.2.3 FX: BAKI [krak]
163.3.1 FX: DOBA [woosh]
163.3.2 FX: GYAA [aieee]
163.3.3 FX: BUMOOH [arrrr]
163.4-5 FX: ZUDODODODO [whud whud whud whud whud]
163.5 FX: DOON [boomsh]

164.2.1 FX: GARA [thrak]
164.2.2 FX: GYAAA [aieee]
164.2.3 FX: BUMOOHH [moooo]
164.3 FX: GARA GARA GARA [klak klak klak]
164.4.1 FX: WAAAH [aieeee]
164.4.2 FX: GARAN [twunk]
164.4.3 FX: DOGAAN [thwudd]

165.2.1 FX: GYAA [aieee]
165.2.2 FX: BAKI [krak]
165.3 FX: GUWA [arrrr]

166.1-2 FX: ZUDOU!! [booomsh!!]

167.1 FX: BISHI [zwipp]
167.2 FX: KUWA [arr!]

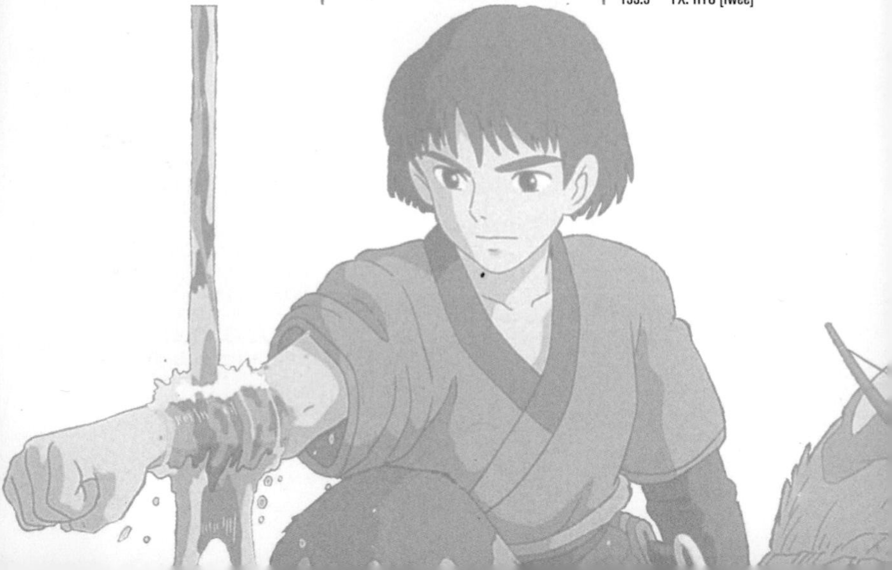

This book should be read in its original Japanese right-to-left format.
Please turn it around to begin!

# PRINCESS MONONOKE

## Volume 1 of 5

Original story and screenplay written and directed by
**Hayao Miyazaki**

Film Comic Adaptation/Yuji Oniki
Lettering/Rina Mapa
Design/Hidemi Sahara
Editor/Eric Searleman

Managing Editor/Masumi Washington
Editor in Chief/Alvin Lu
Sr. Director of Acquisitions/Rika Inouye
Sr. VP of Marketing/Liza Coppola
Exec. VP of Sales & Marketing/John Easum
Publisher/Hyoe Narita

Printed in China

Published by
VIZ Media, LLC
295 Bay St.
San Francisco, CA 94133

First printing, September 2006

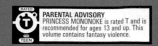

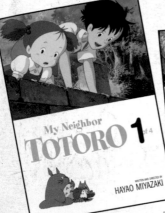
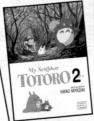
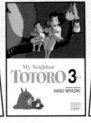
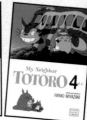
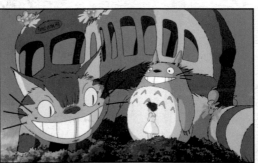

THE ART OF
KIKI's
DELIVERY SERVICE
A FILM BY HAYAO MIYAZAKI

KIKI's
DELIVERY SERVICE
1
FROM THE NOVEL BY EIKO KADONO
HAYAO MIYAZAKI

KIKI's
DELIVERY SERVICE
2
FROM THE NOVEL BY EIKO KADONO
HAYAO MIYAZAKI

KIKI's
DELIVERY SERVICE
3
FROM THE NOVEL BY EIKO KADONO
HAYAO MIYAZAKI

KIKI's
DELIVERY SERVICE
4
FROM THE NOVEL BY EIKO KADONO
HAYAO MIYAZAKI

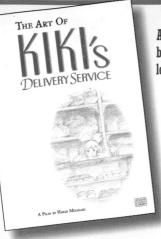

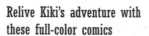

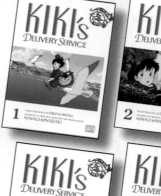

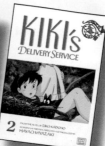

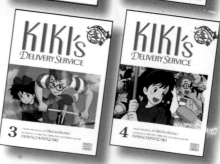

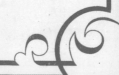